Complete Book of Brainteasers
Table of Contents

P9-CPX-333

How to Use
The Complete Book of Brainteasers

The Complete Book of Brainteasers is a collection of puzzles, riddles and other challenges to get your mind in gear and exercise your mental muscles.

The book is divided into four sections. Level 1 contains the easiest brainteasers. Level 3 contains the most challenging. The last section is made up of brainteasers that tie in with the various seasons and holidays that wc all celebrate.

Levels 1, 2 and 3 each contain a section of brainteasers related to language arts, math, social studies, science and creative arts. The answers for all these brainteasers and the ones that relate to the seasons can be found in the back of the book beginning on page 305.

Brainteasers can be used in any way that is helpful to you. However, if you're looking for a suggestion of how to use the book, work your way page by page through Levels 1, 2 and 3 in order. Enjoy the seasonal brainteasers as the holidays and seasons occur during the year.

What Level 1
Is All About

Some people say that the brainteasers in Level 1 are best used by boys and girls around eight or nine years old. But you never know until you try them if you can actually do them. Accept the challenge! Puzzle them out! Work with a friend! You may be surprised at how much you can do. Even if you're older, you might have fun doing the brainteasers in this level.

Language Arts

Language is made up of sounds, words, spellings and meanings. In the brainteasers in this section, you can have fun using what you already know about language and learn even more.

If you want, you can become a writer yourself by making up even more examples of what you do in each brainteaser. Then, you can share these new puzzles and riddles with your friends and family.

Mirror, Mirror, on the Door

Mirror, mirror, on the door
Bounces words back off the floor.
A word comes up,
And it is found
With letters switched all around! **pat** - -
loop - -

▶ Find the word in each sentence that can be spelled backwards to make a new word. Circle the word in the sentence. Then, write the new word on the line to complete the sentence.

Example: I can use a (net) to catch **ten** fish.

1. I will get into the _____ , but I don't want a bath!

2. Who put _____ on my mug?

3. Please get me the top _____ .

4. Now, we have finally _____ the game.

5. Losing _____ made the balloon start to sag.

6. The _____ for cutting wood was very sharp.

7. Would you like to ride on a _____ or a bus?

8. They used a _____ to get the loot!

9. Don't step on my _____ !

10. Pam drew a _____ for the trip.

11. The hardest part is to _____ the mouse.

12. My cat is my _____ when it sits on my lap.

What do you notice about the words "MIRROR RIM"? _____

_____

Stretch and Grow

Gladys has some goofy glasses. They have springs on them which stretch out words to make room for more vowels.

▶ Add a vowel to each word below to make a new word Gladys can see through her glasses.

1.	pa_l	9.	s_it
2.	fe_d	10.	h_at
3.	ch_in	11.	b_ad
4.	ra_n	12.	fl_at
5.	c_at	13.	b_it
6.	Jo_n	14.	p_in
7.	sh_ut	15.	me_n
8.	bra_n	16.	s_ap

Alphabet Soup

Nan Cook has a special way of making alphabet soup. She mixes two boxes of soup together. Then, she adds two secret ingredients—mystery and fun. After the soup is cooked, a strange thing happens. All the vowels rise to the top of the pot.

▶ Write the consonant that can be used in both the front and back of each vowel or pair of vowels to make a word. One has been done for you.

Everything in Its Place

Tillie likes everything to be in its place. When things are not just so, she waves her magic feather duster around the room and says five times, "You cannot beat a place that's neat!" The pictures and words below would make Tillie very unhappy. Each picture is missing something, and the word that tells what is missing has its letters jumbled.

▶ First, unscramble the letters and write the word on the line. (The first letter of each word is underlined.) Then, write the number of the word by the picture where it belongs.

1. pes<u>g</u>ar _____

2. ar<u>c</u>any _____

3. lo<u>d</u>l _____

4. se<u>b</u>an _____

5. b<u>f</u>oltoal _____

6. sr<u>h</u>mate _____

7. eos<u>r</u> _____

8. rao<u>c</u>yn _____

Level 1, Language

Flip-Flop

save = vase

Professor Turnabout is teaching his class new vocabulary words. However, he seems to be a little mixed-up. When he gives the students a word, he actually means another word that has the same letters but in a different order.

▶ Look at the words below. Help the students figure out which words the professor really wants them to have.

1. deal – _____

2. not – _____

3. grab – _____

4. felt – _____

5. shop – _____

6. ate – _____

7. hips – _____

8. team – _____

9. read – _____

10. may – _____

11. pace – _____

12. rate – _____

13. cabs – _____

14. trap – _____

15. fate – _____

16. race – _____

17. tub – _____

18. part – _____

19. net – _____

20. tab – _____

Name _____

Spelling As Easy As ABC

A boy named PT likes to take shortcuts when he has a lot to write. On this page, he will show U an EZ way to spell. B prepared to B the NV of all your friends. R U ready?

▶ Use the clues and the Word Bank to help you. Write these words like PT would.

1. A kind of tent   _____
2. An insect   _____
3. A hot drink   _____
4. A vegetable   _____
5. A question word   _____
6. A banana's skin   _____
7. A word that
    means slippery   _____
8. A kind of meat   _____
9. Not difficult   _____
10. To look   _____
11. A period of time   _____
12. Pass cards to players   _____
13. Nothing in it   _____
14. A girl's name   _____
15. Pep   _____
16. I am, he is, you __   _____
17. A bird that is blue   _____
18. A water mammal   _____

tepee TP

Word Bank

are	empty	pea	Katie
bee	veal	tea	deal
icy	seal	while	easy
see	why	tepee	jay
	peel	energy	

Name _____

Vet to the Rescue

Dr. Helppets is very busy. All day long, animals come to see him about many different illnesses.

▶ Match each animal to its illness by writing a letter on the line.

1. _____
2. _____
3. _____
4. _____
5. _____
6. _____
7. _____
8. _____
9. _____
10. _____

a. many cavities

b. lost stripes

c. chicken pox

d. stiff neck

e. only eight lives

f. gives chocolate milk

g. cold in nose

h. no voice

i. allergy to cheese

j. sore feet

The Puzzling Print-Out

Professor Gizmo built his own computer. But sometimes the professor is a little absentminded, and he pushes the wrong buttons. Today, he printed some "Funny Food Facts."

▶ Read each fact. Cross out the noun that doesn't make sense. Find a noun in another sentence that fits but still makes a silly sentence. Write it above the crossed-out word. The first one has been done for you.

Funny Food Facts

1. Lazy people eat ~~chili~~. meatloaf

2. The Easter Bunny's favorite vegetables are chicken.

3. The best fruit to drink is strawberries.

4. If you're scared, don't eat dough.

5. Jellybeans must be a cold food.

6. Dancing cows make blueberries.

7. Cavemen ate meatloaf.

8. Bread is rich because it has watermelon.

9. Milkshakes are an unhappy fruit.

10. Club sandwiches grow on the floor of a barn.

Hot Stuff

To become king, the brave, young prince had to have his picture painted with a dragon. He set out on his journey and came upon a cave in which a fire-breathing dragon lived.

The prince called in, "To become king I need to have you pose with me for a painting."

The dragon laughed and answered, "If you can solve the puzzle on the rocks around the entrance to my cave, I will do as you ask."

Word Bank

roast	hot
dogs	bring
me	peppers
and	up
hot	we'll
fire	chili
and	them

▶ Each rebus stands for a word listed in the Word Bank. Help the prince solve the puzzle by writing one word on each line. You will have to respell some words.

_____ _____

_____ _____ _____

_____ _____ _____

_____ _____ _____

Name _____

Pucker Power

One day, a princess walked in the forest. She met a bullfrog who croaked loudly, "Every time you kiss me, I will turn into something different. By the seventh kiss, I will have what I need to be your prince."

▶ On each line write the word that is pictured.

▶ Each word above makes a compound word when combined with the word before or after it. The last compound word tells what the frog needs to become a prince. Write the compound words.

_____ , _____ , _____

_____ , _____ , _____

Level 1, Language

Word Magic

Maggie Magician announces, "One plus one equals one!" The audience giggles. So Maggie puts two words into a hat and waves her magic wand. When she reaches into the hat, Maggie pulls out one word and a picture. "See," says Maggie, "I was right!"

▶ Look at each picture below. Use the Word Bank to help write a compound word for each.

_____

_____

_____

_____

_____

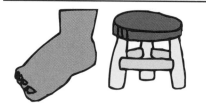

_____

_____

_____

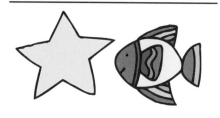

_____

_____

_____

Word Bank

ball	door	rain
basket	ear	shirt
bell	fish	shoe
book	foot	star
bow	lace	stool
box	light	sun
cake	mail	tail
cup	phone	worm

_____

Name _____

Alike, But So Different

Jim and Tim are twins, but they do not look alike and often don't think alike. The boys like to speak in rhymes and finish each other's sentences using words with opposite meanings.

▶ Read each sentence. Then write the missing words. The first one has been done for you. You can use the Word Bank to help find the words.

Jim says . . .

Word Bank

fall	frown
push	old
sink	small
slow	up
long	pull
new	float
smile	short
rise	fast
down	big

Tim says . . .

1. The gold was ____**cold**____ , but the pot was ____**hot**____ .

2. The bush couldn't _____ , but the bull could _____ .

3. Her eyes would _____ , but the ball would _____ .

4. The blast was _____ , but the toe was _____ .

5. The pup stood _____ , but the clown fell _____ .

6. The ball was _____ , but the pig was _____ .

7. The song was _____ , but the fort was _____ .

8. The gold was _____ , but the stew was _____ .

9. The goat could _____ , but the ink would _____ .

10. Kyle would _____ , but the clown would _____ .

Name _____

Puppy Power

An **analogy** is a sentence in which two sets of ideas are compared in the same way. Look at these examples:

Big is to **small** as **day** is to **night**. (Words are opposites.)
Robin is to **bird** as **spaniel** is to **dog**. (Kind of bird; kind of dog)

▶ Complete these five analogies. Then use the words you wrote to answer the question.

1. **Here** is to **there** as **then** is to _____ .

2. **Tack** is to **stack** as **pot** is to _____ .

3. **Net** is to **ten** as **saw** is to _____ .

4. **Down** is to **up** as **bottom** is to _____ .

5. **Siamese** is to **cat** as **poodle** is to _____ .

Why was the spotted dog happy?

| 1 | 2 | 3 | 4 | 5 |

▶ Complete these analogies. Then, use the words you wrote to answer the question below.

6. **We** is to **our** as **they** is to _____ .

7. **Front** is to **heads** as **back** is to _____ .

8. **Is** is to **are** as **was** is to _____ .

9. **Auto** is to **car** as **cart** is to _____ .

How did the other dogs show they were happy?

| 6 | 7 | 8 | 9 |

Take the challenge of the brainteasers in this section. You will see that mathematics is connected to many more things than just pages of number problems. The fact is, there are few things you do in life that are not touched in some way by mathematics.

As you work through the pages of this section, be alert to other ways that you use mathematics in your daily life.

Too Dog-Gone Tired

Ty Half-awake has trouble sleeping. His mother suggested that he try counting puppies. So night after night, he lay awake counting puppies.

▶ Each set of three numbers below contains the actual number of puppies Ty counted on a given night and two other numbers. The number he counted will always be the greatest number of the three. Circle the number of puppies in each row that is the greatest number. Then, circle the letter above the greatest number in each group, and use it to spell out the cause of Ty's sleeplessness.

s	l	p
110,001	110,010	110,100

l	u	a
221,112	222,111	212,211

g	p	t
523,567	523,746	523,476

p	r	e
991,991	919,911	991,191

g	t	y
432,342	423,432	432,423

m	l	n
955,449	959,454	959,445

e	a	o
723,327	772,332	773,223

s	v	t
401,401	410,410	410,401

e	l	r
883,833	838,388	838,833

The cause of Ty's sleeplessness was _____.

Name _____

Share and Share Alike

A certain farmer had a vegetable garden. He did not need all the lettuce and carrots that he grew, so he shared part of his crops with six friendly rabbits.

The farmer followed certain rules:

- Each rabbit would be given one bag of vegetables.
- Each bag had to have one carrot and one head of lettuce.
- All the bags had to weigh exactly the same.

▶ Help the farmer choose which carrot and which head of lettuce to put together in each bag. Write the weight on each carrot and each head of lettuce in the bags at the bottom of the page.

"Bee" Ware

▶ Help Papa Bear find the shortest route in and out of this honeycomb without going through or next to any cell where a bee is. Add the numbers in each cell that your path goes through. The path with the lowest sum is the shortest.

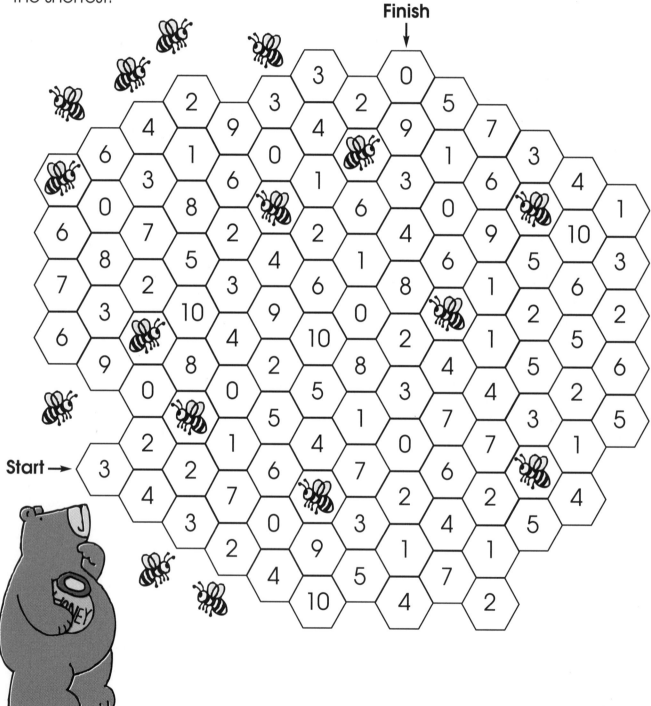

Grab Bag of Numbers

▶ Each of the bags on this page contains several numbers. Your job is to use them in a mathematical sentence so that you can get the given answer. You may use **+**, **−**, **x**, or ÷ between numbers and arrange these numbers in any order.

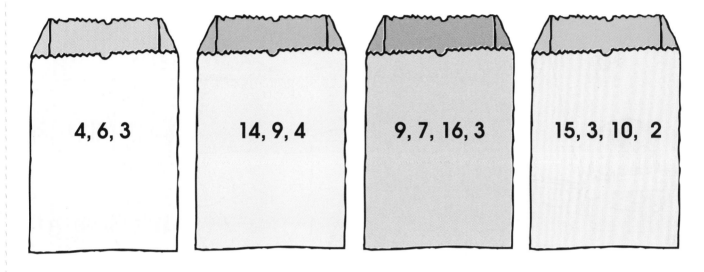

4, 6, 3

14, 9, 4

9, 7, 16, 3

15, 3, 10, 2

_____ = 5   _____ = 9   _____ = 12   _____ = 25

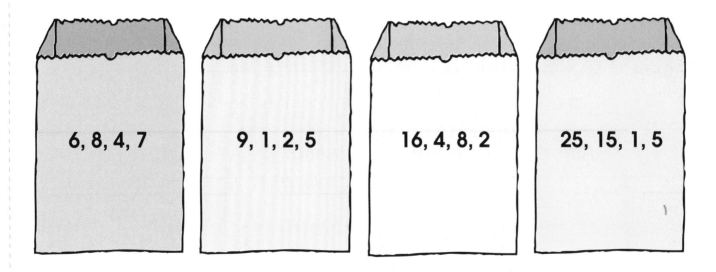

6, 8, 4, 7

9, 1, 2, 5

16, 4, 8, 2

25, 15, 1, 5

_____ = 19   _____ = 15   _____ = 4   _____ = 6

Name _____

Aim to Please

After Jean read a book about Robin Hood, her father took her to an archery range so that she could learn to use a bow and arrow.

Jean took three turns. Each turn she shot four arrows, and each time she got a score of 91. The combination of numbers was different with each turn.

▶ Examine the target below.

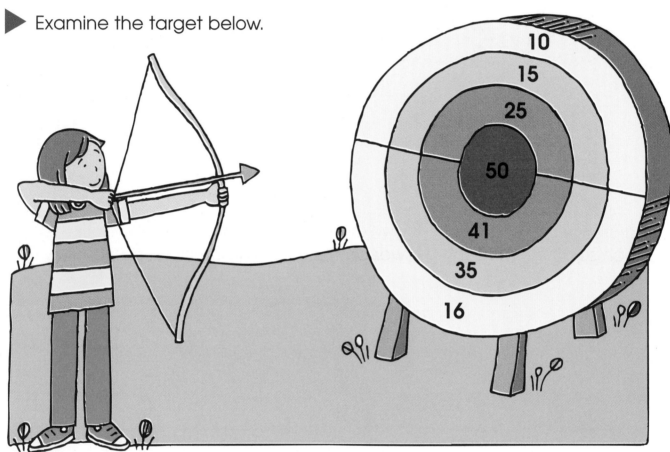

▶ Fill in the chart with the numbers Jean might have hit for each try.

	Arrow 1	Arrow 2	Arrow 3	Arrow 4	Score
Try #1	_____	_____	_____	_____	91
Try #2	_____	_____	_____	_____	91
Try #3	_____	_____	_____	_____	91

Magic Squares

A magic square is one in which the sum is the same no matter which way you add the numbers. You can add across any row, down any column or either way on the diagonal and you will get the same total.

▶ What is the sum of this magic square? _____

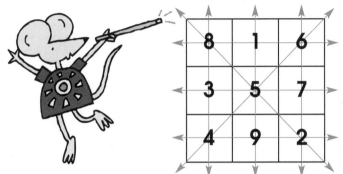

8	1	6
3	5	7
4	9	2

▶ All these magic squares are made from the nine counting numbers. None of these numbers are repeated in any magic square. Add the numbers across, down, and diagonal. What is the sum of each set of numbers in each square? Write the answer on the line next to each square.

10	3	8
5	7	9
6	11	4

_____

12	5	10
7	9	11
8	13	6

_____

▶ The last square needs to be finished. Study the other squares for a pattern which will help you discover and write in the missing numbers.

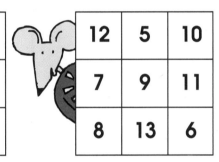

14		12
	11	13
10	15	

▶ What is the sum for each set of numbers? _____

Level 1, Math

Name _____

This Side Up

These cubes are six-sided. The sum of the numbers on opposite sides of each cube always equals 7.

▶ Complete the mathematical sentences on the 3 sides of each cube that can be seen. Then, write and complete a mathematical sentence for the 3 sides that can't be seen. You can use addition, subtraction, multiplication or division. Remember, the answers on opposite sides must have a sum of 7.

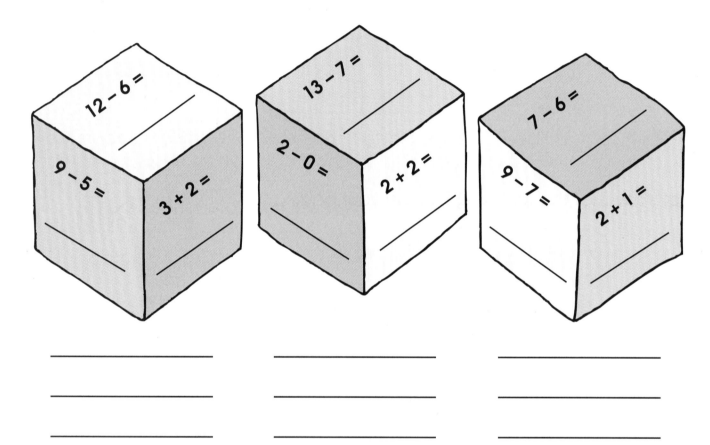

Cube 1: 12 – 6 = ___, 9 – 5 = ___, 3 + 2 = ___
Cube 2: 13 – 7 = ___, 2 – 0 = ___, 2 + 2 = ___
Cube 3: 7 – 6 = ___, 9 – 7 = ___, 2 + 1 = ___

_____ _____ _____

_____ _____ _____

_____ _____ _____

Now, answer these questions about the cubes.

What number is always on the opposite side of 6? _____

What number is always on the opposite side of 5? _____

What number is always on the opposite side of 4? _____

What is the sum of the all answers on a cube? _____

Name _____

A Bag of Sweets

The candy store is having a sale and you decide to stock up on your favorites.

Candy Sticks 2 for 10¢

Hard Candy 5 for 25¢

Rock Candy 10 for $1.00

Saltwater Taffy 5 for 50¢

Chocolate Bonbons 3 for 25¢

Let's say that the following is inside your bag.

- 10 candy sticks
- 15 pieces of hard candy
- 25 pieces of rock candy
- 20 pieces of salt water taffy
- 9 chocolate bonbons

▶ Answer these questions about your bag of candy.

How many pieces of candy are you buying? _____

What is the total cost of all the candy? _____

If you have a twenty, a ten and a five-dollar bill,

which would you use to pay for the candy? _____

How much change will you receive if you use this bill? _____

What candy could you buy with the left-over change?

_____   _____

Feeding Time

Ken and Angie enjoy watching the animals being fed at the zoo. However, when they arrive, they are a little confused by the signs.

▶ Help them figure out the feeding time for each kind of animal, and write it below the description. Be sure to include A.M. or P.M.

Seals: Feeding time is two hours after the monkeys.

_____ : _____

Tigers: Feeding time is two hours after 9:00 A.M.

_____ : _____

Lions: Feeding time is 1:00 P.M.

_____ : _____

Giraffes: Feeding time is one hour before the elephants.

_____ : _____

Monkeys: Feeding time is three hours before the giraffes.

_____ : _____

Elephants: Feeding time is three hours after the lions.

_____ : _____

▶ Now, trace the path in the zoo that Ken and Angie should take, so that they can see all the animals being fed.

Name _____

Fast Foods

Jamie noticed that some restaurants call their food "Fast Food." He decided to see which food is the fastest. He attached small paper plates onto three remote-controlled cars. He put one fast food on each plate. Car 1 is called "Hot Rod Dog." Car 2 is called "Cheeseburger Champion." Car 3 is called "French Fry Fury." Then, Jamie put them at the Starting Line of the track you see below.

▶ Carefully study the dark tracks and all the ways each car can go. Trace the shortest path for each car. Then, decide who the winner of the race is. Use the number of squares to help you.

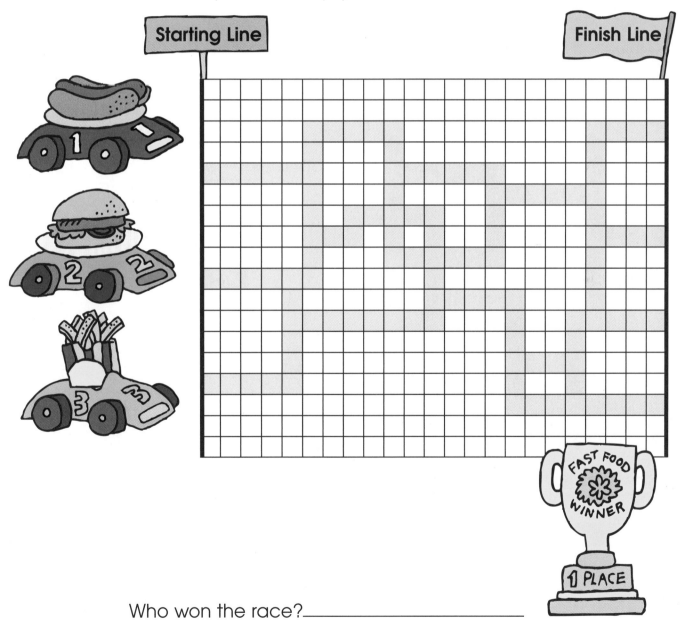

Who won the race?_____

Level 1, Math

Plainly a Plane

A **plane figure** is a shape on a flat surface. The most common plane figures are shown below:

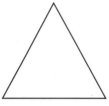

Triangle   **Circle**   **Square**   **Rectangle**

▶ Find and label any shapes in the pictures below which remind you of any of these plane figures. Some of the pictures might suggest more than one plane figure. Label them all.

1.

_____

2.

3.

_____

4.

_____

5.

_____

6.

_____

7.

_____

▶ Now, find a picture in a magazine or newspaper that suggests each of these plane figures. Either cut out and glue them or draw them on another sheet of paper. Label the plane figures.

Name _____

A Picture Diagram

In the diagrams on this page, the outside rectangle stands for a whole set of things. The inside circle or circles stand for part or parts of the whole set.

Example: This rectangle stands for all the dishes in your cupboard. Circle A stands for all the plates in the cupboard. Circle B stands for all the glasses there.

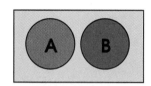

▶ Use this diagram to tell if these sentences are true or false. Write TRUE or FALSE on each line.

1. All the plates are in the cupboard. _____

2. Some of the glasses belong in the set of plates. _____

3. All of the things in the cupboard are plates. _____

4. None of the glasses are in the cupboard. _____

Now, look carefully at this diagram. The rectangle stands for all the children in your class. Circle C stands for all the boys in the class. Circle D stands for all the children in the class who are 10 years old or older.

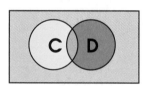

▶ Use this diagram to tell if these sentences are true or false. Write TRUE or FALSE on each line.

5. All of the boys are 10 years old or older. _____

6. All of the boys are in the class. _____

7. Some of those who are 10 years old or older are boys. _____

8. None of the boys are younger than 10 years. _____

9. None of the boys are 10 years old or older. _____

Gordon Gopher

Gordon Gopher wanted a new home. After many days of hard work, he finished a long tunnel. In the tunnel, he hid nuts for the long winter months ahead according to a particular pattern.

▶ Continue the pattern below by drawing the correct number of nuts at each spot marked with an **X**. Then, count the total number of nuts hidden by Gordon Gopher.

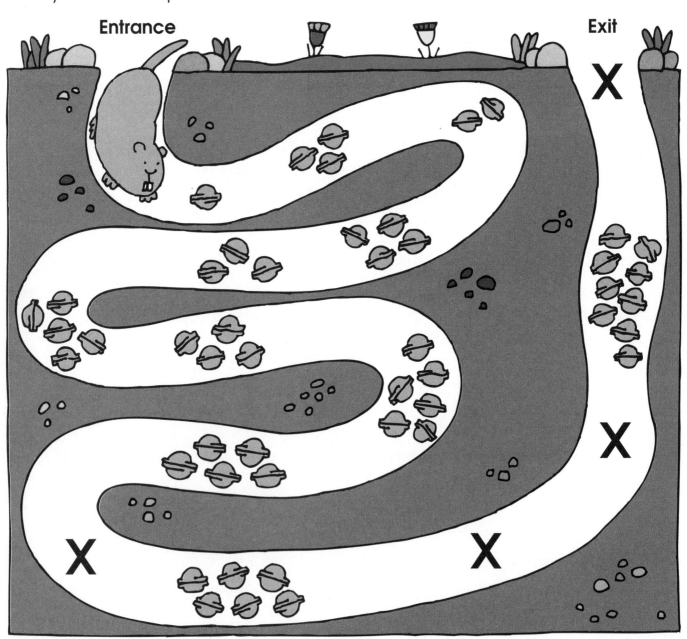

The total number of nuts is _____ .

Social Studies can be fun because this is where you can learn more about how other people live, even people who lived long ago. The more you know about other people and other countries, the better you will be able to live successfully in the place you call home.

Perhaps, as you complete pages in this section, you may find topics you wish to know more about. There are all kinds of sources like books, magazines, maps and even the Internet, that can help you satisfy your curiosity and lead you to great knowledge.

Name _____

The Adventure Begins

A good place to learn about the world around you is to visit a museum or other place where large collections have been gathered. Imagine that one rainy Saturday morning, you have the opportunity to do just that. Study these ads from the telephone book, and then decide where you will go.

Aquarium

Open weekdays from
10:00 A.M. to 6:00 P.M.
Closed weekends
Call 555-FISH

Museum of American History

Open Monday–Saturday
from 9:00 A.M. to 5:00 P.M.
Closed Sundays
Call 555-FLAG

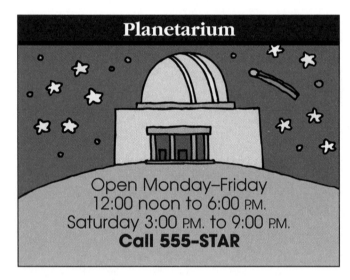

Planetarium

Open Monday–Friday
12:00 noon to 6:00 P.M.
Saturday 3:00 P.M. to 9:00 P.M.
Call 555-STAR

Zoo

Open daily from
9:00 A.M. to 5:00 P.M.
Weather permitting
Call 555-LION

▶ Complete these sentences.

I will probably choose to go to the _____

because _____

_____

Name _____

Home Sweet Home

If you visit a museum of American history, you may see exhibits about Native Americans and their historic homes like those pictured below.

▶ Use the rebuses to discover which nation of Native Americans lived in each kind of home. After you sound out your answer, find the correct spelling in the Word Bank, and use it to complete each sentence.

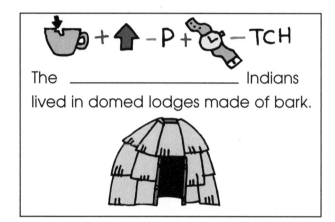

The _____ Indians lived in domed lodges made of bark.

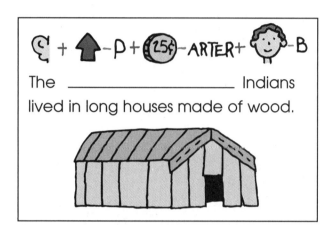

The _____ Indians lived in long houses made of wood.

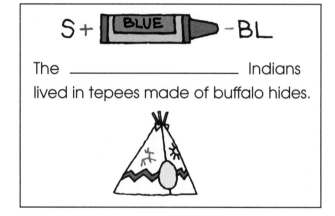

The _____ Indians lived in tepees made of buffalo hides.

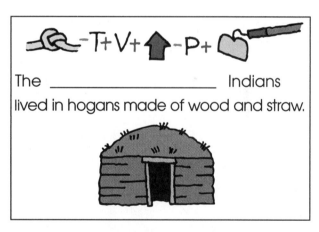

The _____ Indians lived in hogans made of wood and straw.

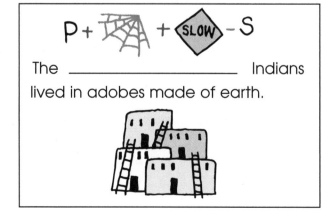

The _____ Indians lived in adobes made of earth.

Word Bank

Pueblo
Iroquois
Sioux
Navajo
Chippewa

Name _____

Dinner Time

Eskimos live in the cold lands of northern North America. In this region, people eat a lot of fish because fish are so plentiful. The children on this page caught many fish. Read the clues given by each Eskimo. On the line below each child, write the number of fish he or she caught.

Hint: When an Eskimo speaks of his or her right or left, it is his or her right or left, not yours. Put an L or R on their left and right arms to help you.

1. Circle the person who caught the most fish.

2. Put a check next to the two whose fish added together equal 21.

Name _____

A Family of Friends

The Native Americans lived in America long before anyone else. When the Pilgrims came from England in 1620, they landed in a place called Plymouth. They survived that first hard winter because the Native Americans helped them to hunt and grow and harvest food.

▶ Read each riddle. Use the Word Bank to write the name of a food that the Native Americans helped the Pilgrims find or grow.

1. Water doesn't stick—
   It rolls off my back;
   And when it does,
   I loudly say, "Quack, quack!"

   I am _____ .

2. I'm not inside a whale,
   But I'm found in a "wheel."
   You'll also find me
   In a piece of "steel."

   I am _____ .

3. When your roof "leaks,"
   You may want to cry.
   You'll do the same thing
   When I'm near your eye.

   I am _____ .

4. Boil me or pop me
   When I am ripe.
   Cook me in bread
   Or use my cob as a pipe.

   I am _____ .

5. I like to "honk,"
   And I can fly.
   Ask the lady who rode me,
   Reciting rhymes in the sky.

   I am _____ .

Word Bank

a goose   a leek
a duck   corn
an eel

Level 1, Social Studies

Then and Now

Many of the things which were commonly used in the past are no longer used by us today. We now have modern things that do the same jobs more easily.

▶ Unscramble the words in column two using the underlined letter as the first letter in each word. Then, write the number of this modern thing next to the object that was used for the same purpose in the past.

Past

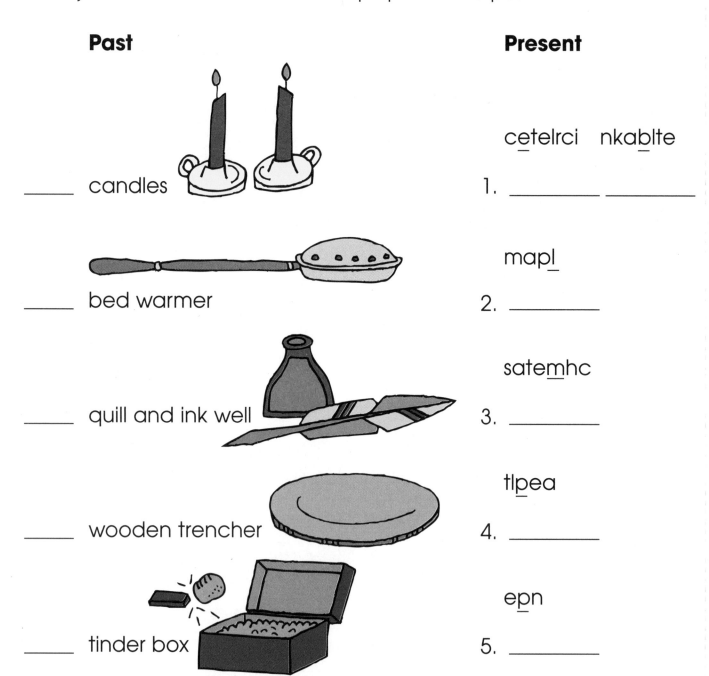

_____ candles

_____ bed warmer

_____ quill and ink well

_____ wooden trencher

_____ tinder box

Present

c<u>e</u>telrci   nkab<u>l</u>te

1. _____ _____

map<u>l</u>

2. _____

sate<u>m</u>hc

3. _____

tl<u>p</u>ea

4. _____

<u>e</u>pn

5. _____

Name _____

Sew What?

A favorite activity of colonial women and girls was getting together for a quilting bee. The quilts, made from scraps of linen, wool and cotton, were frequently sewn together in a pattern.

▶ Look carefully at the pattern in the unfinished quilt below. Then, continue the pattern by drawing pictures in the blank sections to complete the quilt.

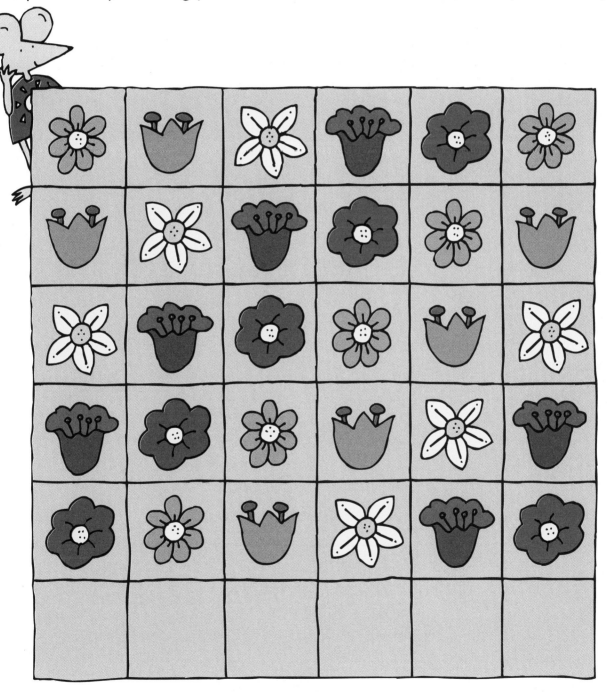

Level 1, Social Studies

Go West, Young Man!

In the first half of the nineteenth century, many pioneers moved westward across the United States. They traveled in big covered wagons called Conestoga wagons.

Some of the trails that the pioneers took in their Conestoga wagons are marked on the map below.

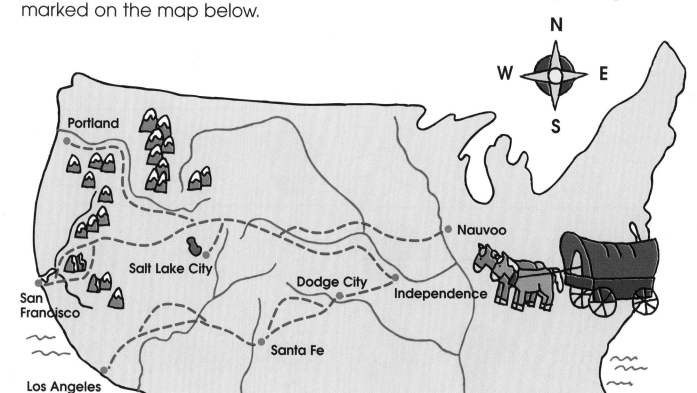

▶ Look closely at the trails. Then, answer these questions.

1. If the pioneers started at Nauvoo and traveled west,
   how many different trails could they take? _____

2. If the pioneers began at Independence and traveled west,
   how many different trails could they take? _____

Name _____

Signs of the Times

In Pennsylvania, there is an area called the Pennsylvania Dutch Country. Many of the people who live there try to live simple lives much like their ancestors did long ago. Some people still use a horse and buggy for transportation.

▶ Look carefully at the paths from the farmhouse to the barn. Count how many different ways a horse and buggy could travel.

They could travel _____ ways to get from the farmhouse to the barn.

Level 1, Social Studies

Name _____

What's Your Brand?

Cowboys were very important in the development of the American West. They went on long cattle drives that lasted two or three months at a time and covered hundreds of miles. Cowboys were often in danger from rattlesnakes, stampedes, wild horses and horse thieves.

During cattle roundups in the spring and fall, cowboys branded the newborn calves to show which ranch owned them.

▶ Look at the brands below. Use the Word Bank to help you write what each brand means.

_____

_____

_____

Word Bank

Twin Snakes
Double Z
Pair of Aces
Sunrise
Too Easy
Rocking Chair
Extra X
Big Deal
Sunset
Barbecue
Broken Wheel
Lazy S
Starlight
Tall Hat
Two Bees

_____

_____

Name _____

R-r-r-r-r-ing!

The Liberty Bell in Philadelphia, Pennsylvania, was rung to announce important events during the early days in America. Today, we often use a telephone to tell others about events in our lives. You can also use the numbers and letters on a telephone to write a secret message.

▶ Use the numbers to decode the sentence below. Remember, for each number you have a choice of three letters.

						B			T						
_	_	_		_	_	_	_	_	_	_		_	_	_	_
8	4	3		5	4	2	3	7	8	9		2	3	5	5

	T					S						E			O	
_	_	_	_	_	_		_	_	_		_	_	_	_	_	_
7	8	2	6	3	7		3	6	7		3	7	3	3	3	6	6

Use this code system to write a message of your own, and try it on a friend.

Name _____

It Was a Great Year

At the end of every year, we usually like to recall the major events that took place during the past twelve months. For example, at the end of 1888, Americans might have read articles about these events.

October 1888						
Sunday	Monday	Tuesday	Wednesday	Thursday	Friday	Saturday
	1	2	3	4	5	6
7	8	9 National Monument to George Washington opened	10	11	12	13
14 John Philip Sousa wrote the Marine Hymn	15	16	17	18 First school for agriculture set up in Minnesota	19	20 American baseball teams go on world tour
21	22	23 William S. Burroughs made the first successful adding machine	24	25 Double-decker ferryboat launched in New York	26	27
28	29	30 J.J. Loud develops ballpoint pen in Plymouth, Mass.	31			

▶ Write the date for each of these headlines. Then, write your own headline for two other events on the calendar.

"Piggyback Ride Across River" _____

"A Hit `Round The World" _____

"First President Honored" _____

"New Invention Makes Mark" _____

"Learning to Farm Is Fun" _____

_____ _____

Name _____

The United States is sometimes called a nation of immigrants because it has people from almost every country in the world.

▶ Print the letters of the alphabet in order in the boxes. Then, complete the name of each country using the suggestions listed in the Word Bank.

1. _ _ _ _ □ _ _ _
2. _ _ _ _ _ □ _ _ _
3. □ _ _ _ _ _
4. _ _ _ _ _ □ _
5. _ _ _ _ _ □ _
6. _ □ _ _ _ _ _ _ _
7. _ □ _ _ _ _ _ _
8. _ _ □ _ _ _ _ _
9. □ _ _ _ _
10. □ _ _ _
11. □ _ _ _ _
12. _ _ _ □ _
13. _ _ _ □ _ _
14. _ _ □ _ _ _
15. _ □ _ _ _ _
16. □ _ _ _ _ _
17. _ _ _ □ _ _ _ _ _ _
18. _ □ _ _ _ _ _ _ _ _ _
19. _ _ □ _ _ _ _
20. _ □ _ _ _ _
21. _ □ _ _ _ _ _ _ _ _
22. □ _ _ _ _ _
23. _ _ □ _ _ _ _ _ _
24. _ _ □ _ _ _ _ _ _
25. _ _ _ _ _ _
26. _ _ _ _ □ _ _

Word Bank

Afghanistan
Australia
Canada
China
Cuba
Egypt
France
Germany
Greece
India
Iraq
Ireland
Israel
Italy
Japan
Kenya
Korea
Mexico
Mozambique
Netherlands
Norway
Philippines
Poland
Puerto Rico
Venezuela
Vietnam

Where's Our Mummy?

▶ Many museums, like the Field Museum of Natural History in Chicago, have great exhibits of Egyptian mummies. Look carefully at the mummies pictured below. Think about word clues that could help someone identify each mummy. Then, write three words to describe or name something about each mummy that makes it different from the others.

_____ _____

_____ _____

_____ _____

Name _____

Getting Better With Age

Like many inventions, the automobile, bicycle, airplane and telephone are constantly being improved to make them more useful.

▶ Show that you know how these inventions have developed by numbering each set of three pictures in the correct order.

Automobile

Bicycle

Airplane

Telephone

Level 1, Social Studies

Name _____

Getting the Job Done

America is often called the "Land of Opportunity." This means that its people may choose from many types of work to make a living.

▶ From the Word Bank, write two different workers who have the following characteristics in common.

1. Place importance on books   _____ _____

2. Consider water an important tool _____ _____

3. Work with needle and thread   _____ _____

4. Work with food   _____ _____

5. Make sure people follow rules   _____ _____

6. Deliver mail and packages   _____ _____

7. Take care of medical needs   _____ _____

8. Work with animals   _____ _____

9. Use numbers quite often   _____ _____

10. Provide entertainment   _____ _____

Word Bank

mathematician	veterinarian	teacher	chef
actor	police officer	nurse	doctor
accountant	mail carrier	seamstress	gardener
musician	firefighter	librarian	tailor
delivery person	farmer	umpire	zookeeper

Science teaches you a lot about the things around you. Learning about animals, plants, weather and the Earth itself can be both interesting and helpful.

If you find any topics in this section that are particularly interesting to you, make note of them and find more material about them at the library.

Name _____

Inside Out

Animals whose skeletons have backbones or spines are called **vertebrates**.

▶ Look at each skeleton below. Read the riddle. Then, decide from the Word Bank which vertebrate is pictured. Write its name to complete the sentence.

1. 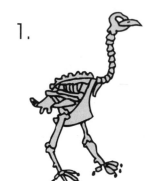 I am thankful to be alive at holidays. People might "gobble me up!"

I am a _____ .

2. 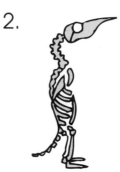 I have wings, but I cannot fly. I love to strut around in my "tuxedo."

I am a _____ .

3.  I am not a bird, but I can fly. I work at night and sleep all day.

I am a _____ .

4. 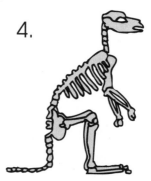 My legs and tail are very strong. I even come with a pocket.

I am a _____ .

5. 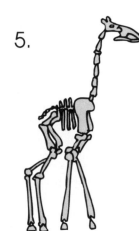 I stand tall and proud. So please don't ask me to eat from the ground.

I am a _____ .

6.  They say I have no hair, and they're right. I represent a great country.

I am a _____ .

Word Bank	
bald eagle	kangaroo
turkey	penguin
giraffe	bat

Name _____

Amazing Amphibians

Amphibians are cold-blooded vertebrates (animals with backbones). They have no scales on their skin. Most amphibians hatch from eggs laid in water or on damp ground. Many amphibians grow legs as they develop into adults. Some live on land and have both lungs and gills for breathing. Frogs and toads are examples of amphibians.

Santjie, a South African sharp-nosed frog, holds the record for the longest triple jump. It jumped a total of more than 33 feet!

▶ The frogs below won 1st, 2nd and 3rd place in a recent triple-jump contest. Each succeeding jump was 2 feet shorter than the jump before. How many total feet did each frog jump?

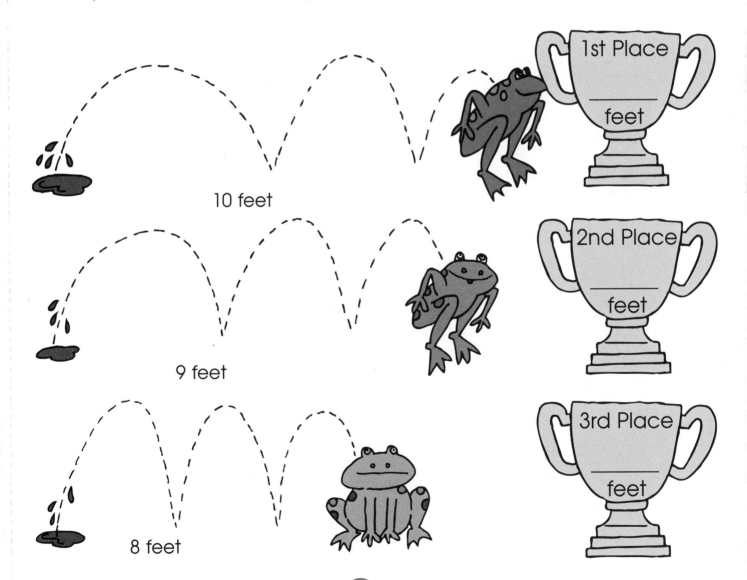

10 feet

9 feet

8 feet

1st Place

_____ feet

2nd Place

_____ feet

3rd Place

_____ feet

The Reptile House

There are about 6,000 different kinds of reptiles. They come in all sorts of shapes and colors. Their sizes in length range from 2 inches to almost 30 feet. Reptiles can be found on every continent except Antarctica. Even though reptiles can seem quite different, they all . . .

- breathe with lungs.
- are cold-blooded.
- have dry, scaly skin.
- have backbones.

▶ Look at the pictures of these five reptiles and read their descriptions. Then, use these clues to write the name of each reptile in its correct home.

Komodo Dragon

is a dragon-like reptile. It is the largest living lizard.

Reticulated Python

is the longest snake. One was almost 33 feet long.

Giant Tortoise

can live over 100 years. It can hide under its shell for protection.

Tuatara

is closely related to the extinct dinosaur.

Saltwater Crocodile

is one of the largest reptiles. It can weigh 1,000 pounds.

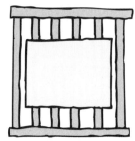  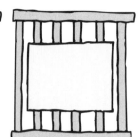  

Clues:
- The reptile which carries its "home" is in the middle.
- A relative of animals that are no longer on Earth is on the far-left side.
- The snake is between the largest lizard and a member of the turtle family.

Name _____

Invertebrates are animals that have no backbone or inside skeleton. Some have soft bodies protected by shells. Others have soft bodies that are not protected. Some invertebrates are so small that they can only be seen with a microscope.

▶ Below are the names of some invertebrates. Use the rebuses to help complete each one.

_____ i p e d e   s _____ f _____

e _____ w _____   j _____ f _____

s _____ d _____   s _____

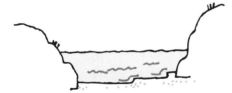

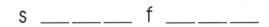

s _____ c _____

Dynamic Dinosaurs

Dinosaurs were reptiles that lived millions of years ago. Some of them were the biggest animals to ever live on land.

Scientists have given names to the dinosaurs that often describe their special bodies, sizes and habits.

▶ Match these dinosaurs with their names in the Word Bank. Use the objects pictured with the dinosaurs as clues to help you.

t r i c e r a __ __ __ __ __

__ __ __ __ __ e o s a u r u s

__ __ __ __ t r o d o n

__ __ __ __ __ a s a u r u s

__ __ __ __ __ o s a u r u s

Word Bank

Saltasaurus
Triceratops
Plateosaurus
Dimetrodon
Lambeosaurus

Name _____

The Mighty Bear

Bears are large and powerful animals. Depending on the type of bear, they can weigh from 60 to 2,000 pounds.

▶ Listed below are four different kinds of bears. The average heights of these bears are 3 feet, 5 feet, 8 feet and 9 feet in no particular order. Use the clues to match each bear to its average height. Write the answers in the blanks.

Clues: Combined, the average heights of the:

Alaskan brown bear and American black bear are 14 feet.

Polar bear and Alaskan brown bear are 17 feet.

American black bear and Sun bear are 8 feet.

The Alaskan brown bear averages _____ feet in height.

The American black bear averages _____ feet in height.

The Polar bear averages _____ feet in height.

The Sun bear averages _____ feet in height.

Butterflies and Moths

People sometimes confuse butterflies with moths, but there are some important differences.

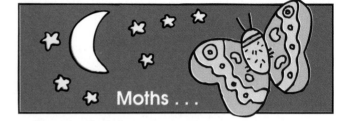

Butterflies . . .
- fly by day.
- have knobs on their antennae.
- have thin hairless bodies.
- rest with their wings held upright.

Moths . . .
- fly at night.
- have no knobs on their antennae.
- have plump, furry bodies.
- rest with their wings spread out flat.

▶ Name three characteristics that butterflies and moths have in common.

_____

_____

_____

▶ Now, name three characteristics in which butterflies and moths differ.

_____

_____

_____

▶ Use one or two words to answer these questions about butterflies and moths.

When would you probably find a butterfly? _____

Which has a longer body, a butterfly or a moth? _____

If a butterfly's wings are sticking straight up, what is it doing? _____

If there is fur on the body, is it a butterfly or a moth? _____

Name _____

The Chocolate Tree

Have you ever thought about chocolate growing on a tree? Actually, chocolate is made from the seeds of tropical trees called cacao trees. Most of these trees grow in the warm, wet climate of western Africa.

▶ Make a list of all the things which are made of chocolate that you could put in this basket. Then, draw some items from your list in the basket.

_____   _____

_____   _____

_____   _____

_____   _____

_____   _____

Level 1, Science

Name _____

Weather Watch

Weather is the condition of the air around the earth for a period of time. A weatherman's job is to predict the weather.

▶ There were some very unusual weather patterns recorded for a recent month. Use the key to draw the correct weather symbols for each day.

- Every Monday and Tuesday, it rained. Then, it was sunny for the following three days.
- On the first and third weekends, the first day was cloudy, and the second day was snowy.
- On the second and fourth weekends, it was just the opposite.

Key

 sunny

cloudy

rainy

snowy

Sun.	Mon.	Tues.	Wed.	Thurs.	Fri.	Sat.
		1	2	3	4	5
6	7	8	9	10	11	12
13	14	15	16	17	18	19
20	21	22	23	24	25	26
27	28	29	30	31		

▶ Write the word that tells about the weather on these dates:

- 6th day of the month _____

- 13th day of the month _____

- last day of the month _____

Travel Light

Earth's closest neighbor in space is the Moon. The Moon is very different from the Earth. It has no wind, no air and no water. The sky around the Moon always looks black, and stars can always be seen. Because there is a lot less gravity on the Moon, astronauts can jump much farther there than on Earth. There are large holes, called craters, on the Moon.

▶ If you were invited to spend a few days on the Moon, imagine what you would pack for the trip. Complete these lists with things that you would need and use during your time on the Moon, and write a few words to tell why you would need them.

Clothes	Reason
_____	_____
_____	_____
_____	_____

Tools	Reason
_____	_____
_____	_____

Other Things	Reason
_____	_____
_____	_____

Level 1, Science

Name _____

What's the Matter?

All things are made of matter. **Matter** takes up space. It can take three forms—solid, liquid or gas.

Solids have shape and volume. They do not change shape easily.

Liquids have volume, but they have no shape of their own. They take the shape of the container they are in.

Gases have no shape or volume. Most gases are invisible.

▶ Find and circle the words in each word search that are examples of that form of matter. Then, write the words on the lines.

SOLIDS

T A B L E
E R A T L
T O E I B
U P B E E
L E A F S

LIQUIDS

A P O P K
B C O L A
J U I C E
A M L I T
W A T E R

GASES

A B T O E P
C I G L T O
E B R A H D
O X Y G E N
W O T E R T
H E L I U M

_____

_____   _____

_____   _____

_____   _____

_____   _____

_____   _____   _____

_____   _____   _____

_____   _____   _____

Magnetic Attraction

The word "magnet" begins with the same three letters as the word "magic," and sometimes magnets do seem a little magical.

Every magnet has two poles—north and south. The north pole of one magnet attracts, or pulls toward, the south pole of another magnet. Two poles that are the same (two north poles or two south poles) do not attract each other. Instead, they repel, or push away from, each other.

▶ Using the information above, continue labeling the horseshoe and bar magnets below with N (for north) and S (for south).

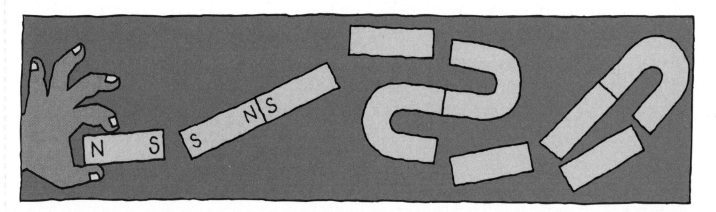

Level 1, Science

Name _____

Man's Best Friend

Dogs are often called "Man's Best Friend," and there are many good reasons for this. Dogs help with hunting and herding. They help guide visually–impaired people and also help the police do detective work. Most often, they are kept as pets and provide both friendship and protection to their owners.

There are over 130 breeds of dogs in the United States. According to one source, the following were the most popular breeds:

| Golden Retriever | Cocker Spaniel | Rottweiler | Poodle | Labrador Retriever |

▶ Use the clues below to discover the order of the dogs' popularity. Then, write each dog's name on the correct ribbon.

Clues: • This dog is the third most popular. His name sounds like something that forms during a rainstorm.

• This dog's name includes one of man's most precious metals. It ranks fourth.

• This dog has the most vowels of all the names. It ranks second.

• This dog doesn't consider it a rotten deal to be last.

• This dog ranks first. It is as proud as a peacock.

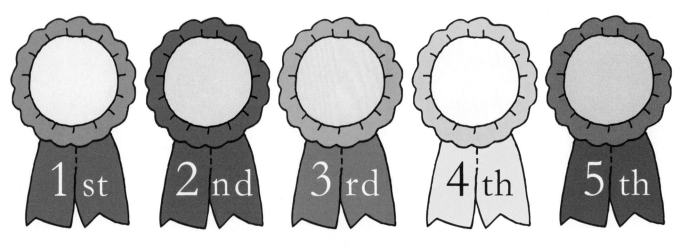

Name _____

Hot solids, liquids and gases sometimes erupt from the Earth in places called volcanoes.

▶ Use the clues below to locate six volcanoes in North America which erupted in the last century. Write the name of each volcano by the flag which indicates the year of its last eruption.

Clues: • El Chichón erupted a year before the volcano called Pavlof.
      • Colima is not in the United States.
      • Shishaldin last erupted 2 years before El Chichón did.
      • Iliamna last erupted 3 years before one of the volcanoes and 8 years before another.
      • Mount St. Helens erupted the same year as the one in Mexico.

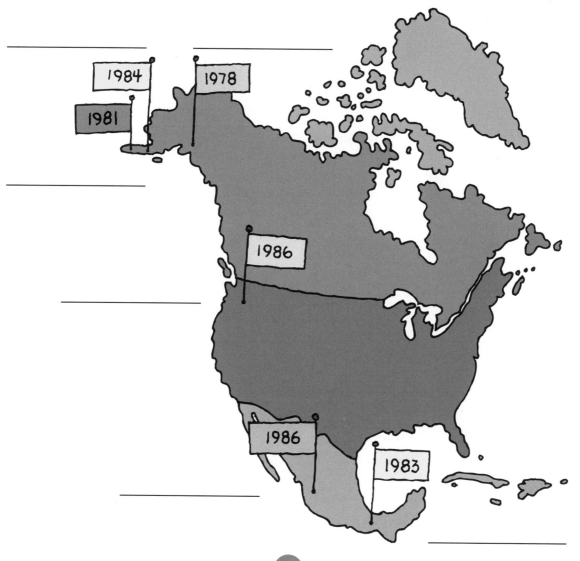

Name _____

Plant, Animal or Mineral?

▶ Things on the Earth can be sorted into three categories—plants, animals or minerals. Read the description of each of them and sort the things listed into their correct category. Then, list other things that belong in each category.

Plants: It includes all living things that can't move on their own, like trees, plants, vines, bushes and herbs.

Animals: It includes all living things that can move on their own, animals big or small, alive or dead, simple or complex.

Minerals: It includes all non-living things on the Earth that are neither plants nor animals.

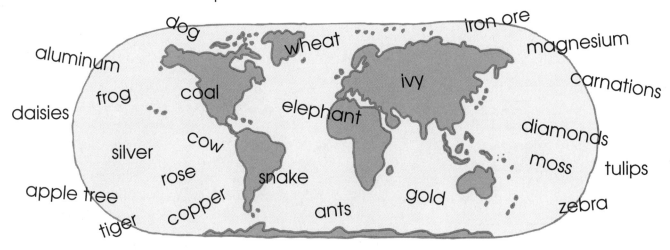

Plants	Animals	Minerals
_____	_____	_____
_____	_____	_____
_____	_____	_____
_____	_____	_____
_____	_____	_____
_____	_____	_____
_____	_____	_____
_____	_____	_____

Creative Arts

In this section, you will complete brainteasers about many different areas of life, such as art, music, poetry and theater. The idea is to see how other people use their own ideas to make things beautiful. Have fun discovering how they do it, but don't forget to use your own ideas as well.

Art That Moves

Below are examples of mobiles that could hang from the ceiling in your room. Something is missing from each mobile.

▶ Select things from the Picture Bank at the bottom of the page and draw them to finish each mobile.

Picture Bank

Name _____

A Funny Message

A **cartoon** is a drawing whose purpose is to make you laugh. This cartoon also has a message. There is a hidden letter in each picture below. Find each letter and write it on the line under the picture.

▶ When you have all the letters in place, you will know what the artist is trying to say.

_____ _____ _____ _____

_____ _____ _____ _____ _____

_____ _____ _____ _____ _____

Name _____

A Rainbow of Colors

The three primary colors are red, yellow and blue. If an artist mixes two of these colors together, the result will be a secondary color.

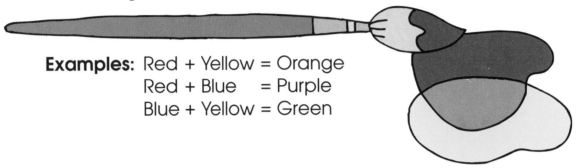

Examples: Red + Yellow = Orange
Red + Blue   = Purple
Blue + Yellow = Green

▶ See how the artist has mixed the paints on the palette pictured below. Label the new secondary colors that have been made. Then, use crayons to show how this happens.

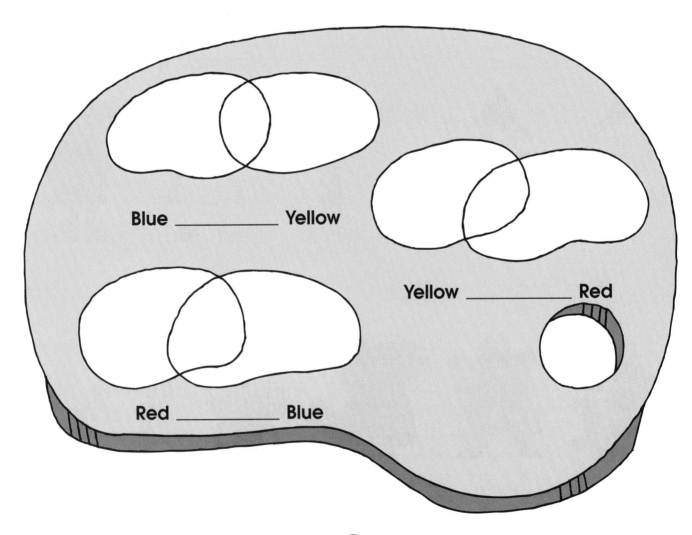

Blue _____ Yellow

Yellow _____ Red

Red _____ Blue

Name _____

Families of Instruments

There are five main groups of musical instruments.

- **Stringed instruments** make sounds when someone makes their strings vibrate.

- **Wind instruments** make sounds when someone blows into them.

- **Percussion instruments** make sounds when someone shakes them or hits them with a stick or mallet.

- **Keyboard instruments** make sounds when someone strikes their keys.

- **Electronic instruments** make sounds using electricity. However, someone still has to strike their keys or make their strings vibrate.

▶ Think about how musical sounds are made by the instruments shown in each of the grids below. Then, draw a straight line through three instruments in a row that belong to the same group.

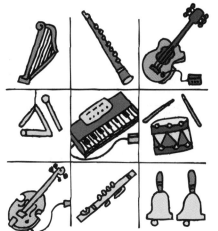

Instrument Chatter

▶ Use the Word Bank to help solve each riddle about musical instruments.

1. Grab the sticks
    And take a seat
   Hit my head
    You'll make a beat!

   I am a(n) _____ .

2. In my triangle-shaped body
    Many strings have I.
   The notes I play
    Are from low to high.

   I am a(n) _____ .

3. I'm the biggest horn
    With a deep, deep voice.
   You must be strong
    If I'm your choice.

   I am a(n) _____ .

4. High sounds you'll hear
    When you play me.
   A long tube with holes
    Is what you'll see.

   I am a(n) _____ .

5. Strum my strings
    And sing in a band.
   I play rock and roll
    In a way so grand!

   I am a(n) _____ .

6. You'll hear a clang
    When you hit my top.
   Once you shake me,
    It's hard to stop.

   I am a(n) _____ .

7. Different sizes
    Are my bars of wood.
   From low to high
    My tones sound good.

   I am a(n) _____ .

Word Bank

electric guitar

tuba

flute

xylophone

harp

drum

tambourine

Name _____

Keys to Spelling

A piano has 88 keys. Fifty-two keys are white, and 36 are black. Each white key has a letter name from A through G. This A–G pattern keeps repeating.

The picture below shows only part of a piano's keyboard. The white C key near the middle is for key number 40.

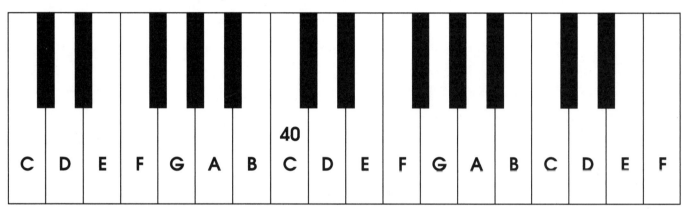

| C | D | E | F | G | A | B | C | D | E | F | G | A | B | C | D | E | F |

40

▶ Number the rest of the keys on the keyboard, but don't forget to count the black keys. Now, use these numbers to spell out some simple words. The last word includes some keys not shown on this part of the keyboard, but you can still find the letters if you use the A–G pattern.

39 49 47 __ __ __

40 37 51 __ __ __

39 49 54 __ __ __

51 44 54 __ __ __

45 49 52 56 __ __ __ __

30 44 37 57 __ __ __ __

Name _____

Let Us Entertain You!

Puppets are dolls. People use strings, wires, rods or their hands to make them move.

▶ Below are five animal hand-puppets. Match each puppet to its job description by writing the puppet's name on the line

| Millie
Monkey | Christy
Crocodile | Ollie
Octopus | Katie
Kangaroo | Danny
Dragon |

1. I am a mail carrier. It is easy for me to carry letters and packages in my own built-in mail pouch.
   My name is _____ .

2. I have one of the greatest jobs in the world. I taste-test candy while it is still hot so that only the best is sold in the stores.
   I am _____ .

3. I have a very important job. I am a firefighter. My climbing skills help me go quickly up a ladder.
   My name is _____ .

4. As a dentist I am proud of my set of perfect teeth.
   I am _____ .

5. I am a painter. I like to paint several pictures at a time. Watercolors are my favorite.
   They call me _____ .

Name _____

Playing the Part

You are starring in a play about nursery rhymes. The director has given you a list of props, one for each nursery rhyme.

▶ Match each prop to the correct nursery rhyme title by writing its number in the star.

An Old Woman

Three Little Kittens

Humpty Dumpty

Hey Diddle Diddle

Mary, Mary, Quite Contrary

Jack Be Nimble

Little Boy Blue

Peter, Peter, Pumpkin-Eater

Jack and Jill

Mary Had a Little Lamb

Old King Cole

Old Mother Hubbard

Props:
1. bone
2. candlestick
3. fiddle
4. flowers
5. horn
6. lamb
7. mittens
8. pail
9. pipe
10. pumpkin
11. shoe
12. wall

▶ Select your favorite nursery rhyme, and write its name here along with a prop that might help you play the part.

_____

Name _____

Dressing the Part

People who act in plays are called actors. For each play, costumes and masks are chosen that make the characters in the story seem more realistic.

Below is the inside of a costume closet.

Dragon   Mouse   Cowboy   Firefighter   Lion   Princess   Ghost   Gorilla   Dog   Football Player

▶ You want to act in some silly plays. Look at the titles of each play below. Write the names of the costume and mask you would combine to fit the main character of each play.

1. "The Protected Ape" _____ _____

2. "The Invisible Man on His Horse" _____ _____

3. "The Cat Who Squeaked" _____ _____

4. "Her Royal Highness Barks up the Wrong Tree"

_____ _____

5. "The Fire Eater Puts Out the Fire" _____ _____

Name _____

A Sweet Dream

The *Nutcracker* is a popular ballet. It is the story of a little girl named Clara who is given a wooden nutcracker for Christmas. The nutcracker looks like a soldier. While everyone is sleeping, it comes to life. It takes Clara to many wonderful places. One special place they go is called the "Kingdom of Sweets."

▶ Choose from the Word Bank names of treats that Clara might enjoy in the "Kingdom of Sweets," and write them on the sign in front of the kingdom. Cross out the six foods listed in the Word Bank that she probably wouldn't find in the kingdom.

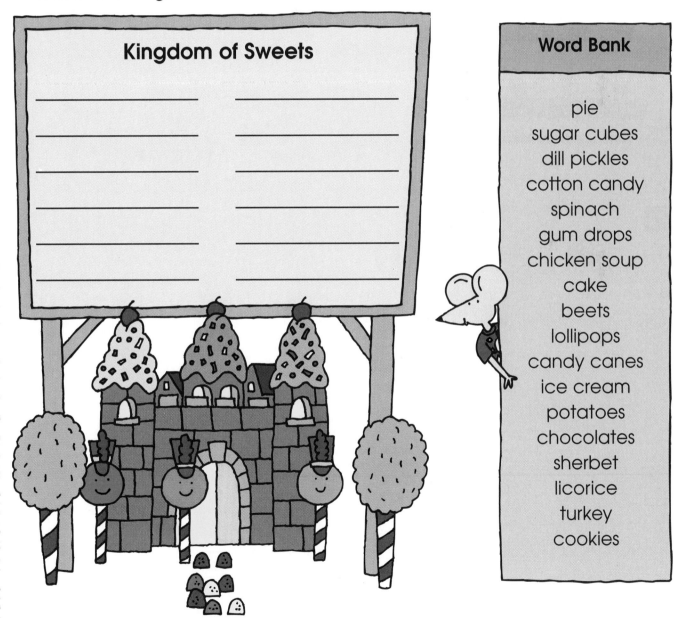

Kingdom of Sweets

_____ _____
_____ _____
_____ _____
_____ _____
_____ _____

Word Bank

pie
sugar cubes
dill pickles
cotton candy
spinach
gum drops
chicken soup
cake
beets
lollipops
candy canes
ice cream
potatoes
chocolates
sherbet
licorice
turkey
cookies

Classy Clay

A potter is an artist who makes plates, vases, jars, bowls and even cooking utensils as works of art.

▶ Carefully examine the pattern blocks on each of these two pieces of pottery. Then, decide which of the blocks continues the pattern. Draw that pattern in the empty box.

 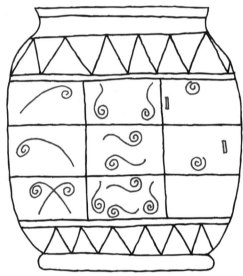

▶ Now, draw your own pattern in the blocks of this piece of pottery. Make it different from the patterns used above.

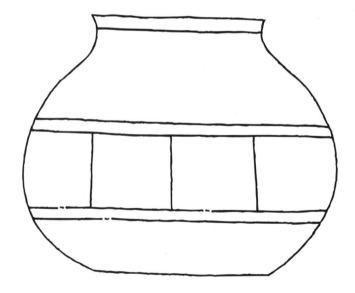

Name _____

A Rhyme at a Time

Some poetry rhymes. Each set of two lines ends with words that rhyme.

Example: Goodness, I would like to be
Nobody else, but just me.

▶ Finish each of these short poems by selecting and writing a word from the Word Bank that makes sense and also continues the rhyme.

1. I can't decide what to say,

   And yet I talk all the _____ .

2. One, two, three, four,

   Please, may I have some _____ ?

3. I can't swim outside in the winter;

   I can't go sledding in spring;

   But when autumn comes in September,

   I can hear the school bells _____ .

Word Bank

tee	see
kite	sing
more	day
best	fun
tore	may
nest	ring
me	we
son	run

4. The wind is blowing through the tree,

   Waving its branches for all to _____ .

   The leaves are dragging one by one

   Playing in them in fall can be _____ .

▶ Now, try to create your own 2- or 4-line rhyme.

_____

_____

_____

_____

What Level 2
Is All About

Some people might say that the brainteasers in Level 2 should be used by girls and boys around nine or ten years old. That doesn't mean that the brainteasers cannot also be solved and enjoyed by those younger and those older. Try them one at a time. Before you know it, you will become an expert at solving brainteasers.

Language is made up of sounds, words, spellings and meanings. In the brainteasers in this section, you can have fun using what you already know about language and learn even more.

Don't be afraid to try your own hand at creating brainteasers. You can make puzzles and riddles like those you find in this book or create some of your own. Then, you can share these with other people who like to act like brainteaser detectives.

Presto Chango!

Marvo the Magician likes to do word tricks. He takes two word cards and drops them into his magic hat. When he pulls the cards out, a letter from one word has traded places with a letter from the other word and two new words appear.

▶ Become as clever as Marvo! Exchange one letter from each pair of words to make two new words. **Example:** l**o**st — **p**ace becomes **p**ost — l**a**ce. **Hint:** the letter will not always be the first letter of each word.

1. hat — point _____ — _____

2. meat — nail _____ — _____

3. brain — get _____ — _____

4. like — bat _____ — _____

5. dear — way _____ — _____

6. reach — pail _____ — _____

7. tray — rage _____ — _____

8. brown — cat _____ — _____

9. cake — book _____ — _____

10. robe — dear _____ — _____

11. hide — creep _____ — _____

12. lamb — cop _____ — _____

13. fin — master _____ — _____

14. letter — gab _____ — _____

Name _____

Fascination With Nations

When most people think of "nations," they probably think of countries like Canada, the United States and Mexico. However, on this page you are asked to name another kind of "nation."

▶ Use the clues to help select the correct "nations" from the Word Bank and write them on the lines.

Nation that uses creativity

_____

Nation that rids itself of pesky critters

_____

Nation that gives reasons

_____

Nation that tries very hard

_____

Nation that's very bright

_____

Nation that gives tests

_____

Nation that pretends to be somebody else

_____

Nation that ends

_____

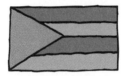

Nation that's going places

_____

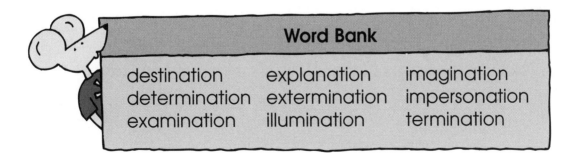

Word Bank

destination	explanation	imagination
determination	extermination	impersonation
examination	illumination	termination

▶ **Challenge!** On another sheet of paper, see how many other "nations" you can add to this list.

Name _____

Word Building

A **compound word** is made up of two or more small words. Together, these small words make a new word with its own meaning.

▶ Some of the words in the figure below can be combined with other words next to them to form compound words. There are 18 possible combinations. Can you find and write them all?

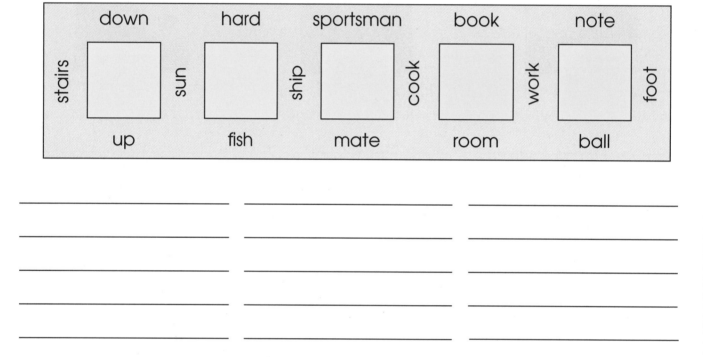

_____ _____ _____

_____ _____ _____

_____ _____ _____

_____ _____ _____

_____ _____ _____

▶ Some of the words in each circle below can be combined with those in a circle next to it to form compound words. There are at least 10 possibilities.

_____ _____

_____ _____

_____ _____

_____ _____

_____ _____

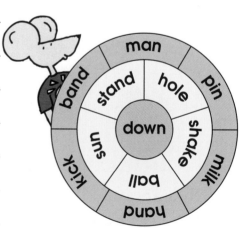

Name _____

An Amazon Adventure

▶ Trace a path through this Amazon jungle by stepping from one stone to another so that each two words make a compound word.

Example: base → ball
↓
room → mate

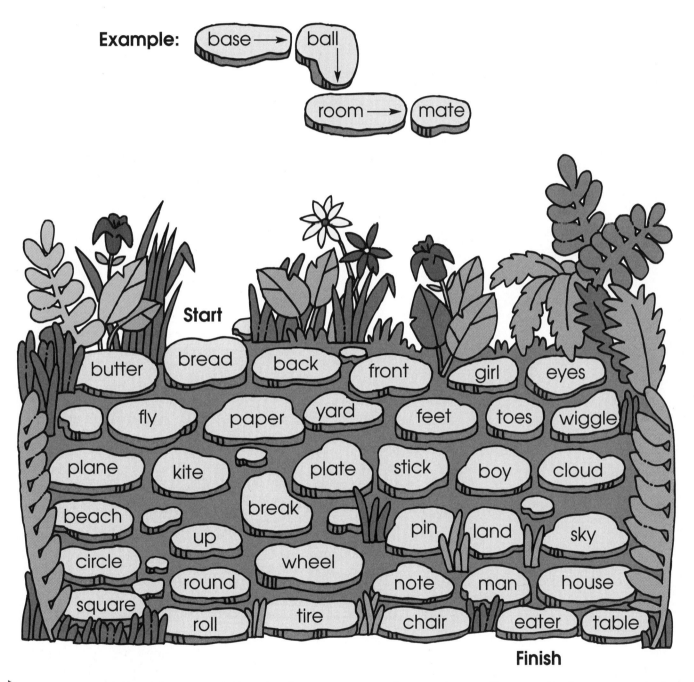

Start

butter   bread   back   front   girl   eyes

fly   paper   yard   feet   toes   wiggle

plane   kite   plate   stick   boy   cloud

beach   break   pin   land   sky

up

circle   wheel   note   man   house

round

square   tire   chair   eater   table

roll

Finish

▶ Now, use the first and the last compound words on the path to complete this sentence.

Maybe the _____ you saw was a _____!

Name _____

Wheel of Nouns

▶ Try your hand at creating "Wheels of Nouns." Here are the rules.

1. Begin with the first word in each circle.

2. Continue clockwise around each circle by adding a word that is spelled like the previous word except for one letter.

3. Make sure that the last word you choose can again turn into the first word with a one-letter change.

The first wheel has picture clues to help you. The other wheels contain no clues. Remember, all the words must be nouns.

Name _____

Quick and EZ

I was so tired last night I took some shortcuts with my homework. Today, I have to do it all over again the right way.

▶ Can you help me rewrite each sentence as it should be?

1. The homework assignment was EZ for a Y's person.

   _____

2. Although KT, LN and LC XL in 10S, they were B10 in the final round.

   _____

3. The BD eyes of the blue J stared at the MT nest.

   _____

4. The DK in the K9's teeth was XSive.

   _____

5. Did NE1 T's the new boy in R classroom?

   _____

6. His XLNC, the king, did not XQ's the conduct of his NME.

   _____

7. 4T pounds of honE had the B's in XTC.

   _____

8. Y do U NV the NRG of an electric EL?

   _____

9. The AV8R flew the jet in XS of 4T5 hundred mph.

   _____

10. I threw salt on the IC sidewalk.

   _____

Level 2, Language Arts

Name _____

Using a Magnifying Glass

Palindromes are words that are spelled exactly the same, forward and backward, like "mom" and "dad."

▶ Read this story. The clues will suggest palindromes that can be found in the story. Circle each palindrome in the story. Then, write it on the line next to the clue. The first one has been done for you.

Captain's Diary—Day 83

After the meteor shower, our spaceship Adventurer was badly damaged. Many of the ship's functions began to slow down or stop. Operations were definitely limited. Our ship continued to hurtle through space.

One of my crew, Jim, knew everything about our spacecraft, or so he thought. Other ships had shut down under such conditions. "Is it already too late for repairs?" he wondered.

"Emma, damage this severe can cause the entire ship to explode!" Ed exclaimed.

While Jim worked to repair the engines below, the cabin seemed extra dark. My crew stood motionless above. Would Jim fail? No—only if he didn't remain calm.

"Use established escape procedures if necessary!" I ordered.

As the crew prepared to exit the ship, they suddenly felt the turbulence stop. A sense of calm returned. The spaceship was repaired in record time.

"I hope episodes like this never occur again!" stated Emma.

As we continued our journey to other planets of destination, a question arose in many of our minds, "Are ferocious beasts awaiting us?"

---

1. soda **p o p**

2. female sheep ___ ___ ___

3. small child ___ ___ ___

4. short for sister ___ ___ ___

5. document showing property ___ ___ ___ ___

6. a method of tracking airplanes ___ ___ ___ ___ ___

7. middle of the day ___ ___ ___ ___

8. homophone of seas ___ ___ ___ ___

9. chick's sound ___ ___ ___ ___

10. to direct to a source for information ___ ___ ___ ___ ___

Not What It Seems

The most important thing to a person in a desert is water. Travelers tell stories of how they have seen ponds of beautiful clear water only to find, upon getting closer, that what they saw was a mirage. A **mirage** is an optical illusion caused by the bending of the sun's rays as they pass through different temperatures in the air.

▶ Imagine that the sun has distorted these words, making anagrams, words formed by reordering the letters of other words. Reorder the letters of each word below and write a new word. The first has been done for you.

1. heart — **earth**

2. rail — _____

3. lemon — _____

4. sleet — _____

5. wasp — _____

6. star — _____

7. snap — _____

8. canoe — _____

9. shoe — _____

10. parsley — _____

11. steak — _____

12. stream — _____

13. gear — _____

14. spine — _____

Level 2, Language Arts

Making Comparisons

▶ An **analogy** is a sentence in which two sets of things are compared. The relationship of the first thing to the second is the same as the relationship of the third thing to the fourth. To solve an analogy, study how the first two parts are related. Then, write a word for the missing part so that the second set is related in the same way. The first one has been done for you.

1. **Any** is to **anyone** as _____ what _____ is to **whatever**.

2. **Come** is to **came** as **do** is to _____ .

3. **Her** is to **she** as **their** is to _____ .

4. **Sang** is to **sing** as **got** is to _____ .

5. **T** is to **then** as **W** is to _____ .

6. **N** is to **M** as **B** is to _____ .

7. **Adult** is to **coffee** as **baby** is to _____ .

8. **Convertible** is to **car** as **pickup** is to _____ .

9. **Bad** is to **fad** as **bell** is to _____ .

10. **In front of** is to **behind** as **out of** is to _____ .

11. **Skin** is to **ski** as **they** is to_____ .

12. **Stream** is to **river** as **pond** is to _____ .

13. **Drop** is to **crop** as **dream** is to _____ .

14. **In** is to **if** as **on** is to _____ .

15. **Scientist** is to **robot** as **Dr. Frankenstein** is to _____ .

16. **Greed** is to **seed** as **group** is to _____ .

▶ **Challenge!** Write the words from the blanks in order to find a riddle about the Loch Ness Monster.

_____ _____ _____ _____ _____ _____

_____ _____ _____ _____ _____ _____?

_____ _____ _____ _____!

Name _____

▶ **Antonyms** are words that are directly opposite in meaning. Choose from the pot the antonym of each of the words listed below. Then, write it on the line.

false _____

joined _____

light _____

frown _____

fact _____

give _____

weak _____

easy _____

open _____

empty _____

poor _____

cool _____

sorrow _____

gone _____

frequently _____

full   closed   rich   happiness   take   warm   seldom   strong   opinion   heavy   here   true   difficult   smile   apart

▶ **Challenge!** Think of several more pairs of antonyms that are not listed here and write them below.

_____   _____

_____   _____

_____   _____

_____   _____

Name _____

The Case of the Missing Capitals

Captain Smith got this note in the mail. He noticed that the writer used no capital letters.

▶ Help Captain Smith interpret the letter by circling the words that need to start with a capital letter. Then, write each word correctly on the lines below. Try to find all twenty-six words.

dear captain smith,

i am writing this note in a special way so that you will not recognize who i am. i was present on the corner of main and elm street on september 15, when doctor john b. jones was robbed of his wallet. other people who saw the robbery were wanda wendle and her husband ben. they work for the zane bakery nearby. the wendles will be happy to give you a description of the robber, but i think you will still have trouble finding him.

sincerely,
the robber

_____ _____ _____ _____

_____ _____ _____ _____

_____ _____ _____ _____

_____ _____ _____ _____

_____ _____ _____ _____

_____ _____

Name _____

In Other Words

An **idiom** is a way of expressing an idea with a group of words. Usually the words themselves in an idiom have different meanings, but when they are put together, their meaning becomes something else.

For example, "It's raining cats and dogs!" is an idiom. You know what rain is. You also know what cats and dogs are, but put together in an idiom, the words become a way of saying that it is raining hard. It has nothing to do with actual cats and dogs.

▶ Match the idioms below with their meanings by writing the letter of the meaning next to the idiom.

1. Too many cooks spoil the broth. _____
2. I have big shoes to fill. _____
3. I'm knee-deep in work. _____
4. The mice do play when the cat's away. _____
5. She's a bookworm. _____
6. You're up to bat. _____
7. He was as quiet as a church mouse. _____
8. It's an oven in here. _____
9. Mind your own P's and Q's. _____
10. He is a bear before breakfast. _____

A. It's your turn.
B. He has a hard time waking up.
C. She likes to read a lot.
D. The person before me did a very good job.
E. It is hot.
F. Be careful.
G. I am very busy working.
H. He was very still.
I. It's too crowded in here.
J. We sometimes act differently when we are watched.

I Smell an Onion!

Once there was a king who loved to eat! In fact, he ate anything that was edible—anything, that is, except onions. He absolutely hated onions!

One day, he sat down at his table to eat his lunch—a large red apple, a batch of golden French fries and a burger with the works (except onions, of course). He took a large bite from the apple and then nibbled on a few fries. Finally, he lifted the burger, bit down and screamed, "Who put onions on my burger?"

Immediately, he called for the three royal cooks, Silly Nilly, Dipsey Doodle and Noodle Head. The cooks knew that trouble lay ahead. When they entered the royal dining room, each cook had a sign hanging around his neck.

Silly Nilly
"Dipsey Doodle did not put onions on the king's burger."

Noodle Head
"I put the onions on the king's burger."

Dipsey Doodle
"I put onions on the king's burger."

▶ The cooks admitted that two signs were true and one sign was false. They hoped to confuse the king.

Look at the information and decide who put the onions on the king's burger.

The guilty cook was _____ .

The brainteasers you will solve in this section deal with only a few of the many mathematical situations that are all around you.

Get ready to strengthen your mental math muscles, but at the same time, have lots of fun.

Name _____

Video Venture

Vincent likes to play games at the Video Adventure Arcade.

▶ Use the following information to help write all the answers. The scores on each video game increase by 100 on each successful try. Whenever the score reaches 1,000, the price of a game is refunded.

1. If Vincent played each game once and it cost him $1.80, on which

   game did he score 1,000 points? _____

2. Another time Vincent played each game twice. He scored 1,000 points

   only once, and the games cost him $3.15. Which game was free?

   _____

3. On another day Vincent played each game once.
   - His highest score was 1,000.
   - His lowest score was 100.
   - His Roll-A-Coconut score was 2 times his Monster Mania score.
   - His Amazon Adventure score was 2 times his Roll-A-Coconut score.
   - His Roller Skate Rock & Roll score was 3 times his Monster Mania score.
   - His Space Hockey score was 100 points more than 3 times his Roller Skate Rock & Roll score.

▶ Write his scores for each game and the amount of money he spent on the games on this day.

Amazon Adventure = _____ points   Monster Mania   = _____ points

Space Hockey   = _____ points   Roller Skate Rock & Roll = _____ points

Roll-a-Coconut   = _____ points   Cost of the games   = _____

Set Your Watches

Dawn and Meagan were at the entrance of the amusement park with their parents. The girls wanted to go on some rides by themselves. Dad said the present time was 11:30 A.M., and they were to meet back at the entrance by 1:00 P.M.

▶ List four different combinations of rides the girls could go on and still be back between 12:45 and 1:00 P.M. Allow a 5-minute walk between each ride and from the entrance to a ride.

The girls could ride on _____

_____and return at _____.

The girls could ride on _____

_____and return at _____.

The girls could ride on _____

_____and return at _____.

The girls could ride on _____

_____and return at _____.

Level 2, Math

Telephone Time

Tatiana, Michele and Rita loved to talk on the telephone. They would talk for hours at a time! Finally, their parents decided to limit the amount of time that they could use the phone.

Michele's parents limited her telephone conversations to Tuesdays and Thursdays from 7:00 P.M. to 8:00 P.M. and Saturdays from 1:00 P.M. to 2:00 P.M.

Tatiana could talk on the phone only on weekends from 12:00 P.M. to 3:00 P.M.

Rita was allowed to use the phone only on weekdays from 6:00 P.M. to 8:00 P.M. and on Sundays from 2:00 P.M. to 3:00 P.M.

▶ If all the girls followed the telephone rules set by their parents, list the times they could speak to each other on the phone.

Tatiana and Michele could talk on _____ from _____ to _____ .

Rita and Tatiana could talk on _____ from _____ to _____ .

Michele and Rita could call each other on _____ from _____ to

_____ and on _____ from _____ to _____ .

Name _____

Hard Work Pays Off

The little ant wanted to help the other ants make tunnels in the sand. A big ant came by and laughed, "You're too little to dig a tunnel!" The little ant did not listen. She started digging, lifting out one grain of sand each minute.

The big ant was strong, but lazy. He could lift two grains of sand at the same time, but he took 5 minutes to do this.

▶ Determine how many grains of sand each ant had removed after one hour. Finish drawing each ant hill below with the correct number of grains of sand, and complete the sentences below.

Little Ant's Hill   **Big Ant's Hill**

The _____ made the larger hill. It contained _____ more grains of sand than the smaller hill.

Age-Old Questions

The Taylor family went to a carnival. A man in a straw hat yelled out, "I bet I can tell you the correct ages of all five of your children!"

Mr. Taylor thought for a moment and decided to accept the man's challenge. He knew that the children's sizes were deceiving and felt this would help stump the challenger.

The man's five guesses were all incorrect. "What are their actual ages?" he inquired.

"If you can solve this puzzle, you will know their ages," Mr. Taylor answered.

1. Each was born one year apart. One is 6 years old. The product of their ages is 6,720. The ages are _____, _____, _____, _____ and _____.

2. Match each child with his/her correct age by closely examining each name and using these clues:

   • Every letter in their names represents a different number from 0 to 9.

   • Find the value of each letter by using the following information.

a = 3	t – o = a	v + r = 9
a + e = a	m + h = a	r > v
a + a = o	m < h	s = odd number

   a = _____   h = _____   m = _____   r = _____   t = _____

   e = _____   i = _____   o = _____   s = _____   v = _____

   • Now, exchange the letters in each child's name for numbers. Add the numbers. Write the sums before the names. The largest sum is the oldest child, the second largest sum is the second oldest child, and so on. Combine this knowledge with the ages you found above. Now, you know each child's age and name!

Sum: __ Thomas is _____ years old. __ Trevor is _____ years old.

__ Travis is _____ years old. __ Theresa is _____ years old.

__ Tamara is _____ years old.

Spinning a Web

▶ The spider has woven its web according to number patterns. Can you discover them? Fill in the missing numbers. Then, explain the pattern on the lines below.

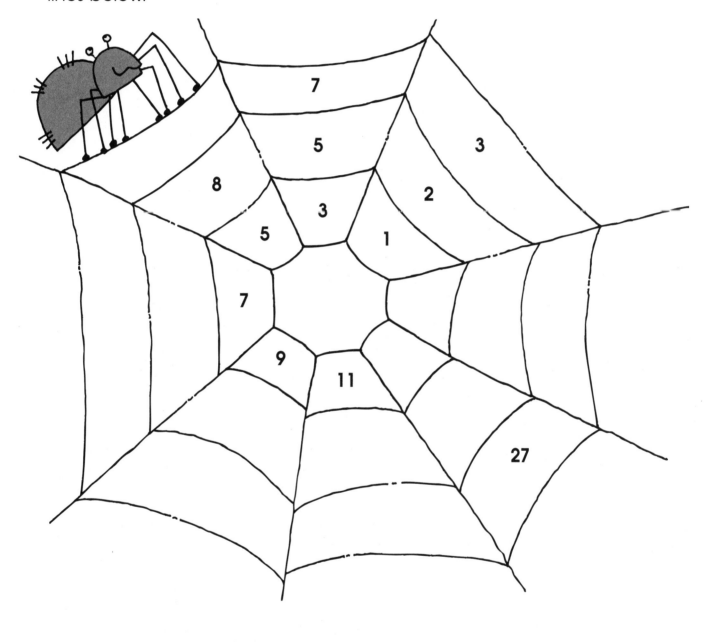

_____

_____

_____

Level 2, Math

It All Adds Up

Think carefully before you answer Mrs. Integer's question about these stacks of cubes. Remember that the sum of opposite sides of any cube always equals 7.

"What is the sum of all the sides you CAN'T see?"

The total number of dots that you cannot see is _____.

Name _____

▶ This is a magic square. If you add the numbers in every direction, including diagonally, the sums will be the same.

In this magic square the sum is always _____ .

▶ Now, fill in each of these boxes with the numbers 1 through 9 to make the numbers in each direction add up to a sum of 25. All the digits should be used, but some of them can be used more than once. There are at least three different ways to solve the problem. Can you find them?

Level 2, Math

Dessert Included

Brenda and Doug really like chocolate—chocolate-covered raisins, chocolate candy, chocolate cake and hot chocolate! Most of all, they are very fond of chocolate sundaes with chocolate chip ice cream. When they find out that the Eats and Sweets Restaurant is offering a free chocolate dessert with any meal costing exactly $5.00, they decide to go there for dinner.

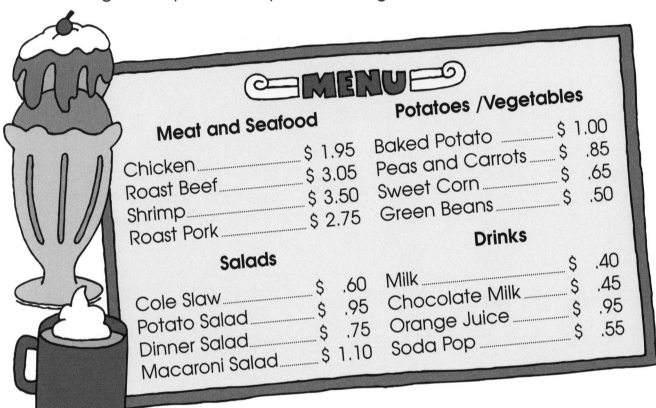

MENU

Meat and Seafood

Chicken .... $ 1.95
Roast Beef .... $ 3.05
Shrimp .... $ 3.50
Roast Pork .... $ 2.75

Salads

Cole Slaw .... $ .60
Potato Salad .... $ .95
Dinner Salad .... $ .75
Macaroni Salad ...... $ 1.10

Potatoes /Vegetables

Baked Potato .... $ 1.00
Peas and Carrots .... $ .85
Sweet Corn .... $ .65
Green Beans .... $ .50

Drinks

Milk .... $ .40
Chocolate Milk .... $ .45
Orange Juice .... $ .95
Soda Pop .... $ .55

▶ Choosing one item from each of the four categories on the menu, list four different meals they could eat for exactly $5.00, and then receive the free dessert. **Hint:** Use each item only once.

Meal # 1 _____ , _____ , _____ , _____

Meal # 2 _____ , _____ , _____ , _____

Meal # 3 _____ , _____ , _____ , _____

Meal # 4 _____ , _____ , _____ , _____

Name _____

Piggy-Bank Countdown

Tomorrow is Mitzi's mom's birthday, so Mitzi empties her piggy bank and finds that she has just enough to buy a special locket that costs $7.43.

She has one 5-dollar bill, one 1-dollar bill and 15 coins. There is at least one quarter, one dime, one nickel and one penny.

▶ There are at least two combinations of coins that Mitzi might have. Use these charts to show them.

1.
	Quarter(s)	Dime(s)	Nickel(s)	Penny(ies)	Total
Number of coins					
Amount					

2.
	Quarter(s)	Dime(s)	Nickel(s)	Penny(ies)	Total
Number of coins					
Amount					

Level 2, Math

Big Discount

The Terrific Toy Company is celebrating its 50th anniversary. All of the toys are discounted.

Original Cost of Toy	Discount
$ 3.00 – $ 5.00	$1.00
$ 6.00 – $10.00	$2.00
$11.00 – $15.00	$3.00
$16.00 – $20.00	$4.00
$21.00 – $25.00	$5.00

As a special bonus, if your bill **after** the discount is exactly $50.00, you also get a free movie video called "Toyland."

Look carefully at the toys and their original prices listed below.

Puzzle — $3.00

Action Figure — $6.00

Board Game — $8.00

Basketball — $10.00

Football — $12.00

Talking Doll — $15.00

Deluxe Blocks — $20.00

Teddy Bear — $22.00

Video Game — $24.00

Remote-Controlled Car — $25.00

▶ Use the discounts to help you decide which four toys you might buy in order to also get the free video. Remember, the discount is the part of the cost that you don't have to pay. Look for two different solutions. Do not choose any toy more than once in a solution.

Solution 1: _____

Solution 2: _____

Name _____

"Cow"nting a New Way

Three children were trying to impress one another with their knowledge of numbers.

"I can count to ten," said Megan. "One, two, three . . ."

"That's really good, Megan, but I can count to one hundred," added Tamara, and she proceeded to count to one hundred.

"Big deal," shrugged Matt. "I can "cow"nt to one hundred by using only 7 of the numbers from 1 to 10."

All of Matt's friends looked puzzled because they didn't understand what he meant.

Here are the numbers Matt used:

2   4   6   7   8   9   10

▶ Use the mathematical signs (**+, −, x, ÷**) on the cow between the numbers and see if you, too, can "cow"nt to 100.

Hints: • There is no mathematical sign between 8 and 9. It is read as the two-digit number 89.
   • The multiplication sign is used 2 times; all the other signs are used only once.
   • The numbers do not have to be used in the order in which they are given.

Thought Diagrams

▶ It's time to exercise your mental muscles. Each rectangle represents an exercise class. Each circle represents a special part of that class. Notice the way the circles are arranged. Then, decide if the following statements are true or false. Write TRUE or FALSE on each line.

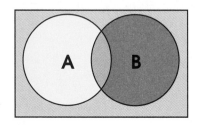

A = All girls in the class
B = All in class who are swimmers

1. All the girls in the class are swimmers. _____

2. All the swimmers are girls. _____

3. None of the girls are swimmers. _____

4. Some of the girls are swimmers. _____

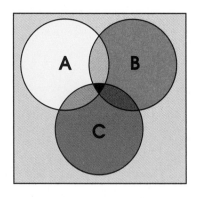

A = All the boys in the class
B = All in the class who are swimmers
C = All in the class who are runners

5. Some of the boys are runners. _____

6. None of the boys are swimmers. _____

7. All of the boys are runners and swimmers. _____

8. Some of the boys who are swimmers are not runners. _____

9. Some of the boys are both runners and swimmers. _____

Life Is Full of Patterns

▶ Each of these series of numbers follows a different pattern. Study each one to help you determine what that pattern is. Then, write the next three numbers according to that pattern.

1. 2   4   8   16   _____ _____ _____

2. 6   8   16   18   _____ _____ _____

3. 5   4   10   9   _____ _____ _____

4. 3   7   15   31   _____ _____ _____

5. 4   12   9   27   _____ _____ _____

6. 7   7   8   16   _____ _____ _____

7. 25   24   22   19   _____ _____ _____

8. 3   6   8   16   _____ _____ _____

9. 18   15   30   27   _____ _____ _____

10. 9   7   10   6   _____ _____ _____

Level 2, Math

Lines of Symmetry

▶ A line of **symmetry** divides a figure into two half-figures which are exactly alike. Not all figures have a line of symmetry. Decide if each of the broken lines in the figures below is a line of symmetry. Write YES or NO below each figure.

1. _____

2. _____

3. _____

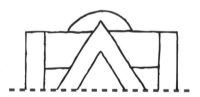

4. _____

5. _____

6. _____

▶ Now, use what you know about symmetry to complete the figures started below. In each partial figure, the broken line is a line symmetry.

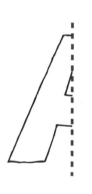

7.

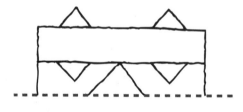

8.

9.

10.

11.

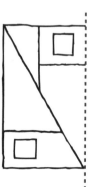

12.

Social Studies

Social Studies can be exciting! Through these brainteasers you can "visit" interesting cities and famous sights and get a taste of what it was like to live long ago.

Social studies is a subject that is constantly changing and affects everyone. You may find topics in these brainteasers that you want to read more about. Visit the library, a good encyclopedia or even the Internet and go exploring.

Name _____

A Family Tree

The Cruise family visited Ellis Island, an old immigration station located in the New York Harbor. Mom and Dad reminded the children that America is a land of immigrants. Immigrants are individuals and families from other countries who have decided to live in America.

The visit prompted the children to be interested in their own ancestry, so Sally, Lee and Jim Cruise decided to create a family tree. It included their names; the names of their parents, Bob and Anita; both sets of grandparents, Tom and Sally Cruise and Sam and Mary Flyer; their dad's sister, Alice; her husband, John Jones; and their two children, Molly and Mark.

► Complete the family tree, starting with the grandparents and writing each person's name on the correct branch. Be sure to label each branch of the family.

Salute to Freedom

The Statue of Liberty has stood in New York Harbor since 1886. It was a gift from the French people to celebrate friendship with the people of the United States and the spirit of freedom for all people.

▶ Work with the clues below to discover some interesting facts about the Statue of Liberty.

The number of steps to the top of the

monument is _____ .

Clues: • The number is between 160 and 170.
• It is an even number.
• If you add the 3 digits in the number, the sum is 15.

The Statue of Liberty is _____ inches tall.

That means it is over _____ feet high.

Clues: • The number of inches in its height is less than 1,820 and more than 1,800.
• It is an odd number.
• The sum of the digits is 13.
• There are 12 inches in a foot.

The Statue of Liberty weighs _____ tons.

That means it weighs _____ pounds.

Clues: • The number of tons is between 200 and 250.
• It is divisible by 5.
• The sum of its digits is 9.
• There are 2,000 pounds in a ton.

Level 2, Social Studies

The Age of Lincoln

One of the most visited sites in Washington, D.C. is the Lincoln Memorial. It is a monument that celebrates the life and work of Abraham Lincoln, the sixteenth president of the United States, who served in that job from 1861–1865.

▶ Look at the events and their dates listed below. Put a **check** after those you think could be closely related to the life and work of this great president. Write **B** on the answer line if you think an event took place before Lincoln became president and write **A** on the line if you think the event took place after he served.

World War II (1941–1945) _____

The signing of the Declaration of Independence (1776) _____

The Civil War (1861–1865) _____

World War I (1914–1919) _____

The landing of the Pilgrims (1620) _____

The discovery of America (1492) _____

Freedom granted to slaves (1863) _____

Man landing on the moon (1969) _____

The American Revolution (1776–1781) _____

The Gettysburg Address (1863) _____

List any other facts or events that you connect with Abraham Lincoln.

_____

_____

_____

Name _____

Totem Poles

Totem poles were created by Native Americans with images of different birds, fish, animals, plants and other natural objects. They carved them into tree trunks.

▶ Shown below are three different totem poles. The objects carved into them follow a pattern. First, discover the pattern. Next, cut out the objects at the bottom of the page. Then, glue them correctly to form Totem Pole 4.

Totem Pole 1 **Totem Pole 2** **Totem Pole 3** **Totem Pole 4**

Level 2, Social Studies

This page intentionally left blank.

Name _____

Viewed From Afar

Jules Verne wrote a book called *Around the World in Eighty Days*. It is the story of a man who traveled for 80 days all over the world in a hot air balloon. Some of the countries he flew over are listed below, but they are written in rebus form.

▶ Match each country from the Word Bank to the correct rebus clues. Write the country on the line.

1. **M** + EXIT − **T** + 🧥 − **AT** _____

2. ⚾ − **T** + 🍖 + GAS − **G** _____

3. 🌿 − **NCH** + **Z** + 😊 − **L** _____

4. 🏠(DOG) − **NEL** + Sweet Potatoes − **MS** _____

5. 🥚 − **G** + 📃 − **R** _____

6. 🥜 − **N** + 🧈 − **I** _____

7. 🛋 − **S** + **AL** + 🐝 − **B** _____

8. 🌭 − **K** + **S** _____

9. 🧂 − **M** + 🍳 _____

10. 🪚 − **S** + **S** + 🐛 + Sweet Potatoes − **MS** _____

Word Bank	
Brazil	France
Japan	Mexico
Italy	Egypt
Kenya	Greece
Australia	Bahamas

117

Level 2, Social Studies

Down Mexico Way

Not far from Mexico City is the famous Pyramid of Quetzalcóatl. It was built over 2,200 years ago and can still be seen today.

▶ Decide if each statement below states a fact or an opinion about this pyramid. Write **F** for fact or **O** for opinion on the line in front of each statement. Then, for the opinion statements, explain why you chose that answer.

_____ 1. The largest pyramid ever built is the Quetzalcóatl at Cholula de Rivadabla.

_____

_____ 2. Ancient pyramids and temples attract many visitors to Mexico.

_____

_____ 3. The pyramids in Mexico are more interesting than those in Egypt.

_____

_____ 4. The Mexican pyramids are flat on the top.

_____

_____ 5. Building the pyramids took great skill and knowledge of architecture.

_____

_____ 6. The base of the largest Mexican pyramid covers an area of nearly 45 acres.

_____

_____ 7. The people who built the pyramids were happy about their accomplishment.

_____

_____ 8. The artists for the Mexican pyramids and temples painted more attractive murals than the Egyptian artists.

_____

Name _____

Native American Heritage

▶ The history of Native Americans is rich with words that are still used today. Use the Native American terms in the Word Bank to complete this word puzzle.

Clues:
1. Part of celebrations
2. Food introduced to early settlers
3. Poles used to honor tribes
4. Corn
5. How baskets were made
6. Decorated dishes
7. Used to travel on water
8. Beads used for money
9. Used to decorate
10. Kind of jewelry
11. Ancestors
12. Shoes
13. Containers
14. Person who cures the sick
15. Shoes worn in winter

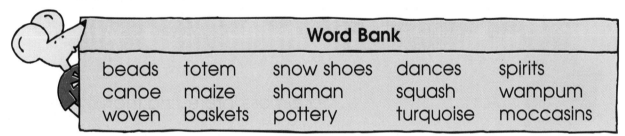

Word Bank

beads	totem	snow shoes	dances	spirits
canoe	maize	shaman	squash	wampum
woven	baskets	pottery	turquoise	moccasins

▶ Read the shaded boxes going down to answer this question:
What is this page about?

1. ___ ___ ___ ___ ___
2. ___ ___ ___ ___ ___
3. ___ ___ ___ ___
4. ___ ___ ___ ___
5. ___ ___ ___ ___
6. ___ ___ ___ ___ ___ ___
7. ___ ___ ___ ___
8. ___ ___ ___ ___ ___ ___
9. ___ ___ ___ ___ ___
10. ___ ___ ___ ___ ___ ___ ___
11. ___ ___ ___ ___ ___
12. ___ ___ ___ ___ ___ ___ ___
13. ___ ___ ___ ___ ___
14. ___ ___ ___ ___ ___ ___ ___
15. ___ ___ ___ ___ ___ ___

Level 2, Social Studies

French Floral Fun

The Palace of Versailles is about 10 miles from the city of Paris, France. It was once a hunting lodge for the French kings. Today, visitors from all over the world come to enjoy the beautiful gardens and stroll the paths surrounding the palace.

▶ Find and circle the names of fourteen kinds of flowers hidden in the garden word search. Write the missing letters in the list below. Then trace the shortest path through the word search from the entrance to the exit. Stay only on letters contained in the flower names.

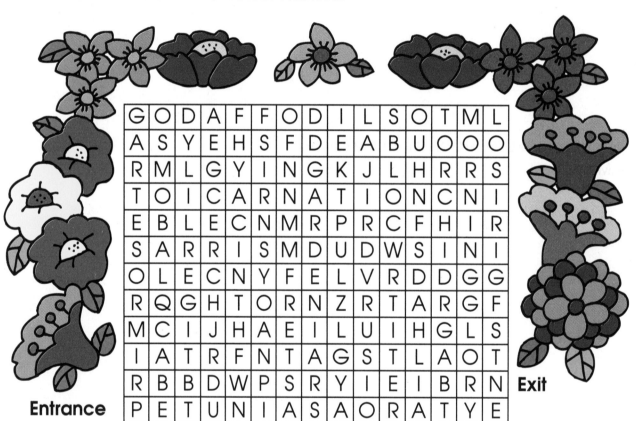

Entrance

Exit

_ e t _ n i a   d a _ _ o d i l   d _ _ _ s y

o _ c _ i d   S _ a p d r a _ o n   i _ i s

_ r i m _ o s e   _ o r n i n g _ l o r y   a _ t e r

_ i g e r _ i l y   c a _ n a _ i o n   _ a _ l i a

_ a r _ e n i a   h _ a _ i n t h

Name _____

Look at the Time

The world is divided into 24 time zones. Beginning at the International Date Line, each zone is one hour ahead of the zone to the west. For example, at 12:00 A.M. at the International Date Line, it is 10:00 P.M. in Sydney, Australia because Sidney is two time zones to the west.

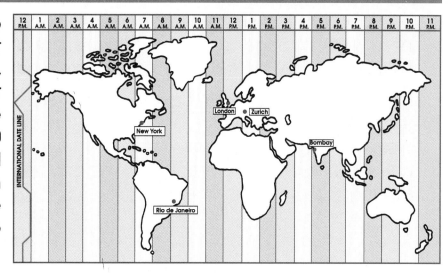

▶ Study the time zone map above and decide what time it is in the listed cities when it is 12:00 A.M at the International Date Line. Draw the hands on the clocks for each city to show its time. Then, write the times including A.M and P.M. below the clock faces.

New York U.S.A.	Rio de Janeiro Brazil	Zurich Switzerland

_____ _____ _____

Bombay India	London England

_____ _____

Level 2, Social Studies

Great Americans

▶ The history of America is filled with tales about the accomplishments of its citizens. On this page, read each achievement and then decide which famous American really did it. Fill in the small circle next to that person's name.

1. I helped lead Lewis and Clark to explore the Northwest.
   - ○ Pocahontas
   - ○ Susan B. Anthony
   - ○ Sacajawea
   - ○ Eleanor Roosevelt

2. I rode to warn the people near Boston that the British were coming.
   - ○ Thomas Jefferson
   - ○ George Washington
   - ○ Sam Adams
   - ○ Paul Revere

3. In 1984, I was the first woman to run for vice-president of the United States.
   - ○ Geraldine Ferraro
   - ○ Sandra Day O'Connor
   - ○ Madeline Albright
   - ○ Martha Washington

4. I led a march on Washington to gain equal rights and freedom for all people.
   - ○ John F. Kennedy
   - ○ Martin Luther King, Jr.
   - ○ Sam Adams
   - ○ Jesse Jackson

5. I was the commander-in-chief of all allied forces for D Day, June 6, 1944.
   - ○ John F. Kennedy
   - ○ Dwight D. Eisenhower
   - ○ Richard Nixon
   - ○ Robert E. Lee

6. I was the first American to orbit the Earth.
   - ○ John Glenn
   - ○ Paul Revere
   - ○ Neil Armstrong
   - ○ Sally Ride

7. I invented the phonograph and the first successful electric light bulb.
   - ○ Thomas Edison
   - ○ Alexander Graham Bell
   - ○ Wilber Wright
   - ○ Albert Einstein

8. I was the first American woman to travel in space.
   - ○ Betsy Ross
   - ○ Sally Ride
   - ○ Amelia Earhart
   - ○ Clara Bart

Name _____

Down Under

Americans and Australians usually speak the same language—English. However, there are times when it is difficult for Americans to understand Australians because of the different words that they use.

▶ Read the sentences below. Use the Word Bank to find and write the words Americans might use for the Australian expressions in bold.

Word Bank		
blanket roll	gasoline	ranches
bucking bronco	herds	elevator
hood	trunk	faucets
interior	wild horses	ranch owners

1. Many **squatters** _____ raise **mobs** _____ of sheep on

    their **stations** _____ in Australia.

2. Others prefer taming **brumbies** _____ and **buckjumpers**

    _____ .

3. If a buckjumper has a **matilda** _____ on its back, it is tame.

4. The **outback** _____ of Australia has a variety of animals.

5. We need to add **petrol** _____ to the automobile.

6. The attendant checked under the **bonnet** _____ as I arranged

    things in the **boot** _____ of the car.

7. Sidney is located near the mouth of a river to provide water for the **taps**

    _____ .

8. We will ride in the **lift** _____ up the side of one of the skyscrapers

    to look over the city.

Name _____

Visitors Welcome

The United States has many national parks, monuments and historical sites. The main purpose of these is to protect the sites and the natural beauty so that all Americans can enjoy them for years to come.

▶ Match the national sites listed below with the natural wonders to be found in them or the events that took place in them. Write the number on the correct line in the second column. If you need help, check an encyclopedia or the Internet.

National Parks and Sites

1. Mesa Verde
2. Grand Canyon
3. Rocky Mountains
4. Kitty Hawk, NC
5. Yellowstone National Park
6. Hawaii Volcanoes
7. Mount Rushmore
8. Yosemite

Natural Wonders and Events

_____ Old Faithful and other geysers

_____ Highest waterfall

_____ Mauna Loa

_____ Faces of four presidents

_____ Colorado River

_____ The Continental Divide

_____ Indian cliff dwellings

_____ Site of the first airplane ride

▶ Write the name of a national park you may want to visit and tell why.

_____

_____

_____

_____

_____

Name _____

Presidential Disguises

The names of ten of America's best-known presidents have been scrambled below. Each name also has a clue to help you identify the president.

▶ Write the name on the line. Try not to use the Word Bank unless you have to.

1. REGGEO GSWOAHNITN _____
   The father of our country

2. HOJN SMAAD _____
   The first president to live in the White House

3. SAMHOT FESNOJFRE _____
   Sent Lewis and Clark to explore the West

4. WARDEN ACJONSK _____
   The first Westerner to be president

5. MABRAAH CNILLON _____
   Freed the slaves

6. EDRETOHO VOTESOERL _____
   Called a "Rough Rider"

7. KNIRFALN SERVOTLOE _____
   Served four times as president

8. YRARH MNRATU _____
   Ordered the White House to be completely rebuilt

9. NJOH YDENNKE _____
   Assassinated after 1000 days in office

10. LANROD GRANEA _____
    Had been a movie star

Word Bank		
Harry Truman	Thomas Jefferson	Abraham Lincoln
Andrew Jackson	John Adams	Franklin Roosevelt
Ronald Reagan	John Kennedy	Theodore Roosevelt
	George Washington	

Level 2, Social Studies

Everything Has Its Place

▶ A time line is a way to show the order of events as they happened. It also helps you to see the relative space of time between events. On the time lines below, beginning and ending dates are given. Your job is to make a mark on the correct line about where you think each event happened and write its name. When you are finished, all the events should be in their places and in order as they happened.

1450 ————————————————————— 1550

1550 ————————————————————— 1650

1650 ————————————————————— 1750

1750 ————————————————————— 1850

Events

- Constitution Approved–1788
- New Orleans Founded–1718
- French and Indian War Ends–1763
- Marquette Explored Mississippi–1673
- Pilgrims Land–1620
- St. Lawrence River Explored–1603
- Georgia Founded–1733
- Jamestown Settled–1607
- America Discovered–1492
- Roanoke Island Settled–1585
- Battle of New Orleans–1815
- Pacific Ocean Discovered–1513
- Declaration of Independence Written–1776

▶ **Challenge!** On another sheet of paper, make a time line of your life so far. On it, mark some of the things that have happened to you.

These brainteasers deal with the natural world, the animals that fill it and the way things work in the world.

When you answer one question on these pages, other questions may come to mind. Don't be afraid to explore these too. That's what makes the study of science so interesting and challenging. Before you know it, you will have become a budding scientist.

Name _____

A Sampling of Snakes

The Snake House is a very popular place to visit at the zoo. There are many different types and sizes of snakes. Some snakes are poisonous while others are not. Some snakes are harmless to most creatures, and some are very dangerous.

The five snakes described here are usually held in the cages below.

▶ Decide which snake belongs in each cage by using the descriptions and clues. Then, write each snake name below the correct cage.

The King Cobra is the longest poisonous snake in the world. One of these snakes measured almost 19 feet long. It is found in southeast Asia and the Philippines.

The Gaboon Viper, a very poisonous snake, has the longest fangs of all snakes (nearly 2 inches). It is found in tropical Africa.

The Reticulated Python is the longest snake of all. One specimen measured over 32 feet in length. It is found in southeast Asia, Indonesia and the Philippines.

The Black Mamba, the fastest-moving land snake, can move at speeds of 10 to 12 miles per hour. It lives in the eastern part of tropical Africa.

The Anaconda is almost twice as heavy as a reticulated python of the same length. One anaconda that was almost 28 feet long weighed nearly 500 pounds.

Clues: • The snake in cage 5 moves the fastest on land.
        • The longest snake of all is between the snake that comes from tropical Africa and the longest poisonous snake.
        • The very heavy snake is to the left of the longest poisonous snake.

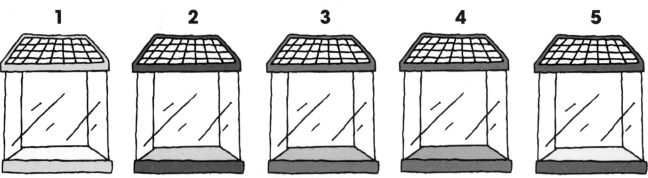

1   **2**   **3**   **4**   **5**

_____ _____ _____ _____ _____

Name _____

Sun Power

Scientists are attempting to efficiently harness the energy produced by the sun. This energy is called solar energy. Every 40 minutes the sun sends enough energy to the earth's surface to equal what the people of the world ordinarily use in one year. We have so far only harnessed a fraction of this solar energy. Scientists are continually trying to discover new means of capturing it and putting it to use.

Listed below are some examples of how scientists so far have used solar energy.

- solar-powered automobiles
- solar-heated furnaces in buildings
- solar air-conditioned houses
- solar power plants
- solar ovens
- solar-generated turbines
- solar-powered calculators and other small electronic devices

▶ Imagine that you are living in the future—a future where solar energy is used in many ways. Describe a day in your life using items operated by solar energy. Be imaginative. (Don't forget that for something to be solar-powered, it must have access to the sun, either directly or indirectly.)

_____

_____

_____

_____

_____

_____

_____

_____

Level 2, Science

Name _____

Fabulous Feathered Friends

Most animals do not talk—at least not in a way that humans can understand. However, some birds can talk quite well. In England, there once was an African gray parrot that won a talking contest twelve years in a row. It knew almost 800 words!

▶ Imagine you are teaching your parrot to talk. Each month your parrot learns a certain number of words. The number of words listed is the total number of words known at that time. Follow the pattern to determine how many months it would take for your parrot to learn as many words as the African gray parrot mentioned above.

First Month   — 50 words
Second Month — 75 words
Third Month   — 125 words
Fourth Month   — 150 words
Fifth Month   — 200 words

It would take _____ months to match the African gray parrot.

▶ Suppose you are teaching words to a very young parrot. This parrot learns slowly. It masters words according to the schedule below. The numbers refer to the total words known at any given time.

First Week   — 4 words
Second Week — 5 words
Third Week   — 8 words
Fourth Week   — 9 words
Fifth Week   — 12 words

How many weeks will it take for the parrot to learn the following? "Polly doesn't

want a cracker. That's for the birds. Give me fruit, nuts and seeds." _____

Name _____

A Crafty Crustacean

The coconut crab is also called the purse crab or the robber crab. This amazing creature climbs coconut palm trees and picks coconuts. Then, it opens the coconuts with its pincer claws and eats them.

▶ In the picture above, each coconut palm tree contains 25 coconuts. Suppose a coconut crab climbs the first tree on the left and takes three coconuts to eat. Then, it climbs each of the next nine trees and each time takes two more coconuts than the tree before.

How many coconuts does the crab take altogether? _____

How many coconuts are left on the trees? _____

Dino Data

Do you like to read about dinosaurs? Some people devour every dinosaur book, movie and article they can find. However, everything they read is not fact. Some things that people write about dinosaurs are opinions.

▶ Read each statement below and write **F** for fact or **O** for opinion on the line.

_____ 1. The first dinosaur fossils were discovered in 1822.

_____ 2. A paleontologist is a scientist who studies animals and plants from the past.

_____ 3. Different sizes and shapes of uncovered dinosaur skeletons show that dinosaurs were not all the same.

_____ 4. A paleontologist knows more about dinosaurs than anyone else.

_____ 5. The Brachiosaurus was the most interesting dinosaur of all.

_____ 6. Dinosaur fossils are often found in solid rock.

_____ 7. The Hypsilophodon was the weirdest-looking dinosaur.

_____ 8. Scientists learn a lot about dinosaurs by studying their bones.

_____ 9. Being a paleontologist is one of the most difficult jobs in science.

_____ 10. Scientists can make copies of dinosaur skeletons using fiberglass so that museums may display and study them.

_____ 11. Everyone in the fourth grade should study dinosaur fossils.

_____ 12. It is more interesting to study about dinosaurs than studying about any other subject.

Name _____

Can you recognize the sounds of a flute? How about the sounds of a violin? Different instruments make different sounds. The sound wave from each instrument makes certain pressure changes in the air. The pressure changes can be illustrated with jagged and curved lines called waveforms.

For example, here's a jagged waveform that shows the sound made by a violin.

Here's a curved waveform that illustrates the smooth sound made by a flute.

▶ Look at the waveforms below. Each contains a pattern that makes it special. Continue drawing each pattern at least once.

A.

B.

C.

D.

Level 2, Science

Name _____

Earth-Shaking News

One morning, Sy Z. Mograff was awakened by pictures falling off the walls. The floor shook as he stood to get out of bed. Later, Sy saw this diagram in the newspaper. It showed what had happened.

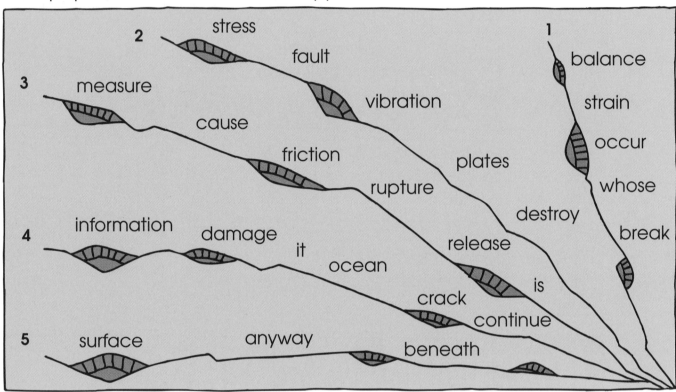

▶ Follow the directions below to see what question Sy wanted answered.

Directions:
1. Cross out all words in the picture containing 3 or more vowels.
2. Cross out all words beginning with st, br, pl, fr or cr.
3. Cross out all remaining two-syllable words.
4. Write the remaining words on the lines to find out what Mr. Sy Z. Mograff asked.

Mr. Sy Z. Mograff asked, "_____ _____ _____

_____ _____ ?"

To answer Sy's question, solve this riddle: "I am your parent, but not your father. Treat me with respect. Look carefully and you'll find me in your heart."

_____ _____ caused the earthquake.

Name _____

Beginnings

Gestation is the time during which a mother animal carries a baby within her body before giving birth. The length of animal gestation periods varies greatly from species to species.

▶ Use the clues below to determine the approximate gestation period for each animal. Write the answers on the correct lines.

Clues: • A giraffe's gestation period = 2 **x** a deer's gestation period.

• 3 **x** a deer's gestation period + 2 months = an elephant's gestation period.

• A whale's gestation period = 5 **x** a beaver's gestation period, or 3 **x** a sheep's gestation period.

• An elephant's gestation period > a whale's gestation period.

• A whale's gestation period > a giraffe's gestation period.

Possible Answers		
3 months	7 months	15 months
5 months	14 months	23 months

Animal Gestation Periods

deer = _____ months giraffe = _____ months

beaver = _____ months sheep = _____ months

elephant = _____ months whale = _____ months

135

Level 2, Science

A Balanced Meal

The foods you eat help you grow and stay healthy. All foods are divided into four main groups: dairy, meat/fish, bread/cereal and vegetables/fruit.

▶ Let's discover the contents of the sandwiches below. Use the Word Bank to write the name of a food that completes each riddle. Not all words will be used. **Hint:** All four food groups will be represented in each sandwich.

Word Bank

bacon   butter
pickle   hot dog
roll   peanut
bun   tomatoes
milk   orange
bread   cheese

Sandwich 1

- A baker uses _____ sticks to play the drums.
- The mouse said, " _____ ," to everyone—not just the photographer.
- A funny _____ could be called a "silly dilly."
- When the cow ate peanuts he made _____ butter.

Sandwich 2

- The pig said he was so hot he was " _____ ."
- The rabbit said to his sweet girl friend, "You're my honey _____ ."
- The unusual farmer planted toes. He harvested _____ .
- One goat bragged to another goat, "I'm a better _____ than you!"

Name _____

Mammal Mix

Mammals are a special group of animals. They live in many different places, but they all have the same characteristics.

Mammals:
- can give milk to their babies.
- are warm-blooded.
- have large, well-developed brains.
- protect and guide their young.
- have hair at some time during their lives.

▶ Below are some silly pictures made from two mammals put together. Write the names of the two real mammals suggested by the picture. The last letter or letters in the name of the first animal are the first letter or letters in the name of the second animal. The first one has been done for you.

1.

   wha<u>le</u>   **<u>le</u>opard**
   _____ _____

2.

   _____ _____

3.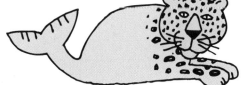

   _____ _____

4.

   _____ _____

5.

   _____ _____

6.

   _____ _____

Level 2, Science

Animal Analogies

Animals have distinguishing features and inherited characteristics. These traits can be discovered in quite interesting and unusual ways.

▶ Use the Word Bank to help complete these analogies. Remember that an analogy is the expression of two like comparisons.

1. A **hill** is to **land** as a **hump** is to a(n) _____.

2. A **hand fan** is to a **human** as **ears** are to a(n) _____.

3. **Four quarters** are to a **dollar** as **four stomachs** are to a(n) _____.

4. **Flypaper** is to **a fly** as an **anteater's tongue** is to a(n) _____.

5. A **needle** is to a **seamstress** as a **beak** is to a(n) _____.

6. **Glass** is to a **window** as **skin** is to a(n) _____.

7. A **mouth** is to a **crocodile** as a **pouch** is to a(n) _____.

8. A **chest beat** is to a **gorilla** as a **shaking rattle** is to a(n) _____.

Word Bank			
kangaroo	cow	glass catfish	camel
tailorbird	ant	rattlesnake	elephant

Name _____

From Egg to Tadpole to Frog

▶ The poem below tells about the changes that occur in frogs during their life cycles. In every line, there is one word that doesn't make sense. Cross it out. Find the correct word in the Word Bank and write it in the puzzle.
Hint: The correct word rhymes with the one you cross out.

The Life Cycle of a Frog

There is jelly on the legs (13 across)
To protect the entire match. (11 across)
It takes tree to twenty-five days (7 down)
Until they're ready to catch. (5 down)

Out comes a pollihog (18 across)
When the time is just bright. (8 across)
It breathes using hills (14 down)
And its size is very tight. (4 across)

It loses its long scale (9 down)
After pegs begin to grow. (1 down)
Digestion and breathing strange (12 down)
In a process fast, yet glow. (2 down)

What helps a frog to seethe (3 down)
Is its thin and moist fin. (6 down)
It also uses rungs (15 down)
To let the hair in. (10 across)

Some frogs can skim like a duck. (6 across)
And some can mop like a rabbit. (16 down)
Others climb bees like a squirrel (7 across)
Which may seem a bunny habit. (17 across)

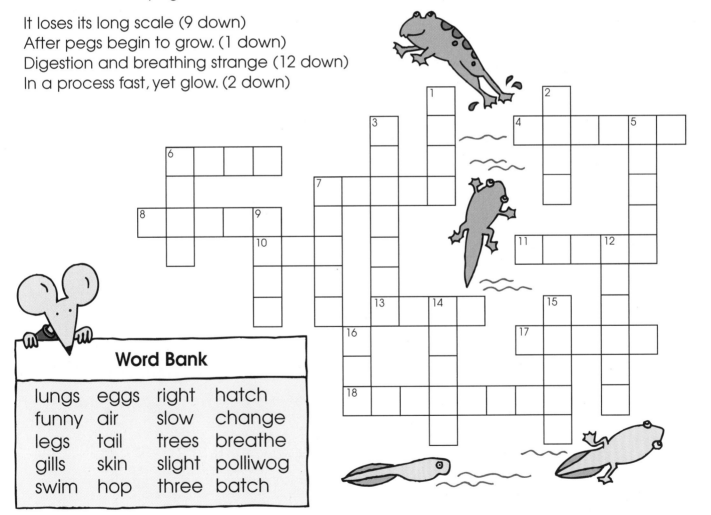

Word Bank

lungs	eggs	right	hatch
funny	air	slow	change
legs	tail	trees	breathe
gills	skin	slight	polliwog
swim	hop	three	batch

Level 2, Science

Weather Watching

Weather describes the condition of the air for a period of time. Weather maps contain symbols that describe the weather.

► Below is a calendar for one month. Beside it is a key for some weather symbols. Read carefully each of the clues listed below the calendar. Then, in the correct boxes, draw the symbols that tell what weather was experienced.

Key

	rain
	snow
	clouds
	fog
	sun
	hail
	sleet

Sun.	Mon.	Tues.	Wed.	Thurs.	Fri.	Sat.
	1	2	3	4	5	6
7	8	9	10	11	12	13
14	15	16	17	18	19	20
21	22	23	24	25	26	27
28	29	30	31			

Clues:
- All days whose sums of digits equal 8 were foggy.
- Two diagonally adjoining even-numbered days whose sum equals 36 were snowy.
- Odd-numbered days that follow a foggy day were rainy.
- All Saturdays except one were sunny.
- The first, middle and last days of the month had weather that began with an s and hasn't been mentioned yet.
- All foggy days except one came after cloudy days.
- Cloudy days followed all snowy days.
- Only two Thursdays were cloudy, and they were two weeks apart.
- Two Sundays of the month had hail.
- The rest of the even-numbered days were the same as the majority of Saturdays.
- The remaining days were cloudy.

Name _____

Feeling Buggy

▶ One the largest of the animal kingdoms is commonly called insects. See how many insect names you can find in the word search. List their names on the lines below.

```
S  L  P  L  A  D  Y  B  U  G  D  R  A  G  O  N  F  L  Y  G
M  O  S  Q  U  I  T  O  J  S  L  D  I  T  F  L  E  A  B  R
B  C  I  S  J  G  F  C  J  D  J  W  P  O  C  L  B  T  F  A
U  U  V  T  D  O  B  C  W  A  S  P  Y  A  A  E  K  D  J  S
T  S  J  I  J  S  Y  C  J  A  S  P  N  N  A  P  B  C  S
T  T  N  C  J  S  E  A  C  W  P  K  A  T  Y  D  I  D  A  H
E  H  Q  K  E  I  D  J  X  B  N  C  T  E  R  M  I  T  E  O
R  J  S  L  C  J  W  U  C  R  I  C  K  E  T  O  F  O  N  P
F  N  S  H  O  N  E  Y  B  E  E  L  J  D  K  T  M  Z  S  P
L  R  U  S  I  L  V  E  R  F  I  S  H  K  A  H  A  C  I  E
Y  B  E  E  T  L  E  I  E  C  O  C  K  R  O  A  C  H  W  R
```

_____ _____ _____

_____ _____ _____

_____ _____ _____

_____ _____ _____

_____ _____ _____

141

Name _____

Fishy Cartoons

Fish live almost anywhere there is water. Although fish come in many different shapes, colors and sizes, they are alike in many ways.

- All fish have backbones.
- Fish breathe with gills.
- Most fish are cold-blooded.
- Most fish have fins.
- Many fish have scales and fairly tough skin.

▶ Some fish have names that remind us of other animals. Use the clues to unscramble these fish names. Write each name correctly on the line. Then, use your imagination to draw each fish in a cartoon.

_____
rpartofish
(a talking bird)

_____
oinlfish
(king of the beasts)

_____
gknifish
(opposite of queen)

_____
tbturelfyfish
(an insect with colorful wings)

_____
ogatfish
(a nanny- or a billy-)

_____
opprucneifish
(animal with quills)

Creative Arts

All the brainteasers in this section have one thing in common—creativity. Perhaps you think you are not creative or it is too difficult to be creative. However, as you are solving the next section of brainteasers, you may just find a creative arts topic you want to further explore.

Name That Key

A piano has 88 keys—52 white keys and 36 black keys. The keys are arranged according to a pattern. After every 7th white key, the pattern is repeated. Each white key is given a letter name from A to G. When you start counting all the keys from the left side of the piano, the 40th key is called "Middle C." Middle C is used as a starting point when positioning your hands on a piano.

The picture below shows part of a piano's keyboard with Middle C labeled.

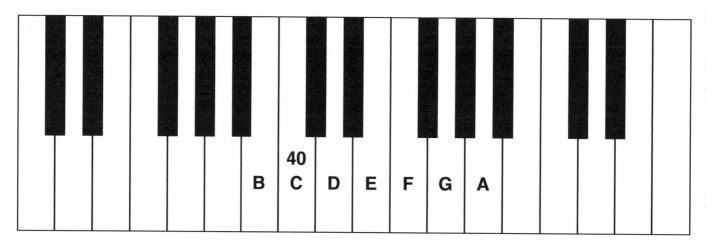

40

B C D E F G A

▶ Label the rest of the white keys with their letter names. Then, number all the keys. Don't forget to number each black key between the white ones. Now, use the keyboard to tell what words are suggested by the following group of keys.

1. 35, 49, 51 _____

2. 54, 49, 39 _____

3. 30, 44, 56, 42 _____

4. 39, 37, 42, 47, 56 _____

5. 51, 56, 32, 45 _____

Name _____

Beating the Rhythm

Musicians use symbols called notes to write music. One of the things that notes do is indicate the rhythm to the musician.

▶ Imagine you are a drummer playing the rhythm of these nursery rhymes. One-syllable words get one note (♩) and two-syllable words get two notes (♫). Match each nursery rhyme to the correct pattern by writing its number before the pattern.

1. Mary had a little lamb . . .   ♫ ♩ ♩ ♩ ♩ ♩

2. Humpty Dumpty sat on a wall . . .   ♫ ♫ ♫ ♩

3. Old Mother Hubbard
   went to the cupboard . . .   ♫ ♫ ♩ ♩ ♩ ♩

4. Little Bo Peep has lost her sheep . . .   ♫ ♩ ♩ ♫ ♩

5. Twinkle, twinkle, little star . . .   ♩ ♫ ♫ ♩ ♩ ♩ ♫

6. Little Miss Muffet sat on a tuffet . . . ♫ ♩ ♫ ♩ ♩ ♩ ♫

▶ Now, use words from the Word Bank to complete each sentence. The musical notes below stand for these missing words. Words may be used more than once. Remember, each note represents one syllable.

Word Bank

melody
musicians
music
pattern
notes
organizing
rises
rhythm
up

7. ♫♩ write ♫ by ♫♫ ♩

   _____ _____ _____ _____.

8. The ♫ of ♩ makes the ♫

   _____ _____ _____ _____.

9. Pitch ♫ as ♩ go ♩

   _____ _____ _____.

Take a Seat!

To achieve a perfect blend of sounds for a symphony orchestra, the conductor decides the seating arrangement for each section of instruments.

- **stringed section** (violin, viola, cello, harp, bass, piano)

- **woodwind section** (flute, oboe, clarinet, bassoon)

- **brass section** (trumpet, French horn, trombone, tuba)

- **percussion section** (kettle drum, bells and cymbals, bass drum, gong, snare drum, triangle, xylophone)

▶ The conductor has the unfinished seating arrangement below. Use the clues to write in the names of the missing sections.

Clues:
- The **percussion** section is directly in front of the **conductor** but as far back as possible.

- The **French horns** are directly in front of the **trombones** and behind the **oboes.**

- The remaining **woodwinds** are between the **oboes** and the **violas** with the **flutes** closest to the conductor.

- The **violins** occupy the largest section in the orchestra.

- The largest **stringed instruments** are in a back corner.

- The remaining **brass instruments** occupy the last section.

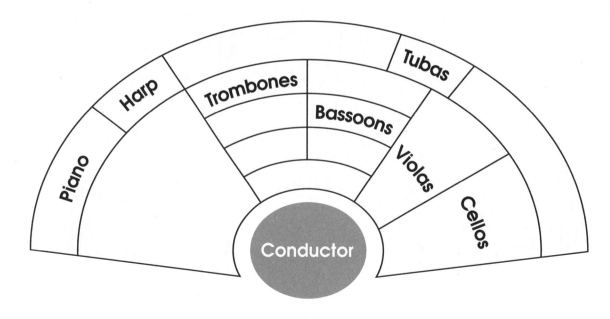

Name _____

Colorful Colors

Many beginning artists have created their first pieces of artwork using only a box of crayons. These colorful sticks of wax come in many different shades.

▶ Use your imagination to create names for the crayons below. The first one has been done for you.

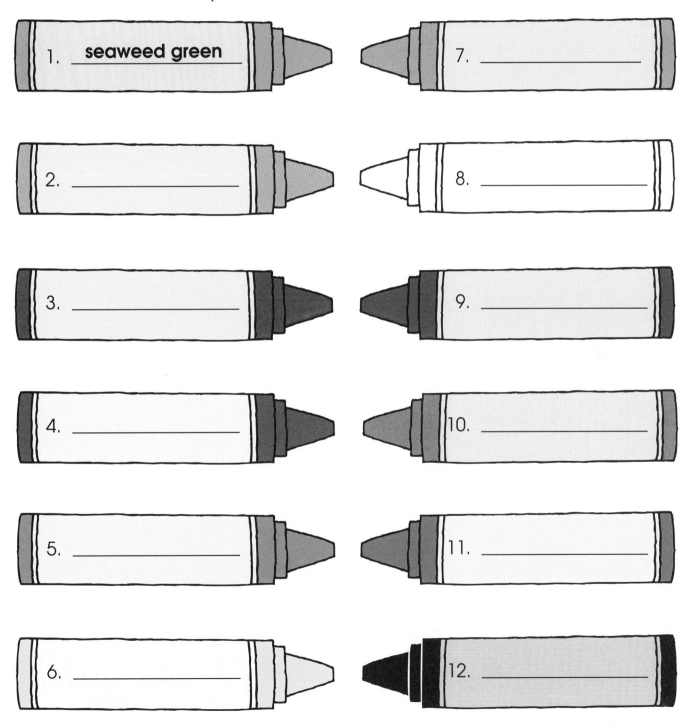

1. **seaweed green**

2. _____

3. _____

4. _____

5. _____

6. _____

7. _____

8. _____

9. _____

10. _____

11. _____

12. _____

Who or What Am I?

A creative person is not afraid to try things that are new, original and different.

▶ Read each riddle below. Use the Word Bank to identify each creative person or product. Write the answer on the line. Each word is used only once.

1. My lips may move,
   But no sound comes out.
   My whole body tells the story,
   It's my movements that shout!

   I am a(n) _____ .

2. I see the world
   Containing colors so vast.
   With a stroke I preserve
   The future, present and past.

   I am a(n) _____ .

3. My words have tones
   From high to low.
   They may be uttered
   Fast or slow.

   I am a(n) _____ .

4. I tell a story
   From beginning to end.
   Actors and actions
   Wonderfully blend.

   I am a(n) _____ .

5. The words I use
   May last a long time.
   Depending on my talents
   They may be prose or rhyme.

   I am a(n) _____ .

6. A tear trickles down
   My face, but it's dry.
   I have no feelings
   Though I appear to cry.

   I am a(n) _____ .

7. I'm frozen in time,
   But I'm not very cold.
   I often reflect history
   In a pose so bold.

   I am a(n) _____ .

8. I can read,
   But I don't see letters.
   Because of me
   The world sounds better.

   I am a(n) _____ .

Word Bank

statue	painter	painting	play
musician	song	mime	writer

Name _____

Pottery Styles

Before beginning a project, an artist who makes pottery must think about how the piece will be used, what type of clay to use and what color and patterns to use. Every artist develops a unique style that can be recognized in the products he or she produces.

The first set of pottery pieces below were created by one talented artist and the second set by another. The third set contains two pieces created by artist number 1 and two by artist number 2.

▶ Number each piece in the third set to show who its creator is.

What helps you to identify artist number 1? _____

_____

_____

149

Level 2, Creative Arts

Name _____

Pretty As a Picture

Still life pictures are drawings or paintings of objects. These objects have no movement or life. They are simply arranged and painted.

▶ Below are three sets of still life pictures. Carefully examine each set. Then, use the lines under each set to write what all three still life pictures have in common.

petunia    pepper    pencil
tulip   tomato   tape
rose   radish   ruler

_____

_____

pumpkin    sunflower    bed
eggplant   carnation   chair
potato   violet   table

_____

_____

apple    asparagus    apples
bread   broccoli   bananas
cheese   carrots   cherries

_____

_____

Name _____

Cakes for All Occasions

You may be surprised to learn that pastry chefs are creative people, too. One of their jobs is to create decorations on cakes made for special occasions.

▶ Look at these three cakes and decide the occasion for which each was made. Write that event on the line below the cake.

_____   _____   _____

▶ Now, it's your turn. Decorate each of these cakes to be used for the indicated celebration. Be as creative as you can, but be sure that the connection between the decorations and the celebration is clear.

Thanksgiving   4th of July   Welcome Home

Level 2, Creative Arts

Name _____

The art of weaving dates back many thousands of years. The colors, types and order of the threads create different patterns. These patterns can be simple or complicated.

▶ Study the weaving pattern below. Finish labeling the colors according to the color patterns.

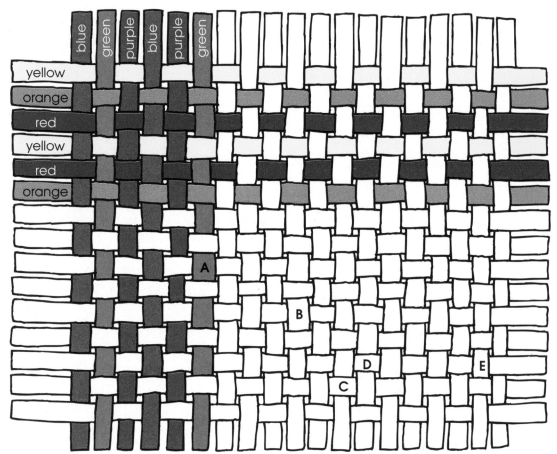

▶ Now identify the top and bottom color of the following points in the patterns.

A — Top color _____   Bottom color _____

B — Top color _____   Bottom color _____

C — Top color _____   Bottom color _____

D — Top color _____   Bottom color _____

E — Top color _____   Bottom color _____

Name _____

Positions, Everyone!

A ballet dancer tells a story with his or her body by using music, dance and mime. All ballet movements begin and end with the feet in one of the positions shown here.

1st position   2nd position   3rd position   4th position   5th position

▶ The positions given below are all set up according to patterns. Examine each one and decide which positions come next. Write the numbers of the missing positions on the lines.

1. ___ ___ ___ ___ ___

2. ___ ___ ___ ___ ___ ___ ___

3. ___ ___ ___ ___ ___

4. ___ ___ ___ ___ ___ ___ ___ ___

5. ___ ___ ___ ___ ___ ___ ___

Level 2, Creative Arts

Name _____

Clowning Around

Clowns entertain audiences through their "large" actions, bright make-up and colorful costumes. Some clowns look happy, while others appear sad. Because the costume is so important to the act, the clown must choose it very carefully. Here is a closet containing some costume items a clown might choose.

▶ Choose one item from each of the three categories—hats, suits and shoes—to create different outfits. How many different combinations can you create? Write the letters in groups of three. Two have been done for you.

ADG, ADH, _____

_____

_____

▶ How many different costumes could the clown create in all? _____

Silence Is Golden

The first movies were silent. Dialogue between the actors was not heard until 1927. Before this, actors had to exaggerate their facial expressions and movements so that the audience could understand the plots. To help tell the stories to the audience, captions were used.

▶ The pictures tell a story. Each caption below contains an incorrect word. Underline the incorrect word and unscramble its letters to find the correct word. Write it on the line. Then, match each caption with the correct picture by writing its number in the circle.

And they slimed lovingly as they gazed into each other's eyes!

◯ _____

"You will be safe in my arms forever, volley Nell!"

◯ _____

"You will never least from the poor again, Dishonest John!"

◯ _____

"Alas, I am so poor that I even had to sell the family livers!"

◯ _____

"I madden your money! Give it to me or you will be very sorry!"

◯ _____

"Help me! Help me! The speeding train is caring down the track!"

◯ _____

155

What Level 3
Is All About

Congratulations! You have reached the top level of Brainteasers in this book. Now you are ready to really shine! Most ten- or eleven-year-old girls and boys will be able to solve these puzzles without too much trouble. However, they are still a challenge.

Keep your eyes open for topics that are of interest to you. You might want to explore some of these ideas further on your own.

Language Arts

Language Arts Brainteasers include such topics as spelling, compound words, word puzzles, abbreviations, homophones, analogies and idioms. Each page stretches what you know to help you learn more and can help you end up with a real feeling of accomplishment.

There will also be opportunities for you to do some writing and thinking which can get your creativity in gear. All in all, you certainly will be a Top-Level Thinker when you are finished.

Top Speller

▶ In each group of words on this page there is one which is not spelled correctly. Cross it out and write the word correctly on the line.

1. either, egg, emty, equal _____

2. moose, moter, move, mumble _____

3. fether, figure, finger, flag _____

4. oficer, often, oil, orange _____

5. read, relative, rattel, return _____

6. slow, sore, stick, steem _____

7. sine, shell, spank, speak _____

8. idiom, igloo, immaculate, Indion _____

9. lion, alive, languge, laundry _____

10. alarm, attend, able, annother _____

11. thin, throw, thum, there _____

12. why, wood, whan, where _____

Name _____

Gears in Motion

▶ Write one word below each gear that could be combined with each word on the large gear to make compound words. The sentences you make will solve the three riddles.

1. What did the mouse that ran down the hickory, dickory, dock clock decide to do?

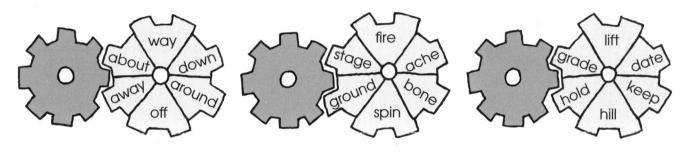

"Now I'll _____ _____ _____."

2. What did Santa say he would do after Christmas?

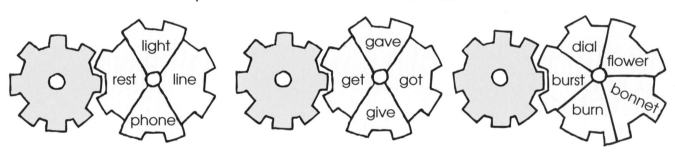

"I'm going to _____ _____ some
_____ shine."

3. What did the visiting South Sea Islander say he would do for fun?

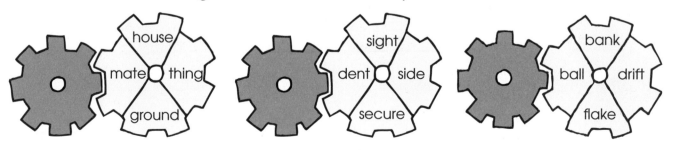

"I think I'll _____ _____ the _____."

Level 3, Language

One Becomes Two

Think of a word that could be the last part of one compound word and the first part of a different compound word.

▶ Write the missing word to make two different compound words.

1. pea _____ cracker

2. snow _____ hunt

3. sun _____ pot

4. cook _____ worm

5. eye _____ room

6. doll _____ fly

7. flag _____ cat

8. cat _____ bowl

9. arm _____ man

10. rain _____ tail

11. sea _____ fish

12. tree _____ coat

13. honey _____ hive

14. bob _____ tail

15. finger _____ brush

16. horse _____ ache

17. bird _____ tub

18. butter _____ shake

19. ear _____ beat

20. grape _____ cake

Unusual Plurals

▶ Most **plurals** are formed by adding "s" or "es" to their singular forms. But some nouns change other letters to make a plural. There are even some nouns that stay the same in both singular and plural forms. Write the plurals for the nouns listed below. You can use a dictionary if necessary.

singular

plural

1. goose _____

2. ox _____

3. fish _____

4. tooth _____

5. spy _____

6. quiz _____

7. factory _____

8. mouse _____

9. foot _____

10. moose _____

11. deer _____

12. brother-in-law _____

13. glass _____

14. sheep _____

15. person _____

Seafood

▶ Each fish below contains the same letters as the fish in front of it plus an additional letter. However, the letters may be in a different order than in the word to the left. The last fish in each group contains a word that relates to the sea. Use the clues to help you figure out these last words first. Then, fill in the missing letters in the other fish.

Clue: plantlike sea animal

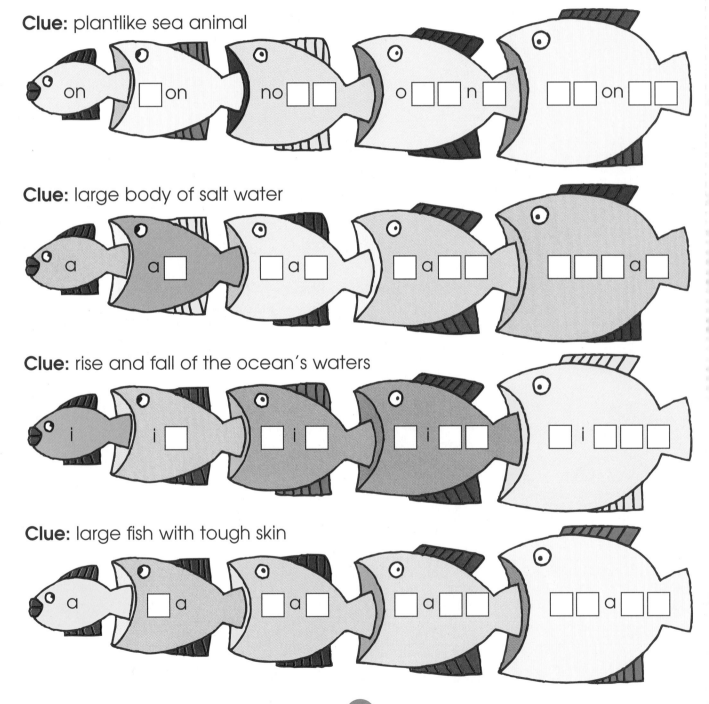

Clue: large body of salt water

Clue: rise and fall of the ocean's waters

Clue: large fish with tough skin

Taking a Shortcut

An **abbreviation** is the short form of a word. It is usually formed by:

a. the first two or three letters of the word followed by a period (A<u>ve</u>nue = Ave.).

b. the first and last letters of the word followed by a period (M<u>iste</u>r = Mr.).

c. the first, middle and last letters of a word followed by a period (B<u>ou</u>l<u>e</u>v<u>ar</u>d = Blvd.).

▶ Here is a story about a ghost. It contains imaginary abbreviations. Periods at the end of sentences will look like this: ⬚. See if you can figure out what the paragraph says. Rewrite the story without any abbreviations.

Onc. upn. a time there ws. a sml. gst. ⬚ Hc frgt. to lok. whr. he ws. ging., and he gt. lst. ⬚ He thot. he knw. whr. he ws., so he trd. to take a shrtct. home ⬚ He sald. ovr. the tres. and undr. a brdge. ⬚ Wen. he cam. to his nbrhd., he thot. he wd. qikly. fl. thrgh. ech. hse. ⬚ At the first hse., he brezd. pst. a napng. dg. who opned. hs. eys. and bgn. brkng. ⬚ At the nxt. hse., the gst. pausd. to wtch. sml. chldrn. plang. a game ⬚ Wen. he entrd. the third hse., the gst. lkd. arnd. and sw. brkn. wndws., a crakd. strcase. and mny. cbwbs. ⬚ Thn. he hrd. a gstly. voice sy., "Yr. lat. !" The sml. gst. rcognzd. hs. mthr. ⬚ "Thr's. no pl. lke. hom.," he thght. ⬚

_____

_____

_____

_____

_____

_____

_____

An Eye for Homophones

Homophones are words that sound alike but have different meanings and usually different spellings.

▶ Use your knowledge of homophones to write titles for these paintings. The first one has been done for you.

a hare with hair
_____
_____

_____
_____
_____

Name _____

Double Duty

Homographs are words that have the same spellings but have different meanings and often different pronunciations.

▶ Use the clues to find the missing homographs. Then, write them on the lines.

Example: The boa constrictor with a __**bow**__ would not __**bow**__ to the baby baboon.
(tied ribbon with loops) (to bend downward)

1. The daring _____ _____ directly downhill.
(bird in pigeon family) (plunged headfirst)

2. A _____ lizard can _____ in limitless localities.
(not dead) (to reside)

3. Watch the clam _____ its shell _____ to the clownfish.
(shut) (near)

4. The dusty dromedary did _____ the dry _____.
(to leave) (sandy region)

5. Don't _____ the _____ between the condor
(to challenge) (competition)
and the cuckoo.

6. The prickly porcupine will _____ the _____ to the
(give) (gift)
patient prairie dog.

7. _____ me, but I thought the _____ given by the
(forgive) (explanation)
elusive elephant was exaggerated.

8. I _____ the _____ of the whimpering wolf with
(wrapped around) (cut)
white gauze.

9. I will _____ a _____ for providing the polar bear
(predict) (plan)
with polka-dotted pajamas.

Level 3, Language

We Don't Have the Foggiest . . .

An **idiom** is a group of words that have a special meaning when they are used together. The cartoons on this page each suggest an idiom.

▶ Write each idiom in a sentence. Then, tell its meaning in your own words.

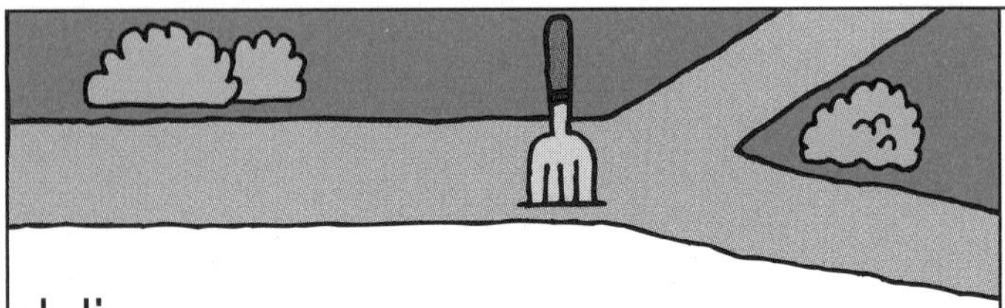

Idiom: _____

_____

Meaning: _____

_____

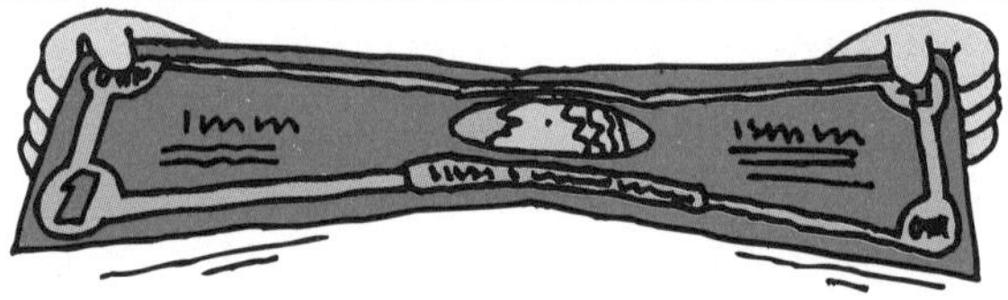

Idiom: _____

_____

Meaning: _____

_____

Idiom: _____

_____

Meaning: _____

_____

Idiom: _____

_____

Meaning: _____

_____

Idiom: _____

_____

Meaning: _____

_____

Idiom: _____

_____

Meaning: _____

_____

Name _____

Alien Visitors

An **analogy** is made of two sets of ideas that are compared in the same way. Think how the first set is compared, and compare the second the same way.

▶ Fill in the lines to complete these analogies.

1. **Nest** is to **bird** as **hive** is to _____ .

2. **L** is to **K** as **B** is to _____ .

3. **Hot** is to **cold** as **enemy** is to _____ .

4. **Day** is to **night** as **follow** is to _____ .

5. **He** is to **him** as **we** is to _____ .

6. **Six** is to **four** as **four** is to _____ .

7. **Paper** is to **pencil** as **chalkboard** is to _____ .

8. **F** is to **G** as **N** is to _____ .

9. **Girl** is to **boy** as **early** is to _____ .

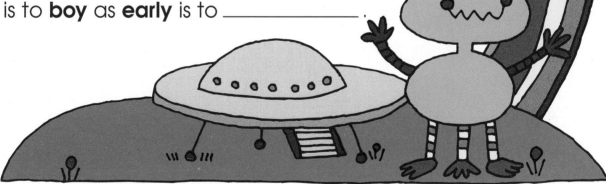

▶ Now, write the new words from the analogies in order to discover what the creature in the picture is saying. Use correct punctuation.

Hint: You will have to respell some words and combine others.

The creature said, " _____ ,

_____ "

Missing Letters in a Letter

When you receive a gift, you usually want to thank the giver right away. One way to do this is to write a thank-you note.

▶ First, fill in the missing letters for certain words. Then, select the correct labels from the Word Bank to name each part of this thank-you note. Write the labels on the correct lines.

_____

_____

_____

January 17, 2002

Dear Uncle Charlie,

Boy w __ s I surpr __ sed today when the mail was delivered to our house. You not only __ emembered my birthday, you sent the __ erfect gift. I know that bui __ ding the model you sent will be a real ch __ llenge, but I can't wait to get started. It is the very model I have bee __ looking for in all th __ catalogs.

Gratefully,

Doug

_____

_____

Word Bank

Closing
Date
Body
Signature
Greeting

▶ Now, answer this question using the missing letters:
What kind of model did Uncle Charlie send to Doug? _____

Nursery Rhyme Gifts

Each of the gift boxes below contains a useful thing for one of the characters in the listed nursery rhymes.

▶ Unscramble the letters in each box. Then, write the name of each present next to the name of the character to whom you would give it. If a box in divided, it contains two words. The number on each box matches the number of the character who receives the gift.

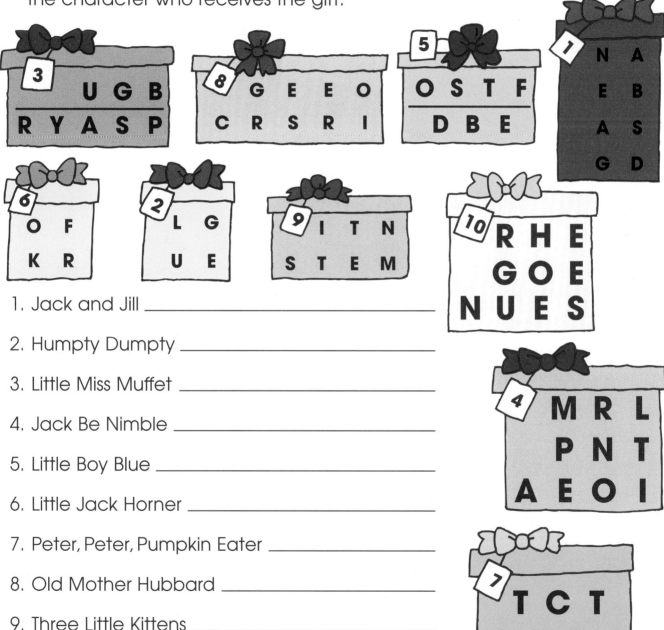

1. Jack and Jill _____

2. Humpty Dumpty _____

3. Little Miss Muffet _____

4. Jack Be Nimble _____

5. Little Boy Blue _____

6. Little Jack Horner _____

7. Peter, Peter, Pumpkin Eater _____

8. Old Mother Hubbard _____

9. Three Little Kittens _____

10. Mary, Mary, Quite Contrary _____

Level 3, Language

Be Wise!

Proverbs are folk sayings that have been used for so long that it is difficult to know who first said them. They are wise sayings whose meanings teach lessons that help people to learn.

Example: "Big oaks from little acorns grow," is a proverb. It means that even great things have small beginnings.

▶ Match each of the proverbs in the first column with its meaning in the second. Write the number of each proverb on the line.

1. Two heads are better than one.

2. A stitch in time saves nine.

3. A bird in the hand is worth two in the bush.

4. All work and no play make Jack a dull boy.

5. Experience is the best teacher.

6. Many hands make light work.

7. You can't judge a book by its cover.

8. Haste makes waste.

9. A penny saved is a penny earned.

10. Misery loves company.

_____ A sad person wants friends to be around.

_____ Doing a job slowly, but carefully, saves time in the long run.

_____ Everyone needs time off from work.

_____ If you hurry with a job, it will not be done correctly.

_____ Outward appearances don't tell you about the kind of person one is.

_____ Be satisfied with what you have.

_____ The more people helping with a job, the faster it is done.

_____ Don't spend money foolishly.

_____ Problems are solved more easily by getting someone's advice.

_____ We learn best by doing.

These brainteasers all have something to do with mathematics. Numbers, relationships, Venn diagrams and even some trick questions will help to keep your math muscles sharp.

Follow the directions carefully in these brainteasers and you will find that math pops up in the most surprising places.

Leaping Frogs

Two large bullfrogs named Lefty and Righty are having a contest. These are the rules for their race.

▶ As each bullfrog passes a square on a domino, he must add the value if it is 5 or more and subtract the value from his total if it is 4 or less. The bullfrog with the greater number at the finish line is the winner.

Which frog won the contest? _____

The winning number of points was _____.

The losing number of points was _____.

Name _____

The Alligator and the Fish

The alligator was hungry. When a school of fish swam by, the alligator shouted, "You will be my lunch today!"

The principal fish said, "You may eat me, my whole school of fish and even my future students if you can solve this riddle."

"How many 3-digit number combinations can you make using these numbers?"

1 6 8

The alligator thought and thought, and finally answered, "That's easy. I can make six numbers."

The principal fish said, "You are wrong," and he showed the correct answer to the alligator.

▶ Write all the 3-digit number combinations you can make using 1, 6 and 8. You know the answer is not six! **Hint:** Turn one number upside-down.

_____

_____

Level 3, Math

Count Your Marbles

Shawn was preparing for the big marble tournament. He opened his marble bag and dumped out the marbles to count them. There were at least 30, but no more than 50, marbles. One-third of the marbles were cats' eyes, one-fourth were aggies, one-sixth were pearlies and one-eighth were steelies. The rest of the marbles were his favorites—the shooters.

▶ How many of each type of marble did Shawn have?
Hint: To find the total number, find a common denominator first.

_____ cats' eyes

_____ aggies

_____ pearlies

_____ steelies

_____ shooters

When the competition was over, Shawn had 1 1/2 times the number of marbles than before. Now, one-third of the marbles were cats' eyes, one-half were shooters, and the remaining marbles were equal amounts of aggies, pearlies and steelies.

▶ How many of each type of marble were in Shawn's marble bag at the end of the tournament?

_____ cats' eyes

_____ aggies

_____ pearlies

_____ steelies

_____ shooters

Name _____

Buy 1, Get 1 Free!

Sparky's Sports Cards Center is offering an unbelievable deal! If you buy one pack of any set of sports cards, you receive a second pack absolutely free!

▶ Figure out how many sets of sports cards Chris, John and Sharon each got by using the clues below.

1. Chris bought twice as many sets of baseball cards as football cards. Ice hockey was his least favorite sport, so he bought only two sets of these cards. Chris purchased three times as many sets of baseball cards as ice hockey.

   With the special offer, Chris went home with _____ sets of sports cards.

2. John bought twice as many sets of football cards as Chris. He bought one–third as many baseball cards as Chris. He bought two more sets of basketball cards than baseball cards. The number of sets of hockey cards he bought was three less than the number of sets of basketball cards.

   With the special offer, John went home with _____ sets of sports cards.

3. Sharon's favorite sport was ice hockey so she bought five times as many sets of hockey cards as John. She also purchased half as many baseball cards sets as Chris. Sharon bought four sets less of football cards than John did.

   With the special offer, Sharon went home with _____ sets of sports cards.

Name _____

Mixed Breeds

Twenty-five puppies lined up next to their masters to march in the "Perkiest Puppy Parade." Five breeds of dogs were represented.

▶ Read the clues to find out how many of each breed were in the parade.

Clues: • The German shepherds outnumbered the Old English sheep dogs by 5 to 1.

• There were twice as many cocker spaniels as German shepherds.

• The number of Dalmatians compared to toy poodles was a ratio of 2 to 1.

• The number of Dalmatians and toy poodles and Old English sheep dogs was the same as the number of cocker spaniels.

_____ German shepherds

_____ Old English sheepdogs

_____ Cocker spaniels

_____ Toy poodles

_____ Dalmatians

Name _____

What a Deal!

The five magician's cards below are arranged according to a pattern.

▶ Write the four missing numbers on the last card in the series.

2 5	3 4	4 3	5 2	
6 3	5 4	4 5	3 6	

▶ Now, complete this set of cards by writing the three missing numbers on the last card in the series.

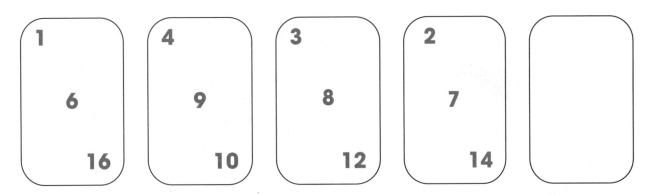

1	4	3	2	
6	9	8	7	
16	10	12	14	

Level 3, Math

Getting Things in Order

Name _____

When numbers are arranged in a pattern, you can continue it once you have identified the rule of the pattern. For example, in the pattern 1, 3, 4, 6, 7, you add 2 to the first number and 1 to the second and then keep repeating this as far as you want to go. The rule is + 2 + 1. The next three numbers in this pattern are 9, 10, and 12.

▶ Identify the rule that was used to form each of these patterns below. Write the next three numbers and the rule you used to find them.

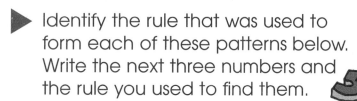

0, 5, 4, 9, 8 . . .   ____ ____ ____ Rule _____

1, 2, 4, 8, 16 . . .   ____ ____ ____ Rule _____

1, 3, 5, 7, 9 . . .   ____ ____ ____ Rule _____

0, 3, 1, 4, 2 . . .   ____ ____ ____ Rule _____

1, 4, 8, 11, 22 . . .   ____ ____ ____ Rule _____

15, 14, 12, 11, 9 . . .   ____ ____ ____ Rule _____

10, 15, 30, 35, 70 . . .   ____ ____ ____ Rule _____

8, 7, 6, 9, 8 . . .   ____ ____ ____ Rule _____

3, 5, 7, 14, 16 . . .   ____ ____ ____ Rule _____

1, 2, 3, 2, 3 . . .   ____ ____ ____ Rule _____

2, 4, 8, 3, 6 . . .   ____ ____ ____ Rule _____

5, 11, 9, 18, 23 . . .   ____ ____ ____ Rule _____

Start Your Engines!

This was the day for the annual Remote-control Car Derby. Five finalists awaited the starting signal. The winner would be determined by the driver who ran the most laps around the track in 30 minutes.

'Round and 'round the track they sped. Finally, the flag came down and the race was over. A total of 137 laps were run by the five drivers.

▶ Use the clues to determine the winners and the number of laps made by each of the five drivers.

Clues:
- Sammy made five more laps around the track than Lucy.
- Greg went around the track twice as many times as Mike.
- Jody and Lucy completed the same number of laps.
- Sammy finished a lap each minute.

Sammy _____ laps   Lucy _____ laps   Greg _____ laps

Mike _____ laps   Jody _____ laps

▶ Write the names of the winners of these trophies.

_____   _____   _____

Racing Chimps

One chimpanzee always liked to brag that it could get more fruit than any other animal in the forest. So, an older and wiser chimpanzee decided to challenge him to a race.

"Let us see who can bring back more bananas in one hour," said the older chimp. And so the race began.

Quickly, the younger chimp picked a bunch of five bananas and carried it back. He continued doing this once every five minutes.

The older chimp was not quite as fast. Every ten minutes he carried back eight bananas.

After 45 minutes, the young chimp decided to stop and eat one of his bananas before continuing. By the time he finished, the hour was over and the older chimp called out, "The race is over. Let's see who the winner is."

▶ Use the information above to figure out how many bananas were in each pile, and which chimp won the race.

The younger chimp had _____ bananas in his pile.

The older chimp had _____ bananas in his pile.

The winner was the _____ chimp!

Try, Try Again

A young mountain goat was learning how to climb. Unfortunately, he fell down a lot. An adult goat saw him and laughed, "You will never be able to climb mountains."

First, the little goat's feelings were hurt. Then, he became angry. "I will show that old mountain goat. I will learn to climb mountains," he said.

The young goat approached the bottom of the mountain and began climbing over the rocks. But, every time he climbed over three rocks, he slipped and fell back one rock. Finally, he made it to the top. "I knew I could do it!" he said proudly.

▶ How many times did the mountain goat have to start to climb to reach the

peak? _____ times

Level 3, Math

Venn Diagrams

A **Venn diagram** is a picture that represents a collection. The rectangle always stands for the whole collection. Any circle inside the rectangle stands for a part of it.

This Venn diagram represents all the trucks manufactured by a certain company. Circle R stands for all the red trucks, circle B for all the blue trucks and circle F for all the four-wheel-drive trucks the company made.

▶ Read each statement about this Venn diagram and identify it as either TRUE or FALSE.

1. All the trucks have four-wheel drive. _____

2. Some of the red trucks have four-wheel drive. _____

3. Some of the four-wheel-drive trucks are blue. _____

4. All of the blue trucks have four-wheel drive. _____

5. None of the red trucks have four-wheel drive. _____

6. All of the four-wheel-drive trucks are either red or blue. _____

7. None of the trucks with four-wheel drive are either red or blue. _____

Name _____

Going Out of Business

The Sunny Surf Shop was going out of business. Everything was marked down in price. On Saturday morning, bargain hunters came to the store looking for good buys.

Stock Up Now on Summer Items!

Sun hats and visors
Subtract $4

T-Shirts
Subtract $5

Double the Savings!

Double the Savings!

Windbreakers

Triple the Savings!

Triple the Savings!

Sandals
Subtract $6

Swimsuits
Subtract $7

Note the extra discounts when you purchase a windbreaker with another item.

▶ Figure out how much each purchase cost.

1. If Carol bought a sun hat that sold for $10 and a windbreaker that was marked $20, how much was her bill? _____

2. If Sally bought a swimsuit that originally sold for $45 and a windbreaker that was marked $28, how much did she spend? _____

3. If Bonnie bought a swimsuit that originally cost $32, sandals marked $20, a T-shirt marked $12 and a sun hat that originally cost $15, what would she have to pay? _____

How much money was spent by all three customers? _____

How much money was saved by all three customers? _____

Level 3, Math

A 24-Hour Clock

In the American military branches and sometimes in other countries around the world, a special way of telling time is used. It is based on a clock that has 24 hours instead of the standard 12. In this system, the day begins at 0000 and ends at 2359.

number   **0000**   number
of hours   **2359**   of minutes

The first half of each day is from 0000 to 1159. The second half is from 1200 to 2359. In this system you do not need to label time with A.M. or P.M. because the numbers themselves tell you if the time is in the first or second half of the day. Look at these rules for writing standard time as 24-hour-clock time.

For all A.M. times and for all 12 P.M. times, the time is written with the same numbers. Note that when the hour has only one digit, a zero is written before it.

Examples: 3:15 A.M. is 0315.
                12:15 P.M. is 1215.

For all other P.M. times, you add 12 to the number of hours in standard times.

Example: 3:15 P.M. is 1515.

▶ Now, you try it. Write the 24-hour-clock time for each standard time.

1. 5:03 A.M. _____   6. 2:00 A.M. _____

2. 7:39 P.M. _____   7. 9:10 A.M. _____

3. 12:00 P.M. _____   8. 9:10 P.M. _____

4. 12:55 A.M. _____   9. 12:00 A.M. _____

5. 6:30 P.M. _____   10. 4:44 P.M. _____

Name _____

Graphing Information

Graphs help picture numerical information. On this page is a horizontal bar graph, a vertical bar graph and a line graph. All three graphs are supposed to be pictures of the same information. Graph 1 is correct. But several mistakes were made in the making of Graph 2 and Graph 3.

▶ Find these mistakes on Graph 2 and Graph 3, and circle each one.

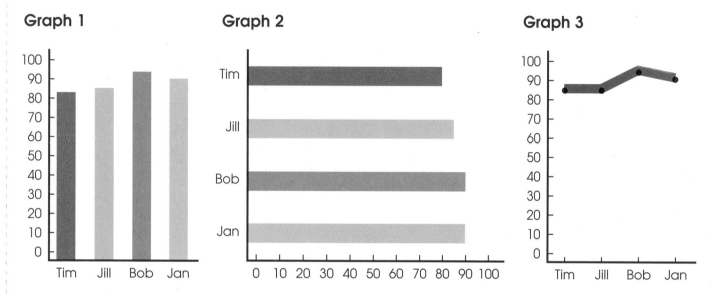

Graph 1

Graph 2

Graph 3

▶ Now, answer the following questions based on Graph 1.

1. What was Tim's math score? _____

2. What was Bob's math score? _____

3. Who had the highest score? _____

4. Who had the lower score, Tim or Jill? _____

5. Who had the higher score, Jan or Jill? _____

6. Who had the higher score, Bob or Jan? _____

7. Which graph, 2 or 3, makes the scores look higher? _____

Don't Be Fooled

▶ There are four answers given for each mathematical question on this page, but only one is correct. Fill in the circle in front of the correct answer.

1. If a mile measures 5,280 feet, how many feet are there in 3 miles?

   ○ a. 10,560   ○ b. 5,280
   ○ c. 5,283   ○ d. 15,840

2. If a farmer has 7 goats and he sells all but 4, how many are left?

   ○ a. 4   ○ b. 3
   ○ c. 7   ○ d. 0

3. If some months have 31 days and others 30, how many months have 28 days?

   ○ a. 2   ○ b. 1
   ○ c. 12   ○ d. 3

4. If a yard contains 36 inches, how many inches are there in half of a yard?

   ○ a. 18   ○ b. 12
   ○ c. 72   ○ d. 46

5. How many 6-cent candies are there in a dozen?

   ○ a. 6   ○ b. 24
   ○ c. 2   ○ d. 12

6. If there are 2 pints in a quart and 4 quarts in a gallon, how many pints are there in a gallon?

   ○ a. 8   ○ b. 6
   ○ c. 16   ○ d. 2

7. If there are 10 pieces of paper and you take away 6 of them, how many pieces do you have?

   ○ a. 4   ○ b. 10
   ○ c. 6   ○ d. 5

8. If you drink a glass of water every half-hour beginning at 9:00, when will you have drunk 4 glasses of water?

   ○ a. 10:00   ○ b. 10:30
   ○ c. 11:00   ○ d. 11:30

9. If February has 29 days in 2000, when were the last two leap years?

   ○ a. 1992 and 1996   ○ b. 1995 and 1999
   ○ c. 1994 and 1998   ○ d. 1980 and 1990

10. If two 2-inch thick books are standing next to each other on a shelf, how many inches are there between the last page of the first book and the first page of the last?

   ○ a. 2   ○ b. 4
   ○ c. less than 1   ○ d. more than 1

Here's your chance to travel to many places near and far. The brainteasers in this section will introduce you to some fantastic places that you may have already visited or may visit some day. You can increase your enjoyment of those experiences by getting to know as much as possible about the places. But even if you never actually see them, you can always dream and be an "armchair" traveler.

A Secret Message

▶ Let's see how good you are at reading rebus sentences. Each line below is one word in the sentence.

L + (✈ – j) + 's = _____

S + (🐝 – b) = _____

(🪤 – rap) + (🐔 – n) = _____

(🦄 – 🌽) + t + (🛏 – b) = _____

(🥪 – pler) + (⊙ – ir) + s = _____

▶ Suppose this suggestion was made to you. The rebus below might suggest your answer. What is it?

Y + (♟ – CH – S) = _____

Name _____

State Wise

▶ Every state in the United States can boast about its famous sites, events that have taken place in it and the well-known people who come from it. See how state wise you are by identifying each of the states hinted at below.

1. I am the Lone Star State. I used to be the largest state, but now I'm the second largest. I was the home of the Alamo and of Sam Houston. My capital is Austin.

   Which state am I? _____

2. I am called the Sunshine State. Many people come to live in my nice warm temperatures during the wintertime. I am the home of the Kennedy Space Center and the Everglades. My capital is Tallahassee.

   Which state am I? _____

3. I am called the Green Mountain State. I was a part of the original thirteen colonies. Now many people come in wintertime to ski on my mountain slopes and enjoy good maple syrup. My capital is Montpelier.

   Which state am I? _____

4. I am called the Keystone State because of my shape. I am the home of Benjamin Franklin, Independence Hall and the Liberty Bell. My capital is Harrisburg.

   Which state am I? _____

5. I am called the Buckeye State. Eight presidents were born within my borders. I am the home of the Football Hall of Fame and the Rock and Roll Hall of Fame. My capital is Columbus.

   Which state am I? _____

Challenge! If your state is not mentioned, write a description of it.

_____

_____

Level 3, Social Studies

Name _____

The Grand Canyon

The Grand Canyon is probably the most popular of America's national parks.

▶ See if you can complete these interesting facts about this site by unscrambling the letters at the end of each sentence. Use the Word Bank if necessary.

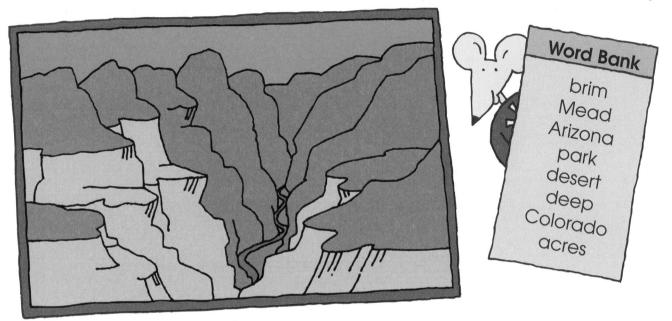

Word Bank

brim
Mead
Arizona
park
desert
deep
Colorado
acres

1. The Grand Canyon has been a national _____ since 1908. (karp)

2. Grand Canyon National park covers 1,218,375 _____ . (caesr)

3. The canyon is 4 to 13 miles wide at its _____ . (rmib)

4. The canyon is between 4,000 and 5,000 feet _____ . (epde)

5. The Grand Canyon is located in northwestern _____ . (zanioar)

6. The canyon was formed by the _____ River. (rodoclao)

7. The bottom of the Grand Canyon is mostly _____ . (seetrd)

8. The Lake that forms at the southern end of the Grand Canyon is called

   Lake _____ . (deam)

Name _____

Plymouth Rock

In Plymouth, Massachusetts, you can see a famous rock that marks the Pilgrims' landing in America in 1620. The graphite boulder with the date carved on it is named "Plymouth Rock." It lies near the water's edge.

▶ See how many things you can find in this word search that might either have been seen by the Pilgrims long ago near Plymouth Rock or by a tourist visiting the area today. Use the Word Bank, if you need to.

```
A D S J L F M K L T Z J P Y
Q N K M B E A V E R S B U I
I E P T M A Y F L O W E R X
C P H O G C F M G O N G I H
O I U U O L L O E T Y R T M
B L H R I F O N Z N F D A W
P G A I J V W P F A D I N K
B R E S V K E L T U S M S X
O I V T C E R U D Q V R Q H
S M A S S A C H U S E T T S
T S T W S E O R B F U W W N
O R H P L Y M O U T H B A Y
N H A I C A P E C O D B A Y
Y R T P P R A Z X A N V X J
Z I Q B S P C O L O N Y O A
M I L E S S T A N D I S H C
```

Word Bank

Pilgrims
ship
Tourists
Cape Cod Bay
beavers
Mayflower
Massachusetts
Plymouth Bay
colony
traps
Miles Standish
Boston
Mayflower Compact
Squanto
Puritans
fish

Level 3, Social Studies

Name _____

Our National Anthem

"The Star-Spangled Banner" has been the National Anthem of the United States since 1931. It was written long before that by Frances Scott Key. During the War of 1812, when the British were bombarding Fort McHenry in Baltimore, Key wrote the words to rejoice that the "Stars and Stripes" still flew over the fort. The flag Key saluted can still be seen in the Smithsonian Institute in Washington, D.C.

▶ Most Americans know the first verse of Key's song from memory. See if you do. Write the missing words in the verses below. You may use the Word Bank to help you.

Word Box

rockets'	glare	banner	stars
light	proof	see	proudly
brave	air	stripes	flag
gallantly	wave	free	gleaming

O say, can you _____ , by the dawn's early _____ ,

What so _____ we hail'd at the twilight's last _____ ?

Whose broad _____ and bright _____ , thro' the perilous

fight, O'er the ramparts we watch'd, were so _____ streaming?

And the _____ red _____ , the bombs bursting in

_____ , Gave _____ thro' the night that our _____

was still there. O say, does that star-spangled _____ yet

_____ O'er the land of the _____ and the home of the

_____ ?

Name _____

Down on the Farm

The colonists were the people who were the first Europeans to come and live in what is now the United States. They needed much help and hard work just to get by in those early days. One of the things they did was to learn how to grow corn. Look at the rows of corn below. Each stalk is numbered from 1 to 24. Notice that the first number has a circle around it, the second a square and the third a triangle.

▶ Continue the pattern of shapes for all the corn.

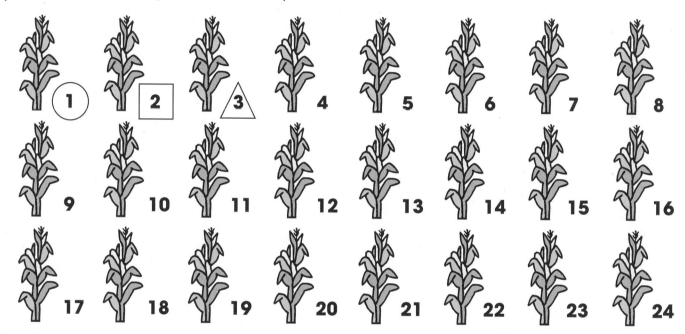

▶ Now, imagine that a colonist named Thomas picked all the corn marked with circles, one named Jonathan picked all the corn marked with squares and one named James picked all the corn marked with triangles.

1. Who picked and husked corn from cornstalk 20? _____

2. Who picked and husked corn from cornstalk 22? _____

3. If all the even-numbered cornstalks had two ears of corn, and all the odd-numbered cornstalks had one ear of corn, how many ears of corn did each boy husk?

Thomas _____   Jonathan _____   James _____

Level 3, Social Studies

Name _____

Inventions and Inventors

What did people do before they had telephones, radios, TV's and airplanes? How did they get along without electric lights, rubber tires and sewing machines? This brainteaser will help you to think about the people responsible for giving us these things.

▶ In the first column of each section is a list of important inventions along with dates in which they were created. In the second column is a list of the inventors. Match the inventors in each section with their invention by writing the number of the invention on the line. If you're not sure about an answer, check an encyclopedia or the Internet.

1. Telescope — 1609   _____ Benjamin Franklin
2. Bifocal lens — 1780   _____ Galileo
3. Telegraph — 1837   _____ Charles Goodyear
4. Rubber tires — 1839   _____ Samuel F.B. Morse

5. Sewing machine — 1846 _____ Alexander Graham Bell
6. Telephone — 1876   _____ Thomas Edison
7. Electric light bulb — 1879 _____ Gottlieb Daimler
8. Motorcycle — 1885   _____ Elias Howe

9. Radio — 1895   _____ Igor Sikorsky
10. Airplane — 1903   _____ Guglielmo Marconi
11. Helicopter — 1939   _____ Edwin Land
12. Polaroid Camera — 1948 _____ Wright Brothers

Challenge! Select one of these inventions. Write a thank-you note to its inventor and tell him how it helps you.

_____

_____

Name _____

Great Land Masses

There are seven continents in the world: North America, South America, Europe, Asia, Africa, Australia and Antarctica. All but the last two of these continents are divided into countries.

▶ Use the outline map below to help you decide on which continent each of the countries listed below belongs. Then, check your answers on a globe or world map.

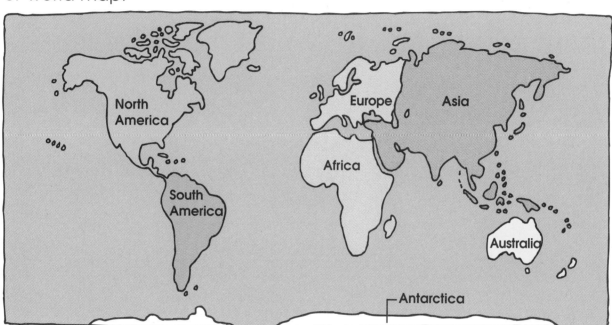

1. Argentina _____   9. England _____

2. Japan _____   10. Brazil _____

3. Italy _____   11. Canada _____

4. United States _____   12. Germany _____

5. Egypt _____   13. Mexico _____

6. Russia _____   14. Chile _____

7. Spain _____   15. Kenya _____

8. China _____

Level 3, Social Studies

Capitals of the World

Every country in the world has a capital city where the leaders of the country live and work. Usually this capital city is large and very busy and has many important buildings where government workers do their jobs. Sometimes capitals are well known for other reasons as well.

▶ Listed below are eight capital cities along with several clues about each. Fill in the circle next to the country of each of the capitals.

1. Rome
   (in the middle of a "boot," the Eternal City)

   ○ France   ○ Italy
   ○ China   ○ Germany

2. Ottawa
   (North of the United States, home of the Royal Mounties)

   ○ Germany   ○ France
   ○ Brazil   ○ Canada

3. Cairo
   (in the same country as the pyramids, on the Suez Canal)

   ○ Egypt   ○ China
   ○ Japan   ○ Italy

4. Berlin
   (once surrounded by a wall, the Rhine River)

   ○ Canada   ○ Japan
   ○ Germany   ○ England

5. Dublin
   (shamrocks, St. Patrick's Day)

   ○ England   ○ Canada
   ○ Ireland   ○ Denmark

6. Jerusalem
   (very old city, home of the temple wall)

   ○ Italy   ○ Israel
   ○ Egypt   ○ England

7. Amsterdam
   (dikes keep back water, windmills)

   ○ United States   ○ India
   ○ Netherlands   ○ Russia

8. Washington, D.C.
   (home of the Washington Monument, on the Potomac)

   ○ Norway   ○ Canada
   ○ United States   ○ Israel

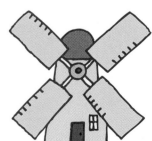

Name _____

A Taste of Italy

Italy is famous for its good food. Chances are that you have enjoyed Italian pizza at one time or another yourself.

▶ Unscramble the letters to spell three different toppings on each pizza.

onpepiper

mah

oomsshmur

_____

_____

_____

vsacnhoei

nsoino

dourng feeb

vslieo

gseauas

energ prseepp

_____   _____

_____   _____

_____   _____

Parthenon Pillars

Greece is one of the countries of southern Europe. It is a very mountainous country. Its most famous mountain is Mount Olympus, the highest in Greece. It stands 9,576 feet above the sea. Athens is the capital and best-known city in Greece. High above Athens are the ruins of the Parthenon, an ancient temple. People from all over the world climb to the heights over Athens to visit this wonderful building. It was built around 400 B.C. and dedicated to the goddess Athena. Beautiful statues and sculptures once filled this magnificent structure. The Parthenon measures 237 feet in length and 110 feet in width. It stands about 60 feet tall. Forty-six Doric columns surround the outer edge of the temple.

▶ How would you answer the questions below?

1. Is Greece in Asia or Europe? _____

2. Is Greece generally flat land or mountainous? _____

3. Is the Parthenon on Mt. Olympus or overlooking Athens? _____

4. Is the Parthenon an old or a new building? _____

5. Was the Parthenon a temple or a fort? _____

Challenge! If there are eight columns on each of the smaller sides of the Parthenon, how many columns can be seen on each of the longer sides?

Hint: The long and short sides share a corner column. _____

Name _____

Chinese Cyclists

China is a large country in Asia. About one-fifth of the world's population lives in China. There is less than one automobile for every 500 people, so people generally use simple means of transportation, such as walking and riding bicycles.

▶ Think about these three problems and see if you can solve them.

1. One bicyclist arranged to meet his cousin at a point midway between their homes. They each had to ride 5 miles. One rode at a rate of 10 miles per hour and the other at only 5 miles per hour. If the cousins wanted to meet at 2:00 P.M., what time should each leave home to arrive on time?

_____

2. If a bicyclist can average 8 miles per hour, when should she leave for a 4:00 P.M. appointment that is 12 miles away?

_____

3. It took 3 hours for a young man to walk 9 miles to his school. How fast was he walking?

_____ miles per hour

The Lion Dance

The Lion Dance, which started in China, became a Japanese folk dance. In this dance many people line up under a long piece of colorful cloth. The person in front wears a mask of a lion's head. As a group, the line of people dance in the streets around the town.

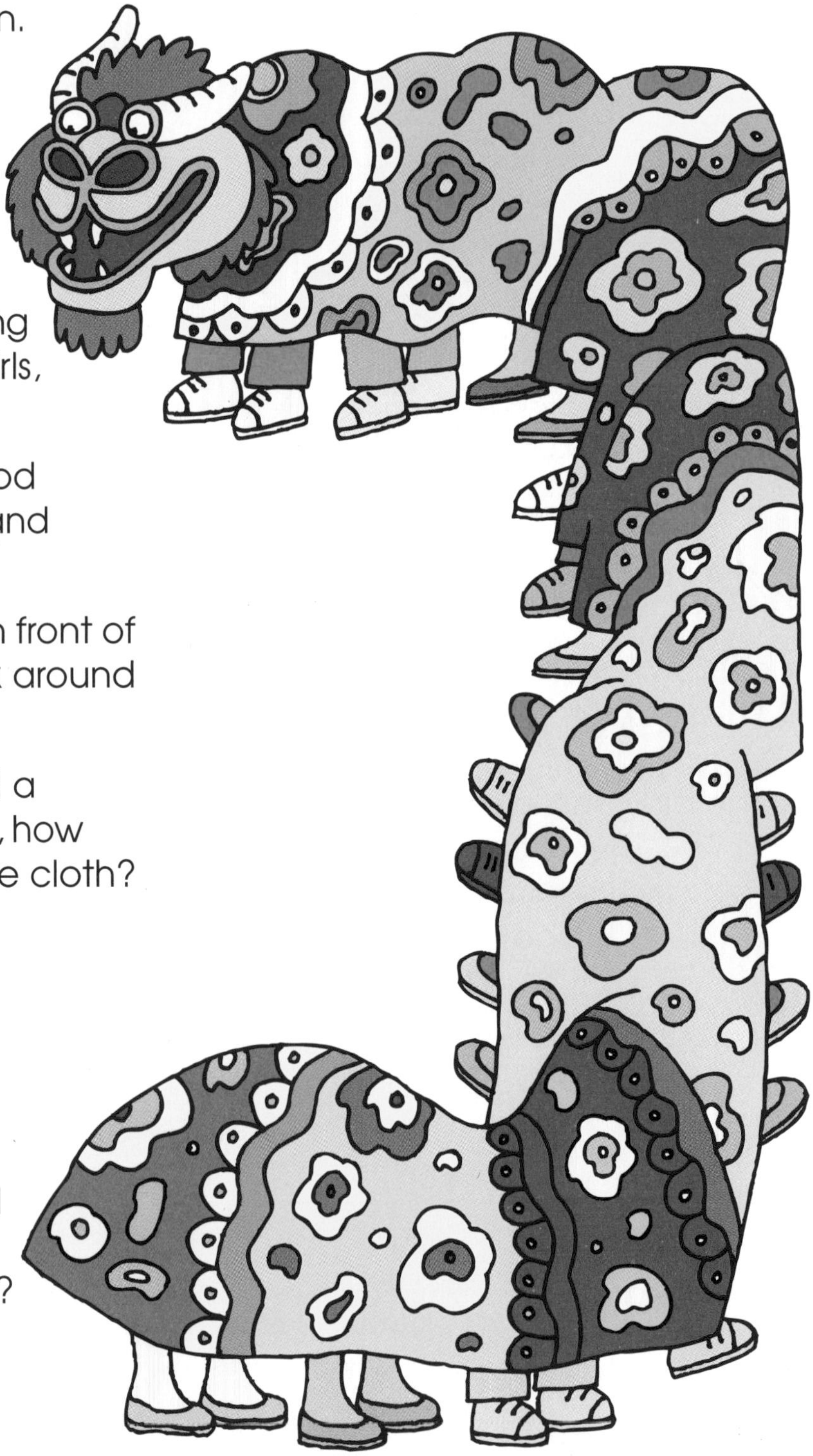

▶ In this Lion Dance, the children lined up according to this pattern: 2 boys, 2 girls, 2 boys, 2 girls, and so on.

- A boy named Masato stood behind the fifth boy. Find and **circle** his left foot.

- A girl named Koko stood in front of the seventh boy. Put a **box** around her left foot.

- If every two children need a 4-foot section of the cloth, how many feet long is the entire cloth?

_____ feet

Challenge! How many yards long is the entire "lion" if the head extends out for another four feet?

_____ yards

Name _____

Oriental Origami

Japan is an island country in Asia. It is sometimes called "The Land of the Rising Sun." One of the things Japan is famous for is the art of origami. This is the art of folding paper to create beautiful shapes and figures.

Suppose Masato and five of his friends fold sheets of paper to create the figures below.

▶ Read the clues and decide who made each origami figure. Write the correct name on the line below each figure.

Clues: • Masato's figure and Yoshiko's figure are both in the middle.
- Both Kenichi's and Takashi's figures are on the ends.
- Yukiko's figure is directly to the right of Kenichi's.
- Masato's figure is separated from Kenichi's by two other figures.
- Manami's figure is separated from Yukiko's figure by two others.

_____ _____ _____ _____ _____ _____

▶ Now, use these clues to discover which one of the figures required the most folds and which one required the least.

Clues: • The frog needed twice as many folds as the tyrannosaurus.
- The walrus was made with 3 less folds than the tyrannosaurus.
- The elephant was constructed with exactly 1/2 as many folds as the lobster.
- The elephant consisted of 6 more folds than the frog.
- The kangaroo needed more folds than the tyrannosaurus and less than the frog.

The _____ needed the most folds, and the _____

needed the least.

Level 3, Social Studies

Name _____

Kenya's Kingdom

Kenya is a beautiful country on the continent of Africa. Large areas of Kenya have been set aside as national parks and wildlife preserves. Tourists come from all over to see many unusual animals in their natural settings. In these parks and preserves, the animals are protected from those who might harm them.

▶ Try your hand at these tricky problems about the animals of Kenya.

1. An ostrich traveled forty miles at a rate of 20 miles per hour. What was its rate of speed?

   _____

2. A crocodile laid 34 eggs and buried them in the mud. Three large lizards found the eggs and carried them away. The first lizard carried 3 eggs every 10 minutes. The second carried 5 eggs every 15 minutes. The third carried 1 egg every 2 minutes. How long did it take the lizards to carry off all the eggs?

   _____

3. Three giraffes nibbled on the leaves of a tree that was 35 feet tall. The first giraffe was 1/5 the height of the third giraffe. The second giraffe was 5 times the height of the first giraffe. The third giraffe's head reached 3/7 of the height of the tree. What are the heights of the three giraffes?

First giraffe   _____

Second giraffe _____

Third giraffe   _____

Name _____

"True" Tales

Three men claimed to have taken a photograph of the mysterious Sasquatch, also known as Bigfoot. Information collected from previous reports states that Bigfoot is from 7 to 10 feet tall, weighs over 500 lbs., has thick fur and long arms, and walks upright on two feet, leaving footprints over 16 inches long.

Mr. T. Rapper's Story

"Last month I was camping in the mountains of Canada. While sitting by my campfire, I saw a huge creature at least 9 feet tall coming towards me. I grabbed my 14-foot-long fishing net, climbed a tree and dropped it, completely covering Bigfoot, entangling his arms and legs. I jumped down, grabbed a camera and snapped this picture. As I turned to look for rope, Bigfoot broke free and ran back into the woods."

Mr. A.D. Venture's Claim

"I went looking specifically for Sasquatch. The last I heard, he was seen in the mountains of Washington. I drove my car on the winding roads hoping to catch a glimpse. I was becoming sleepy, so I pulled off the road and dozed off. I was awakened suddenly by a loud crunching sound. The creature had climbed onto the hood of my car and was staring at me through the windshield. I grabbed my camera and jumped out of the car. Sasquatch thumped down on the ground as I snapped a picture. He ran off into the forest before I could do anything else."

Mr. X. Plorer's Version

"I am an ornithologist. Studying birds is my profession. I was patiently waiting for a rare species of bird to return to its nest in a 13-foot tree when I saw a large, hairy creature. The 10-foot-tall creature bent down in front of the tree, picked up a tiny bird and placed it in the nest. I hastily snapped a picture. Bigfoot heard the click, looked around and then raced out of sight."

▶ Examine the facts and the photographs. Determine which story could possibly be true and explain why.

_____

_____

_____

_____

Beaches 'n' Bonnets

The Bahamas are a chain of about 3,000 coral islands and reefs in the West Indies. If you visit the Bahamas, you probably will spend some time on the beach. So put on your swimming suit, grab a beach towel and prepare to soak up some rays.

The temperatures might seem perfect to you. It will be 85°F by 10:00 A.M. in the morning. It will then rise 1 degree every hour until about 2:00 P.M., when it will begin to decrease 2 degrees every hour until about 7:00 P.M.

1. What will the thermometer read at 4:00 P.M.? _____

2. What will the temperature be at 7:00 P.M.? _____

You will probably want to get a sun hat for the rest of your stay. An open-air market sells a variety of straw hats. The prices vary depending on their structure and design.

▶ What is the actual price of each kind of hat? Add the additional cost to the basic hat price. Write the actual price on the line below each hat.

Basic Hat $2.00 Add $1.50 Add $.75 Add $1.25 Add $1.00

▶ The merchant has 50 hats to sell in the following quantities:

• 2/5 of the hats are of the basic variety with no flowers or bands.

• 3/10 of the hats have floral patterns with no flowers or bands.

• 1/5 of the hats contain geometric patterns with bands, but no flowers.

• 1/10 of the hats are of the basic variety and have flowers, but no bands.

• The merchant has run out of the basic hats with bands.

If the merchant sells all of the hats except for four with floral patterns and no flowers or bands, and two hats with geometric patterns and bands, how much money will he take in? _____

In this section, you will be solving brainteasers about the natural world around you. There is a wealth of information on these pages. When you answer one question, more than likely, other questions will come to mind for you to wonder about. That's what makes the study of science so interesting and challenging. Let these pages be the launch platform for all kinds of neat ideas.

Birds of a Feather

Birds are the only animals that have feathers. All birds have wings, but not all can fly. They all hatch from eggs, have backbones and are warm-blooded.

▶ Fill in the puzzle with the names of the birds you see on the eggs. The last letter of one name becomes the first letter of the next name. Start at the outside edge and spiral in toward the center. The first three names are written for you.

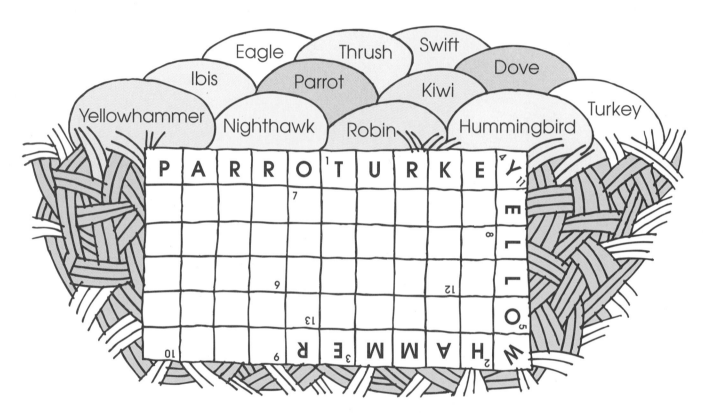

▶ Complete this story. Write the letters that are in the numbered boxes in the puzzle.

A sly and hungry fox quietly crept into the hen house one night. Carefully, he took a basket and began filling it with eggs. As he turned to leave, he tripped on a rake and went tumbling down, eggs and all. The hens awoke, laughed loudly, and said,

" ___ ___ ___   ___ ___ ___ ___ ___ ,   ___ ___   ___ ___ ___ !"
  1   2   3   4   5   6   7   8   9   10   11 12 13

Name _____

No Speed Limits

All animals exhibit some movement during the course of their lives.

The chart below indicates the comparative speeds of various animals:

Animals in the Air

| Housefly | 5 mph | Dragonfly | 50 mph |
| Robin | 30 mph | Peregrine Falcon | 180 mph |

Animals on Land

| Turtle | 1/10 mph | Gazelle | 50 mph |
| African Elephant | 25 mph | Cheetah | 70 mph |

Animals in the Water

| Goldfish | 4 mph | Dolphin | 25 mph |
| Sea Turtle | 20 mph | Sailfish | 30 mph |

▶ Answer the following questions by stating possible explanations.

1. What is there about a peregrine falcon that helps it to fly faster than a common housefly? _____

_____

2. If a tall person can frequently outrun a short person, why can't an elephant outrun a cheetah? _____

_____

3. What factors allow a peregrine falcon to move faster than a cheetah?

_____

_____

4. Although many land turtles are slow, lumbering creatures, the sea turtle can move rather swiftly. What might explain this?

_____

_____

Level 3, Science

Name _____

Animals on Guard

Wild animals in their natural habitats often face many different enemies and dangers. Each species has its own special ways of defending itself.

▶ Use the words in the Word Bank to complete the analogies about animal defenses.

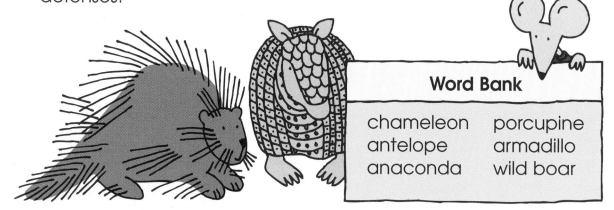

Word Bank

chameleon	porcupine
antelope	armadillo
anaconda	wild boar

1. **Arrows** are to an **archer** as **sharp quills** are to a(n) _____.

2. **Armor** is to a **knight** as **bony plates** are to a(n) _____.

3. **Racing tires** are to a **racecar** as **swift legs** are to a(n) _____.

4. **Disguises** are to a **spy** as **color changes** are to a(n) _____.

5. A **front bumper** is to a car as **tusks** are to a(n) _____.

6. **Powerful muscles** are to a **wrestler** as a **long muscular body** is to a(n)

_____.

Challenge! Now, try writing your own analogies for these animal defenses.

- **Escape down a hole** is to a **prairie dog** as _____

_____

- **Strong claws** are to an **eagle** as _____

_____

- A **pungent odor** is to a **skunk** as _____

_____

Name _____

Here are some more examples of how some plants and animals protect themselves.

Plants

The **teasel** is a plant that forms a moat between two leaves, collects rainwater at that point, and then drowns unsuspecting snails and insects.

The **screw pine**, a tropical plant, has tough, sword-shaped leaves with sharp barbs that can capture curious animals.

The **nettle** has leaves covered with hairs that act like needles that puncture and release irritating chemicals.

The **acacia tree** has hollow thorns that provide both a home and a sugary food for ants that, in turn, attack other animals endangering the tree.

The **sticky sundew** has leaves covered with sticky, glue-like hairs that trap insects.

The **octopus tree** has spines that extend beyond its leaves, providing it with protection from large animals.

Animals

The **armadillo** has a bumpy, worm-shaped tongue and gummy saliva with which to catch its prey.

The **markhor**, one of the largest species of goats, has great corkscrew horns to use as swords against enemies.

The **archer fish** takes aim at insects in the air and shoots water from its mouth to drown them. It then eats the insects when they fall to the ground.

The **spined spider**, a tropical short-legged spider, has sharp, brightly colored spines sticking out from its body to discourage predators from attacking it.

The **clownfish** lives near sea anemones. The clownfish provides food for the anemones and the anemones remove parasites from the clownfish.

The **gaboon viper**, with the longest fangs of any snake, can inject a deadly poison into its victim.

▶ Use the information above and the clues below to pair one plant with one animal that show a similar means of self-preservation. Write their names under the correct clue.

We like to "fence" with our enemies.	Always practice water safety near us.	We've been in many a "sticky situation."
_____	_____	_____
_____	_____	_____
We follow a buddy system.	Our message to intruders has a point!	Be careful! That's poison.
_____	_____	_____
_____	_____	_____

Level 3, Science

The Amazing Amazon

The land around much of the Amazon River in Brazil is a rainforest. There are more species of mammals, birds, reptiles, amphibians and insects living in the rainforest than anywhere else in the world.

▶ Below are statements about some of the animals that live in Brazil's rainforest. The statements are always true. Use the information provided to write a conclusion that is also true. The first one has been done for you.

1. The collared anteater is also called a tamandua. Anteaters eat mainly insects.

   Therefore, __a tamandua eats mainly insects.__

2. A coati is a member of the raccoon family. Raccoons are mammals.

   Therefore, _____

3. A toucan has feathers. Only birds have feathers.

   Therefore, _____

4. Capuchins are intelligent monkeys. Monkeys belong to the group of mammals called primates.

   Therefore, _____

5. A macaw is a species in the parrot family. A parrot is a bird.

   Therefore, _____

6. An iguana is a lizard that eats fruit, flowers and leaves. A herbivore is an animal that eats plants and grass.

   Therefore, _____

7. The capybara is the largest of all rodents. Rodents are mammals with front teeth suitable for gnawing.

   Therefore, _____

8. A falcon is a bird of prey. A caracara is a member of the falcon family.

   Therefore, _____

Name _____

The Mighty Sphinx

The Sphinx is an enormous stone sculpture in Egypt. It measures 66 feet in height and 240 feet in length. It has the head of an ancient Egyptian king and the body of a lion.

The Egyptians built sphinxes to honor kings, queens and other important personalities. The animal chosen to be part of the sphinx, usually the lion, represented characteristics of the honored person.

▶ Imagine you are planning to build a sphinx. Make a list of animals that might represent the characteristics given below. You can use the animals listed in the Word Bank or other animals if you wish.

Word Bank

antelope	dog	eagle
anaconda	cat	shark
tiger	monkey	elephant
gorilla	falcon	whale
chameleon	skunk	rattlesnake

Strength

_____

_____

_____

_____

Intelligence

_____

_____

_____

_____

Swiftness

_____

_____

_____

_____

Bravery

_____

_____

_____

_____

Level 3, Science

Jumbled Dangers

▶ Each set of jumbled letters below represents two possible dangers to explorers. Use the clue to help you unscramble the letters to name the two dangers. Use all the letters, but use each letter only once.

1. **Clue:** Both have nothing inside. Do you dig them?

POETHIL

_____   _____

2. **Clue:** Both are cats, but one is "king."

PLEIALRONDO

_____   _____

3. **Clue:** Both are man-eating and live in or near water.

PIROOEIACCRNDALH

_____   _____

4. **Clue:** Both are part of the Earth's surface, but vary greatly in size.

MTUADUONOEBLRIN

_____   _____

5. **Clue:** Both mammals like to charge, but not with a credit card.

COEHRHIPNLNEAOTERS

_____   _____

6. **Clue:** Both can make you "shake, rattle and roll."

OEVLCTAUAHEORANQK

_____   _____

7. **Clue:** Both like to "monkey around."

BLOBAOIOGRLAN

_____   _____

Name _____

Animals of Action

Here is a puzzle that will make you think.

The first two letters of the verb in each sentence on this page are the last two letters of the missing animal's name.

▶ Read each clue and use the verbs to help discover the names of various animals from around the world. Write each animal's name on the line. One has been done for you.

Example: The baby gorilla tightly latches onto vines.

1. The _____ needs new quills to replace those lost while defending itself.

2. The _____ hungrily feeds on leaves from the tallest trees.

3. The _____ often alarms animals and people with its mournful cry and yapping, usually heard at night.

4. The _____ learns to float in water with only its eyes and nostrils above the surface.

5. The _____ sometimes elects to go without water for days or even months.

6. The _____ quickly charges on two-toed feet.

7. The _____ uses its excellent swimming skills when staying under water for as long as 6 minutes.

8. The _____ goes into water, mud and sand to feed on the shell fish it finds.

Level 3, Science

Name _____

Animal Hints

▶ Complete the crossword puzzle about animals using the clues and the words from the Word Bank.

Word Bank

chinchilla
emperor penguin
gnu
musk ox
sea pen
vulture
yak
kangaroo rat
tarantula

1. No, I do not wear cologne!
2. I can save unchewed food in my stomach and later return it to my mouth for a meal.
3. While some may desire my coat, I need it more than they.
4. Although I am definitely water-based, you couldn't write with me.
5. Things may become a bit "hairy" if I crawl near you.
6. Who needs a president when I'm titled for life?
7. "What's new?" I'm often asked. I only shake my head and smile.
8. I can't talk, although my name may indicate the contrary.
9. Spoilage does not affect my appetite.

Name _____

Fluid Facts

Every living thing must have water to survive. Read the information in the water droplets to discover some important facts about water.

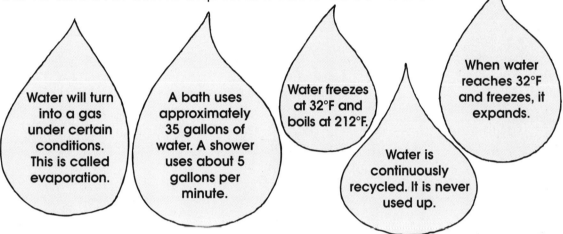

Water will turn into a gas under certain conditions. This is called evaporation.

A bath uses approximately 35 gallons of water. A shower uses about 5 gallons per minute.

Water freezes at 32°F and boils at 212°F.

Water is continuously recycled. It is never used up.

When water reaches 32°F and freezes, it expands.

▶ Use the information and your thinking skills to answer these questions.

1. Consider a family of 8 members. Four take daily baths. Two follow a schedule of 5-minute showers on Monday, Wednesday and Friday, and baths on the remaining days. The other family members take a 3-minute shower every day. How much water do they use for bathing in a week?

_____

2. A glass of ice water is filled to the top with the ice cubes extending over. Why doesn't it overflow when the ice melts? _____

_____

3. If you leave a glass of water on the sink for long enough, the water disappears. Where does it go? _____

_____

4. What happens to water that is boiled for a long time? _____

_____

Challenge! Explain how you would freeze a penny in the middle of an ice cube.

_____

_____

Name _____

Record-Setting Weather

Even though the people who predict weather use all sorts of complicated instruments, their forecasts are never 100% accurate.

▶ Here are some record-setting weather conditions. Look them over carefully. Then, answer the questions below.

Highest Recorded Temperature: 136.4°F

Libya,
September 1922

Lowest Recorded Temperature: –128.6°F

Antarctica,
July 1983

Greatest Snowfall in One Year: 1,224 1/2 inches

Washington state,
February 1971 to February 1972

1. How many degrees difference are there between the two record-breaking temperatures? _____

2. Six inches of wet, heavy snow equals about 1 inch of rainwater. About how much rain would have fallen instead of snow in Washington state in one year if the temperature remained above freezing? _____

3. On the Fahrenheit scale, 32 degrees is the freezing point of water and 212 degrees is the boiling point. About how many degrees from the boiling point was the highest recorded temperature? _____

4. About how many degrees from the freezing point was the lowest recorded temperature? _____

5. If the record snow fell on approximately 120 days in 1971 and 1972, about how many inches of snow were there per day? _____

Name _____

"Association" Power

"Learning all these scientific terms is hard!" said Brad.

"I have an idea!" exclaimed Vonda brightly.

"Let's make up associations for the scientific terms that we want to learn. That will help us remember the terms for tomorrow's test."

▶ Use the Word Bank to help Vonda and Brad choose scientific terms that fit into the situations below.

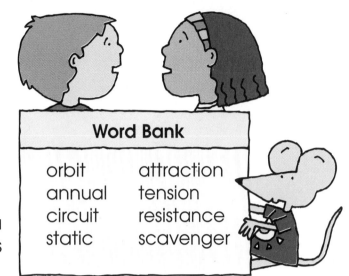

Word Bank

orbit	attraction
annual	tension
circuit	resistance
static	scavenger

1. When Ms. North and Mr. South met at the party, they must have felt an instant _____ because they've been together ever since.

2. After Brenda was rude and rubbed Sandy the wrong way, you could feel lots of _____ in the air.

3. Everyone felt the _____ grow as Ed G. Nerves sat between the two quarreling friends.

4. Sat L. Light seemed to go into _____ as he danced round and round the room.

5. Pat acted like a _____ as he ate everyone's leftovers.

6. Jim seemed excited as he completed a by connecting chairs all around the room. _____

7. Because Lyle's little sister Lilith was sleepy, she put up very little _____ while being carried to her crib.

8. The garden party was so much fun we'll make it an _____ event.

Level 3, Science

Space Lingo

▶ Carefully follow each direction on this and the next page to form words that are important for successful space travel.

1. Write a 3-letter word that means a rule we must obey. ___ ___ ___

   Add the name of the meal you eat at noon. ___ ___ ___ ___ ___

   Remove two letters to form a word that marks the beginning

   of a space trip. ___ ___ ___ ___ ___ ___

2. Write a 4-letter word that refers to a bottle stopper. ___ ___ ___ ___

   Jumble those letters to form a word that means "a stone." ___ ___ ___ ___

   Add "et" for the power source for a spaceship. ___ ___ ___ ___ ___ ___

3. Write a 2-letter word hidden in "that." ___ ___

   Add the abbreviation of Missouri. ___ ___

   Add a 6-letter word that means "a globe." ___ ___ ___ ___ ___ ___

   Combine the letters to form a word for the space around Earth.

   ___ ___ ___ ___ ___ ___ ___ ___ ___ ___

4. Write a 5-letter verb that shows how you might cook turkey or chicken.

   ___ ___ ___ ___ ___

   Add a fish often used in sandwiches. ___ ___ ___ ___

   Jumble the letters and you will have the name of a space crew member.

   ___ ___ ___ ___ ___ ___ ___ ___ ___

Name _____

5. Write a verb that means "to sulk." ___ ___ ___ ___

   Change two letters to form a word that means "to close." ___ ___ ___ ___

   Add a word that means "to allow." ___ ___ ___

   Jumble three letters to name an important space vehicle.

   ___ ___ ___ ___ ___ ___ ___

6. Write a word that names the punctuation used to separate words in

   a list. ___ ___ ___ ___ ___

   Add a word that means the opposite of "over."

   ___ ___ ___ ___ ___

   Remove a letter to show the leader of a space crew.

   ___ ___ ___ ___ ___ ___ ___ ___ ___

7. Write a 6-letter word that means "something very ordinary."

   ___ ___ ___ ___ ___ ___

   Add three letters that refer to the Central Intelligence Agency.

   ___ ___ ___

   Add the suffix in "attention." ___ ___ ___ ___

   Change one "o" to a "u" and jumble. You will form a word that is

   important for transmitted instruction.

   ___ ___ ___ ___ ___ ___ ___ ___ ___ ___ ___

Name _____

Kaleidoscope of Letters

A **kaleidoscope** is a small tube that contains tiny pieces of glass. When the kaleidoscope is turned, different arrangements of the glass are made. The results are beautiful designs.

▶ Each of the pieces of glass in this kaleidoscope contain a letter. These letters can spell a number of valuable treasures.

How many treasures can you form using only letters that are attached to each other by the sides of their triangular shapes? List them on the lines below.

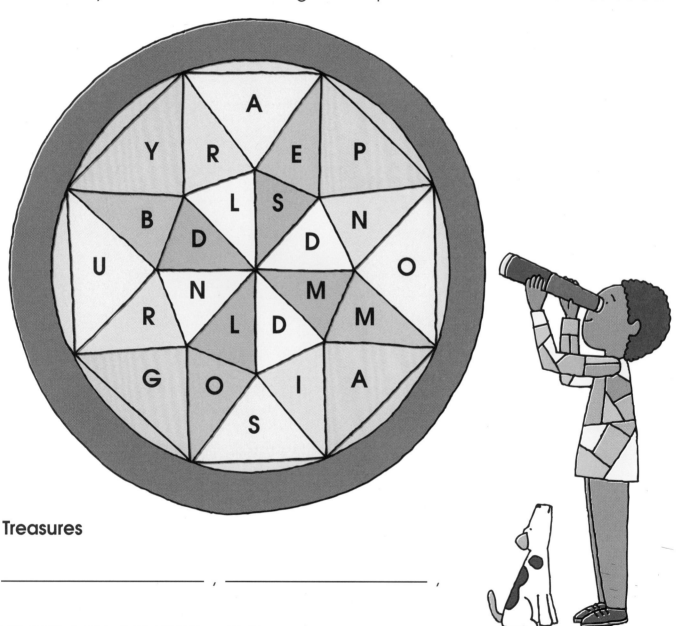

Treasures

_____ , _____ ,

_____ , _____ ,

Creative Arts

Everyone possesses some degree of creativity. Perhaps your work with these creative arts brainteasers will bring out some of yours. You may even find an area of the arts that sparks a special interest in you.

You Oughta Be in Pictures!

Photographs are pictures that capture images at a precise moment. **Movies**, on the other hand, appear to show continuous action. Actually, movies give us the **illusion of movement**. A movie contains thousands of still pictures that move before our eyes so quickly that we cannot detect the individual pictures! The photographs are in sequence with only a tiny change from one to the next. When they are flashed very quickly before our eyes, we see what we think is movement.

▶ Examine the twelve pictures below. Only the first and last pictures are in the correct places in the sequence. Number the other pictures from 2 to 11 so that they are also in the correct order.

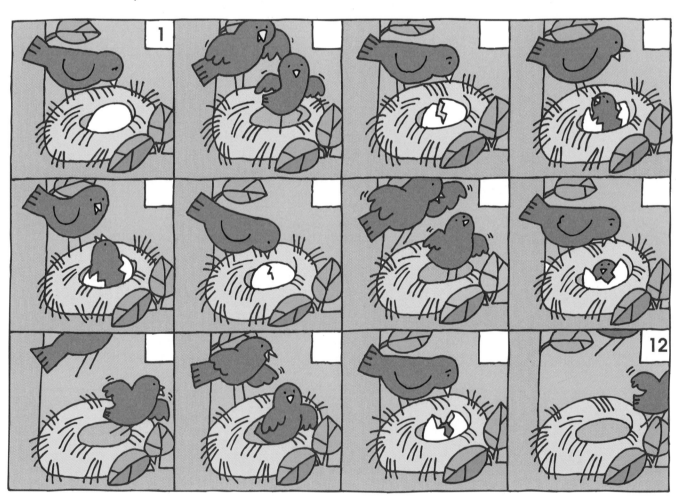

Write a sentence that describes what has happened in this sequence of pictures.

_____

Body Language

Mimes are easily distinguished from other actors by their appearance. They wear white make-up on their entire face with dark lines drawn around their eyes and red paint on their lips. A mime's clothing is simple—often white or black pants with a T-shirt and sometimes a hat.

▶ Here is a list of short skit ideas for a single mime to perform. Study the suggestions carefully. Then, number them from 1 to 10 in their order of difficulty with 1 being the easiest to perform.

_____ An astronaut landing on Mars _____

_____ Walking your stubborn dog to the vet's office _____

_____ Directing traffic at rush hour _____

_____ Running a relay on the moon _____

_____ Climbing the steps in the Empire State Building _____

_____ Feeding a playful baby _____

_____ Being a wind-up doll _____

_____ Making pizza at a restaurant _____

_____ Driving on a tall mountain _____

_____ Eating spaghetti that contains one long noodle _____

▶ Listed below are words that express feelings and emotions. Use these words or others of your choice to describe the feelings a mime might convey in each skit above. Write your choices on the lines above.

anger	diligence	hesitancy	persistency
astonishment	discontentment	hostility	relentlessness
boredom	disgust	impatience	resignation
competitiveness	displeasure	innocence	rigidity
complacency	exhaustion	light-heartedness	surprise
determination	giddiness	obstinance	uncertainty

Level 3, Creative Arts

With Expression

Timmy's teacher kept saying, "Try to read with more expression!" Yet it seemed that no matter how hard he tried, his words came out as flat as the paper on which they were written. Then, after a music lesson, Timmy got a terrific idea! He decided to use some Italian musical terms to help him put expression in his reading.

1. **accelerando** — gradually speeding up the tempo
2. **crescendo** — growing louder
3. **decrescendo** — growing softer
4. **fortissimo** — very loud

5. **largo** — very slow
6. **pianissimo** — very soft
7. **presto** — very fast
8. **tremolo** — quivering or trembling style

▶ Below are some sentences that Timmy had to read. After each sentence, write the number or numbers of the Italian terms that would have helped him read with expression. Use the expressions to help you read the sentences aloud.

1. ". . . Then, in the darkness, I heard heavy footsteps coming closer and closer behind me!" _____

2. "The hot sun in the dry desert seemed unbearable, and so I sat, hoping someone would come soon with water." _____

3. "Because we were so excited about opening our brightly wrapped presents, we slid down the long banister." _____

4. "The innocent baby lay sleeping, totally unaware of her admiring sister and brother." _____

5. "The majestic stallion ran quickly from the stable, looking behind as if something were hiding in the shadows." _____

Name _____

Fancy "Feets"

The feeling spreads
As the music flows,
It makes you want
To tap your toes!

If watching a professional tap dancer makes it look easy, try doing it yourself! It looks like fun, but you need a lot of muscle control and stamina to dance so quickly.

▶ Four dancers decided to have a contest to see who could tap-dance the fastest. Use the chart below to answer the questions.

> Tommy — 10 taps per second
> Rhonda — 150 taps every 15 seconds
> Sammy — 540 taps per minute
> Chris — 3,300 taps in 5 minutes

Which two people tapped at the some rate? _____

Which dancer could tap the fastest? _____

▶ The answer to the riddle below is hidden in the letters. Each vowel equals 1/2 beat and each consonant equals 1 beat. Circle the letters (from left to right) that represent each 5th beat. Then, write them in order on the blanks to solve the riddle.

A G L I S C S E M P Q O X Z N B

R O U D S T N E I G O C A S F H

U J K O P S X Y N T I M H J I Q

B A V W O H L B C N E S D O J S

What two vegetables did the tap dancer grow?

___ ___ ___ ___ ___ and "B" ___ ___ ___ ___ ___ ___

Shapes Within

Some artists paint very realistic pictures—apples that look real enough to eat, people who look as though they could walk off the canvas, and other objects so authentic-looking that a person touches them to see if they are real. Other artists' paintings are more abstract. They paint pictures that give the idea of an object, not a duplication of it. **Cubism** is one type of abstract art. Geometric shapes are a part of these pictures.

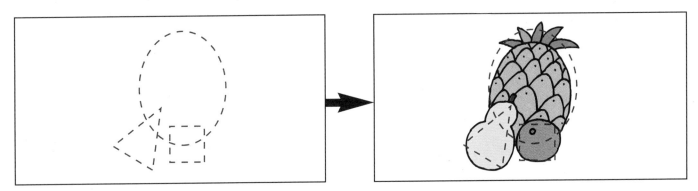

▶ The pictures below contain geometric shapes: circles, rectangles, ovals, squares and triangles. Use your imagination to decide what real objects could be represented by the shapes. Draw the real objects over the shapes in each of these four pictures.

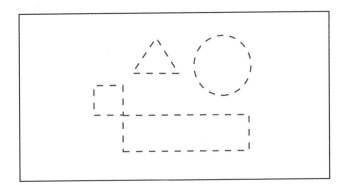
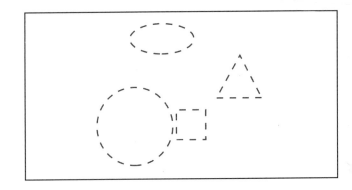

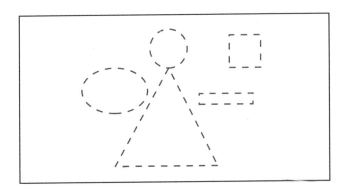
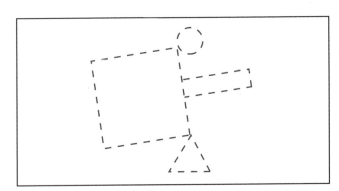

Bits and Pieces

▶ Below are some collages. Each one represents a favorite children's story. This could be tricky! One item is added to each collage that doesn't belong in it. Cross out that thing. Then, write the name of the story on the line. Choose the names from the Word Bank.

_____   _____   _____

_____   _____   _____

Word Bank

Jack and the Beanstalk
Pinocchio
Hansel and Gretel
Wizard of Oz
Three Little Pigs
Peter Pan
Aladdin
Cinderella

_____   _____

Level 3, Creative Arts

Name _____

An Array of Art

Mr. Art Curator was very excited. Today, the new shipment of artwork arrived. Every piece needed to be placed in the correct gallery. Read the title of each piece of art and decide in which gallery the artwork should be placed.

▶ Write the number of each art title in the correct room.

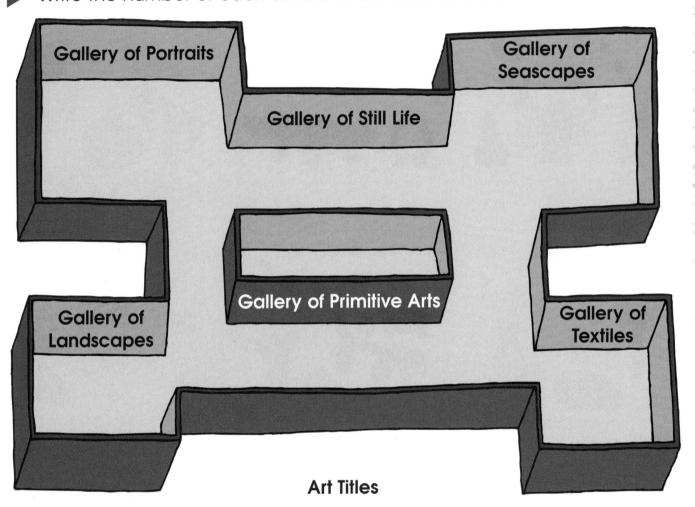

Art Titles

1. African Drum
2. Fruit in a Bowl
3. A Breeze Along the Coast
4. Rug of Twisted Braids
5. Spring Meadow
6. The Golden Violin
7. Adventure on High Seas
8. Chief of Sioux Nation
9. Knotted Wool Weaving

10. The Danube on a Summer Day
11. John Glenn, Astronaut
12. Brazilian Ceremonial Cup
13. Conquering the Peak
14. French Lace
15. City Congestion
16. Purple Vase with Primrose
17. Young Child with Mother
18. Cameroon Mask

Name _____

Mobility at Its Best

▶ Each mobile below needs related items to hang from each string. Choose things from the Word Bank that fit together. Write their names at the end of each string in their mobile. After each mobile is complete, write a title that explains why all of the objects in that mobile are related.

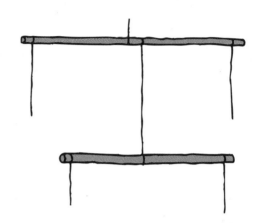

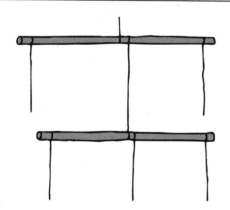

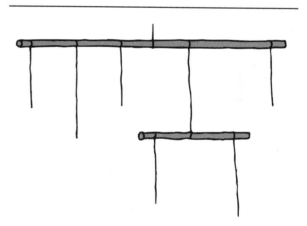

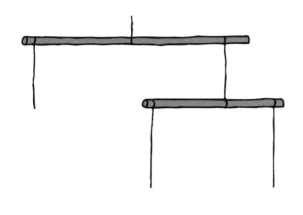

Word Bank

ant	fairy	leprechaun	troll
bee	goldfish	lion	unicorn
boar	gorilla	rhinoceros	whale
butterfly	gnome	rowboat	
elephant	grasshopper	tiger	

229

Level 3, Creative Arts

Name _____

The World Is Not Flat!

By adding a few lines to a square, an artist can make it look like a cube.

square   **cube**

The cube appears to have three dimensions.

▶ Examine the stacks of cubes below. Determine how many cubes each picture represents.

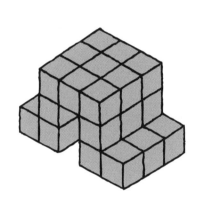

_____ cubes

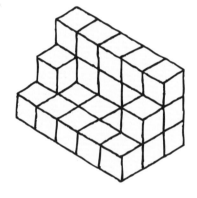

_____ cubes

_____ cubes

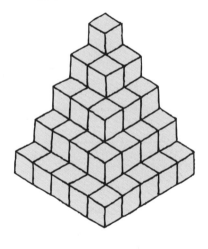

_____ cubes

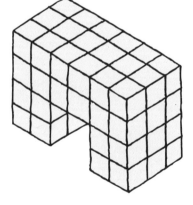

_____ cubes

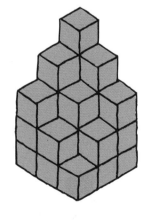

_____ cubes

Level 3, Creative Arts

230

Name _____

"Riddled" With Instruments

▶ In these riddles about musical instruments, one important word is missing in each. Find the word in the Word Bank and write it on the line. Then, in each box, write the letter of the instrument that fits the description.

☐ I have a _____ , but you won't find me on a playground.

☐ I have a large _____ , but don't fill me with groceries.

☐ I need a _____ , but you can't tie it.

☐ My _____ are pressed, not turned.

☐ You wouldn't want to eat me, even though I'm shaped like a _____ .

☐ Although chocolate-lovers crave them and dancers use them, you must strike my _____ to hear me.

☐ I don't require _____ when you bump my head.

☐ Fill me with lots of _____ , and you'll hear my deep voice.

☐ Although I contain lots of _____ , you couldn't use me to fly a kite.

A.

B.

C.

D.

E.

F.

G.

H.

I.

Word Bank		
keys	slide	bow
strings	pear	bars
aspirin	air	bag

231

Level 3, Creative Arts

Name _____

Banding Together

Six friends decide to form a band to play for special occasions. Read the clues to decide which instrument each musician plays. Use the chart to help organize the clues. Each musician plays only one instrument.

Clues:
- Fred plays the larger string instrument in the band.
- Ted plays a keyboard, but it's not electric.
- Patty cannot play the drums or a keyboard instrument.
- Sue must position herself near an electrical outlet.
- Greg uses wooden sticks.
- Melody cannot play drums, keyboard or a string instrument.

	Piano	Electric Keyboard	Banjo	Guitar	Drums	Flute
Melody						
Fred						
Ted						
Sue						
Patty						
Greg						

Melody plays a _____. Sue plays an _____.

Fred plays a _____. Patty plays a _____.

Ted plays a _____. Greg plays _____.

Name three musical instruments you probably would not want to add to this band.

Name _____

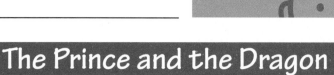

The Prince and the Dragon

In what could be a typical folk tale, the prince came to save the princess who was trapped in a cave by a huge, ferocious, fire-breathing dragon. The prince brought only a rope, a rock and a bucket of sand, but he could also do excellent voice imitations.

▶ Can you think of ways to save the princess from the dragon?

1. _____

2. _____

3. _____

4. _____

5. _____

6. _____

7. _____

8. _____

9. _____

10. _____

Level 3, Creative Arts

Name _____

Curtain's Going Up

Every play has three important elements: characters, setting and plot. The **characters** are the people who act out the play and recite the lines. The **setting** is the location and time in which the play takes place. The **plot** is what happens to the characters or what the characters do in the setting.

▶ There are six plays listed below. Each one has a catchy title. Your job is to briefly list the main characters, the setting and a short description of the plot of each play. The first one has been done for you. Use your own creativity.

1. **Title:** *Blizzard Blindness*
   Main Character: Sam Bravehart and his dog Mack
   Setting: Winter in the Maine woods
   Plot: Sam and his dog are lost in a blizzard. They are rescued by an unexpected twist in the plot.

2. **Title:** *What's Cooking?*
   Main Character: _____
   Setting: _____
   Plot: _____

3. **Title:** *In Search of the Blue Diamond*
   Main Character: _____
   Setting: _____
   Plot: _____

4. **Title:** *Capturing the Great Shark*
   Main Character: _____
   Setting: _____
   Plot: _____

5. **Title:** *The Talented Acrobat*
   Main Character: _____
   Setting: _____
   Plot: _____

6. **Title:** *Mystery of the Sinking Potion*
   Main Character: _____
   Setting: _____
   Plot: _____

Seasonal Fun Table of Contents

What Seasonal Brainteasers Are All About

Do you enjoy celebrating holidays? This section is is packed with activities that are related to holidays and celebrations throughout the year. Use the Seasonal Fun Table of Contents on the previous page to help you locate the holidays that are included in this section.

Seasonal Fun

You can use this section in two different ways. You may want to save pages for the actual holidays they commemorate, or you can complete the activities at any time you wish.

Some of these pages might be easy for you; others might be a real challenge. Try them all, in-season or out, for a year full of celebrations!

It All Begins in January

▶ Use number words to complete this calendar page.   New Year's Day

January						
Sun.	Mon.	Tues.	Wed.	Thurs.	Fri.	Sat.
				one	two	three
____ A	five	____ B	C	eight	nine	____ D
____ E	____ I	thirteen	____ M	____ N	sixteen	seventeen
eighteen	____ R	twenty	twenty- ____ S	twenty- ____ T	twenty-three	twenty-four
twenty- ____ U	twenty-six	twenty-seven	twenty- ____ Y	twenty-nine	thirty	thirty-one

▶ Now, match the letters on the calendar with the numbers to write the answer to this riddle.

Why does a calendar feel sad on New Year's Eve?

___ ___ ___ ___ ___ ___ ___   ___ ___ ___
6   11   7   4   25   21   11   12   22   21

___ ___ ___ ___   ___ ___ ___
10   4   28   21   4   19   11

___ ___ ___ ___ ___ ___ ___ ___ !
15   25   14   6   11   19   11   10

Name _____

We Go Together

▶ Can you find the missing fact from each family? To solve the riddle below, write the letter on the groundhog's shadow that matches the missing fact.

Groundhog Day

6 + 2 = 8
8 − 6 = 2
2 + 6 = 8

H

9 − 4 = 5
4 + 5 = 9
9 − 5 = 4

F

7 + 3 = 10
10 − 3 = 7
10 − 7 = 3

M

1 + 5 = 6
6 − 5 = 1
5 + 1 = 6

K

8 − 3 = 5
3 + 5 = 8
5 + 3 = 8

I

10 − 6 = 4
4 + 6 = 10
10 − 4 = 6

E

4 + 7 = 11
11 − 7 = 4
11 − 4 = 7

W

12 − 9 = 3
3 + 9 = 12
12 − 3 = 9

R

4 + 3 = 7
7 − 3 = 4
3 + 4 = 7

S

5 + 6 = 11
11 − 6 = 5
6 + 5 = 11

O

2 + 8 = 10
10 − 8 = 2
10 − 2 = 8

L

9 + 4 = 13
13 − 9 = 4
4 + 9 = 13

C

6 + 8 = 14
8 + 6 = 14
14 − 8 = 6

X

What do you get when you cross a groundhog with your principal?

| ___ | ___ | ___ | | ___ | ___ | ___ | ___ |
| 7 − 4 = 3 | 8 − 5 = 3 | 14 − 6 = 8 | | 3 + 7 = 10 | 11 − 5 = 6 | 9 + 3 = 12 | 6 + 4 = 10 |

| ___ | ___ | ___ | ___ | ___ | | ___ | ___ |
| 7 + 4 = 11 | 6 + 4 = 10 | 6 + 4 = 10 | 6 − 1 = 5 | 7 − 4 = 3 | | 11 − 5 = 6 | 5 + 4 = 9 |

| ___ | ___ | ___ | ___ | ___ | ___ |
| 7 − 4 = 3 | 13 − 4 = 9 | 8 − 2 = 6 | 11 − 5 = 6 | 11 − 5 = 6 | 8 + 2 = 10 |

Seasonal Brainteasers

Name _____

Heart to Heart

▶ Arrange the numbers on each group of hearts in order from least to greatest. Copy the words in the blank hearts in the same order as the numbers to answer each riddle.

Valentine's Day

What happened to the Valentine sweethearts who wanted to kiss in the fog?

but 411
mist 501
they 482
They 349
tried 361

How do you kiss a hockey player?

pucker 217
need 179
to 190
up 270
You 158

What did the postage stamp say to the envelope on Valentine's Day?

you 115
stuck 101
am 96
I 87
on 110

What did the snake say to his special sweetie?

Give 23
little 54
a 41
hiss 58
me 37

Name _____

Hidden Surprise

▶ To discover the filling in each chocolate candy, solve each problem. Then, color each piece according to the code below.

Valentine's Day

46 — cherry (red)	54 — lime (green)
37 — lemon (yellow)	68 — blueberry (blue)
75 — orange (orange)	83 — solid chocolate (brown)

Name _____

Cards to Send

Many people send fancy cards on Valentine's Day.

Valentine's Day

▶ Match a card with an envelope. Add the numbers on the cards and the envelopes. Then, draw lines between like answers to discover which card and envelope go together.

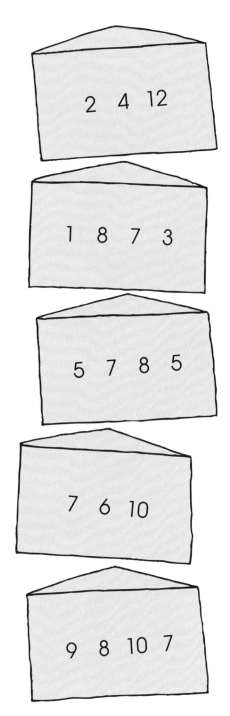

Mending Broken Hearts

▶ Mend the broken hearts by coloring the matching
halves the same color. You will need six different colors.

Valentine's Day

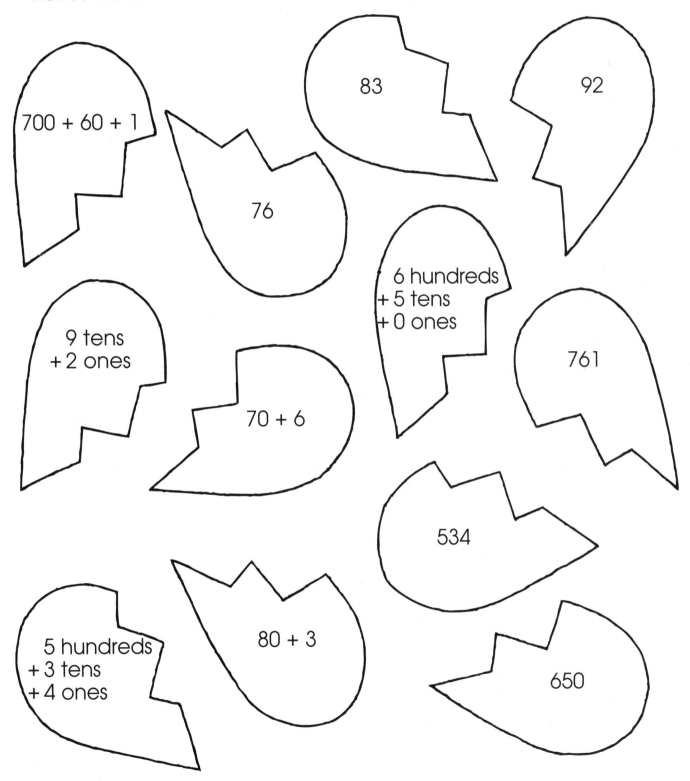

700 + 60 + 1

83

92

76

9 tens
+ 2 ones

6 hundreds
+ 5 tens
+ 0 ones

761

70 + 6

534

5 hundreds
+ 3 tens
+ 4 ones

80 + 3

650

A Presidential Family

▶ Solve the subtraction problems. Then, match the letters with the answers beneath each line to find out which president had the most children.

Presidents Day

A 18 − 9	B 6 −6	C 10 − 2	E 8 −7
F 11 − 9	G 15 − 9	H 12 − 9	I 10 − 5
N 14 − 7	O 9 −5	R 20 − 10	S 16 − 3
T 14 − 2	U 15 − 0	W 18 − 7	Y 16 − 2

___ ___ ___ ___ ___ ___ ___ ___ ___ ___ ,
11   9   13   3   5   7   6   12   4   7

___ ___ ___ ___ ___ ___ ___   ___ ___
0   1   8   9   15   13   1   3   1

___ ___ ___   ___ ___ ___   ___ ___ ___ ___ ___ ___
11   9   13   12   3   1   2   9   12   3   1   10

___ ___   ___ ___ ___   ___ ___ ___ ___ ___ ___ ___ .
4   2   4   15   10   8   4   15   7   12   10   14

Name _____

If a leprechaun's name indicates his worth in gold, how many coins of gold is each leprechaun worth?

St. Patrick's Day

▶ Match the letters in each name with the numbers in the chart. Then, add the numbers together for each name. The first one has been done for you. Color the leprechaun whose name is worth the most.

Code:

A	I	E	L	N	O	D	S	T	Y	U	R
1	2	3	4	5	6	7	8	9	10	11	12

Laddy

Louie

$4 + 1 + 7 + 7 + 10 = 29$

_____

Lennie

Leslie

_____ _____

Lennon

Lester

_____ _____

245

Seasonal Brainteasers

Pure Gold

▶ Help the leprechaun sort his genuine gold coins from the fake ones. Color the coin **golden** (yellow) if the number on it is even. Color the coin **brown** if the number is odd.

St. Patrick's Day

Pots O'Gold

▶ How many coins does each leprechaun have in his pot?   St. Patrick's Day
   Read the clues and write the numbers on the pots.

The number of my coins is an even number. It is greater than 50 and less than 62. The sum of its two digits is 13.

My coins are a factor of 5. I have less than 60 coins. The sum of its two digits is 10.

I'm glad I have 3 more coins than the second highest leprechaun.

I have saved an odd number of coins. It is half of 100 plus 17.

I've collected more than 65 coins but less than 75. The sum of its two digits is 11. The first digit is larger than the second.

Seasonal Brainteasers

Name _____

Rainbow of Colors

St. Patrick's Day

► Help the leprechaun climb over the rainbow to reach his pot of gold. Solve each addition problem. Then, look at the first row of three boxes. Which problem has an answer of 2? Color it any color. Climb to the next row of three boxes. Which problem has an answer of 4? Color it another color. Continue counting and coloring the answers by 2's until you reach the pot of gold. Use a different color for each row.

Name _____

Count the Coins

▶ Each whole pot of gold contains $1.00. Count the money in each half and write the amount on the pot. Then, draw a line to connect the two halves that equal $1.00.

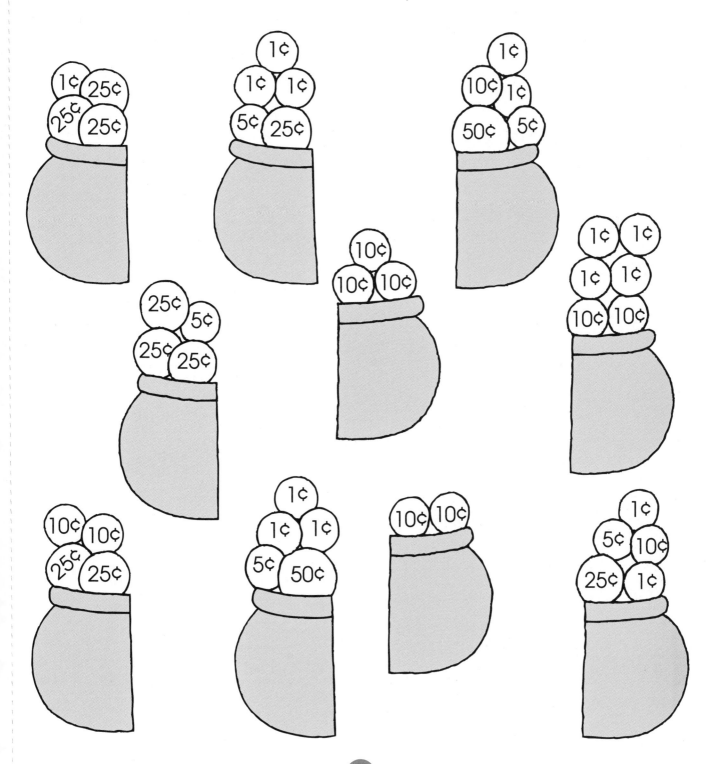

Seasonal Brainteasers

"Dozen" It Make Sense?

▶ Read each clue. Then, color the eggs in each carton as directed.

Color: 3 eggs blue; 2 eggs yellow; all of the rest green and pink, but one more pink egg than green.

Color: 2 eggs purple; twice as many eggs green as purple; 3 times as many eggs yellow as purple.

Color: 3 eggs pink; 1 more egg yellow that pink; 1 more egg orange than yellow.

Color: the same number of eggs blue as green; 2 eggs purple.

Color: 4 times as many eggs yellow as green; 4 eggs blue; 1 less egg purple than blue.

Color: 3 eggs red; twice as many eggs blue as red; half as many eggs yellow as blue.

Easter Mix-Up

▶ Cut out the squares at the bottom of this page and glue them onto the boxes with the same number. Do this one square at a time. The bold lines show the top of the square.

Easter

1	2	3	4	5
6	7	8	9	10
11	12	13	14	15

You will find out what you get when you cross a baby Easter chick and a baby Easter bunny.

seven

fourteen

ten

eight

three

thirteen

five

twelve

one

fifteen

two

eleven

four

nine

six

Seasonal Brainteasers

This page intentionally left blank.

Name _____

A **line of symmetry** divides a figure so that one half of it is exactly the same as the other half.

Easter

▶ Finish drawing these pictures by making both halves the same. Use the grid lines as a guide.

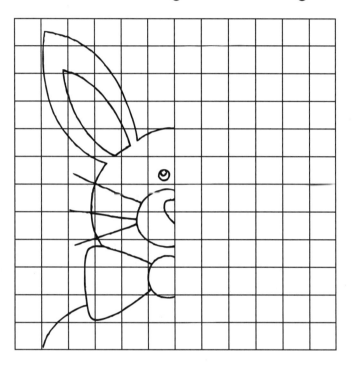

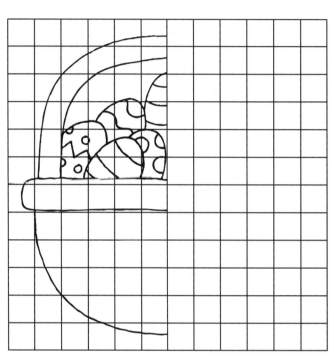

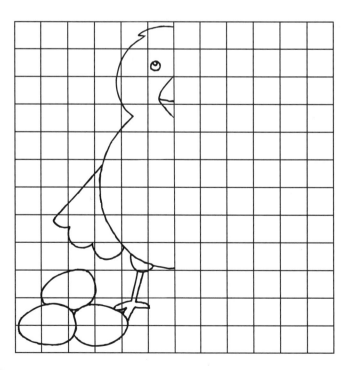

Seasonal Brainteasers

Name _____

Easter

What do
you call ducks
in a crate?
A box
of quackers!

▶ Begin at **50** and count by **5's**. Rearrange and write the letters on the eggs in that order, and you will answer this question.

What happened when the Easter Bunny told a bunch of silly jokes?

l	a	l
60	50	55

f	o
70	65

e	t	h
85	75	80

g	s	e	g
95	105	90	100

e	c	k	r	a	c	d
135	125	130	115	120	110	140

p	u
150	145

▶ Now, connect the dots in the same order for a closer look.

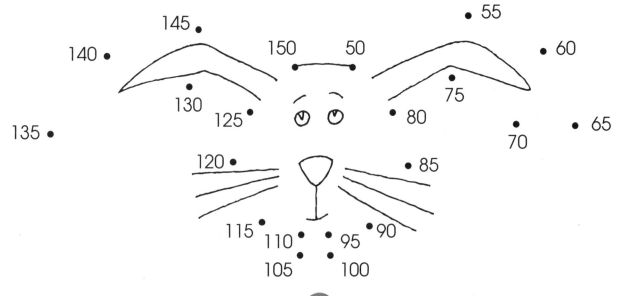

Name _____

No Business Like Shoe Business

Oh, no! A prankster took everyone's tennis shoes and threw them into a big pile. Now, they need to be arranged in pairs. Each pair of shoes contains a pair of consecutive numbers (like 256–257 or 921–922).

April Fool's Day

▶ Write the numbers for each pair on the lines below. Then, color the shoes.

_____ , _____   _____ , _____   _____ , _____

_____ , _____   _____ , _____   _____ , _____

_____ , _____   _____ , _____   _____ , _____

_____ , _____

Seasonal Brainteasers

Name _____

Surprise!

▶ Begin at **68** and count backward by **2's**. Rearrange and write the letters in this same order on the bugs, and you will answer this question.   April Fool's Day

What has two heads, twenty-four legs and sharp, pointy teeth?

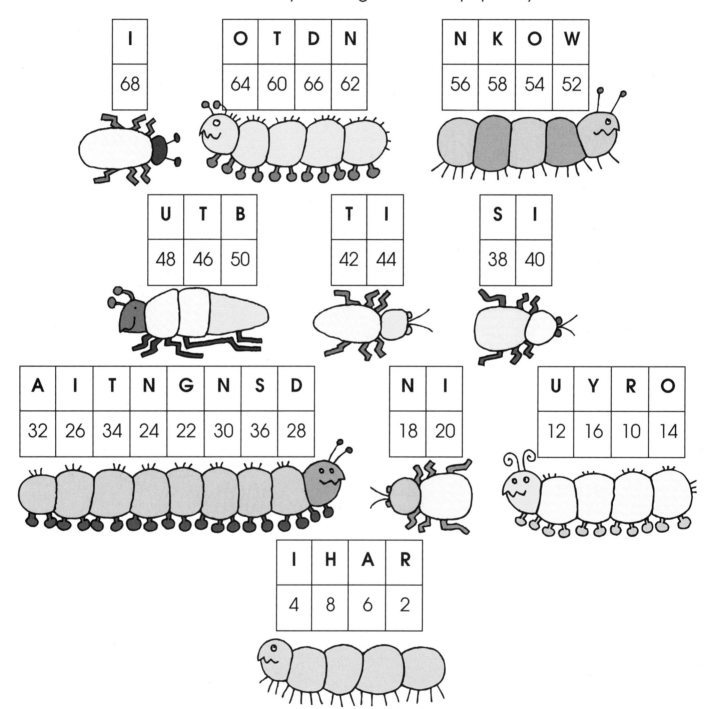

I
68

O	T	D	N
64	60	66	62

N	K	O	W
56	58	54	52

U	T	B
48	46	50

T	I
42	44

S	I
38	40

A	I	T	N	G	N	S	D
32	26	34	24	22	30	36	28

N	I
18	20

U	Y	R	O
12	16	10	14

I	H	A	R
4	8	6	2

Quit Buggin' Me!

Placing candy bugs in clever places is one way to trick your friends.

April Fool's Day

▶ Match like numbers and color each matching half of a bug the same color. You will need six different colors.

seventy

3 tens + 6 ones

ninety-six

1 ten + 7 ones

thirty-six

8 tens + 3 ones

9 tens + 6 ones

eighty-three

4 tens + 8 ones

seventeen

7 tens

forty-eight

Love Our Planet

▶ Use a blue crayon to color all of the spaces with odd numbers. Then begin at the star. Write the letters that you did not color in the spaces below. Move clockwise around the circle.

Earth Day

★

Solution (even-numbered letters, clockwise from the star):

___ ___ ___ ___ _____ .

___ ___ ___

___ ___ ___ ___ ___ ___ ___ ___ ___ .

SAVE OUR EARTH. GET RID OF POLLUTION.

Name _____

Tree-mendous Riddles

▶ Use a calculator to help answer these riddles. Remember to press the equal sign after each direction. If you turn the calculator upside down at the end, you will find the answer.

Arbor Day

Riddle: What does Smokey the Bear always bring when he visits the forest?

Enter: the number of legs on a bear

X	900
−	ninety-six
+	0.514
=	○

Answer: _____

Riddle: Who visited the apple tree on a beautiful spring day?

Enter: the number of pennies in five dollars

X	ten
+	340
−	1.8782
=	○

Answer: _____

Riddle: What did the maple tree do when it wanted syrup on its pancakes?

Enter: the number of one dozen trees

X	300
+	four hundred fifty
−	850
=	○

Answer: _____

Riddle: What do you call a tree that has stopped growing?

Enter: number before seventy

X	ten
+	seven
−	90
=	○

Answer: _____

259

Name _____

Home Sweet Home

▶ Follow the path and solve the problems along the way to discover the number of trees in this forest.

Arbor Day

Start   7   x   7   +   7

+   6   x   8   ÷

8   ÷   5   +   5   x

Answer   =   10   +   6

Name _____

Mother's Day Bouquet

▶ Write each missing number in the counting sequences.   Mother's Day

Color the space **yellow** if the number is from **1–5**.
Color the space **purple** if the number is from **6–10**.
Color the space **orange** if the number is from **11–15**.
Color the space **red** if the number is from **16–20**.
Color the space **green** if the number is from **21–25**.

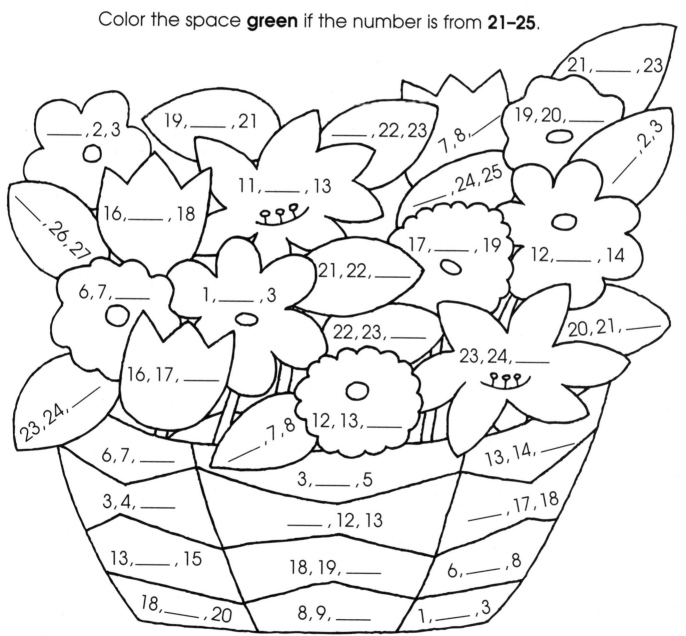

Mother Dear

▶ Use a calculator to help answer these riddles. Remember to press the equal sign after each direction. If you turn the calculator upside down at the end, you will find the answer.

Mother's Day

Riddle: Who is one of the most famous mothers in history?

Enter: number of tentacles on an octopus

+	8,000
−	398
÷	twenty
X	92
=	◯

Answer: _____

Riddle: What mother doesn't lecture her child for "piggy" table manners?

Enter: number of pennies in 3 quarters

X	ten
+	four
−	150
=	◯

Answer: _____

Riddle: What did her children say as Mother read her favorite nursery rhymes?

Enter: the number of inches in 1 foot

X	thirty
+	24
÷	7,680
+	0.01006
=	◯

Answer: _____

Riddle: What did this famous mother call her first child?

Enter: number of years in a century

X	six
÷	two
−	134.0955
X	four
=	◯

Answer: _____

Honor Our Veterans

► Solve these addition problems. Next, write the letter on each star that matches the answer on the line below. Then, answer the question.

Memorial Day

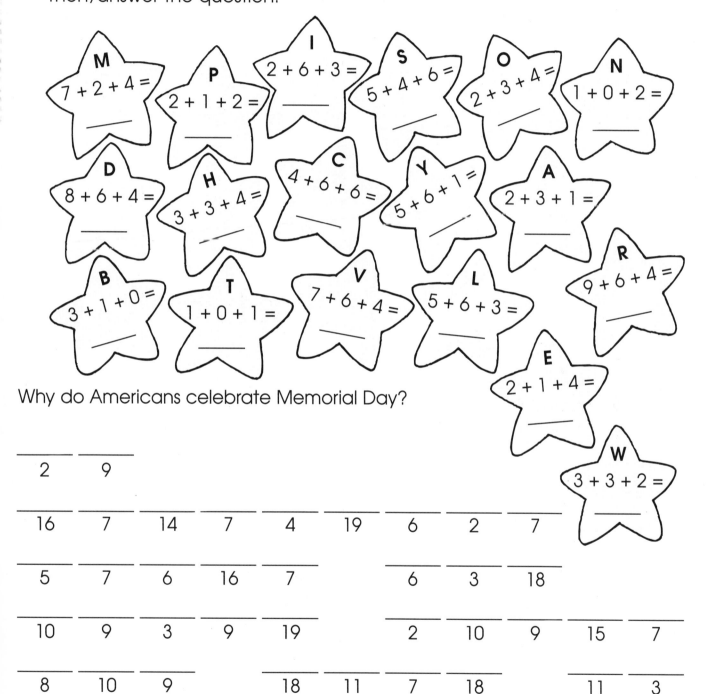

Why do Americans celebrate Memorial Day?

2	9							
16	7	14	7	4	19	6	2	7
5	7	6	16	7		6	3	18
10	9	3	9	19		2	10	9	15	7
8	10	9		18	11	7	18		11	3
8	6	19	15					

263

Seasonal Brainteasers

Salute to Our Flag

▶ Think big! Find the answer to each problem. Then, check it with a calculator.

Flag Day

$$84,956 - 13,042$$

$$53,916 + 45,032$$

$$89,689 - 19,658$$

$$74,201 + 23,478$$

$$81,325 + 13,642$$

$$54,978 - 32,846$$

$$69,858 - 49,827$$

$$44,321 + 52,626$$

▶ Use a calculator to solve the riddle below. Remember to press the equal sign after each operation. When you are finished, turn the calculator upside down to read the solution.

Riddle: What do you get when a cannon is shot on Flag Day?

Enter: half of one thousand

X	10 tens
+	3,800
−	96
+	0.618
=	○

Answer: _____

Name _____

An "Outta This World!" Tie

Dad thinks his tie is very special—because it's from you!

Father's Day

▶ Solve the problems and write the answers.

Color the space **purple**
if the answer is **1–3**.

Color the space **green**
if the answer is **4–6**.

Color the space **blue**
if the answer is **7–9**.

Color the space **orange**
if the answer is **10–12**.

Color the space **yellow**
if the answer is **13–15**.

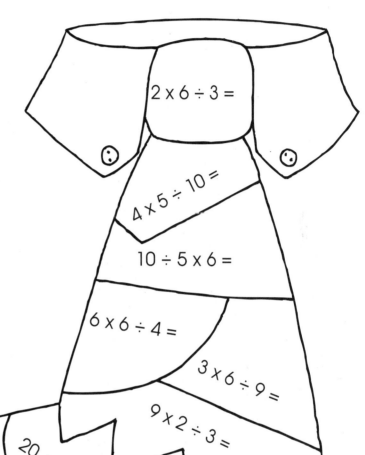

2 x 6 ÷ 3 =

4 x 5 ÷ 10 =

10 ÷ 5 x 6 =

6 x 6 ÷ 4 =

3 x 6 ÷ 9 =

9 x 2 ÷ 3 =

20 ÷ 4 x 3 =

4 x 3 ÷ 6 =

3 x 5 ÷ 3 =

40 ÷ 8 x 3 =

8 x 5 ÷ 4 =

25 ÷ 5 x 3 =

12 ÷ 6 x 5 =

4 x 3 ÷ 2 =

6 x 4 ÷ 3 =

Seasonal Brainteasers

Name _____

Fishing With Dad

▶ Use a calculator to help answer these riddles. Remember to press the equal sign after each direction. If you turn the calculator upside down at the end, you will find the answer.

Father's Day

Riddle: What's the main difference between a father and his young children?

Enter: half of one hundred

+	16,000
÷	five
+	5.514
=	◯

Answer: _____

Riddle: What are Dad's favorite fish to catch?

Enter: eight thousand

+	861
X	six hundred
+	eighteen
=	◯

Answer: _____

Riddle: What is Dad's favorite word to his child on a fishing trip?

Enter: number of cents in one dollar

+	180
÷	0.05
−	1,200
+	forty-five
=	◯

Answer: _____

Riddle: What is a father's least favorite word from his child on a fishing trip in a boat?

Enter: number of cents in two quarters

+	7,000
−	337
X	eight
=	◯

Answer: _____

Name _____

▶ Connect the dots starting at **100** and counting by **10's**.   4th of July

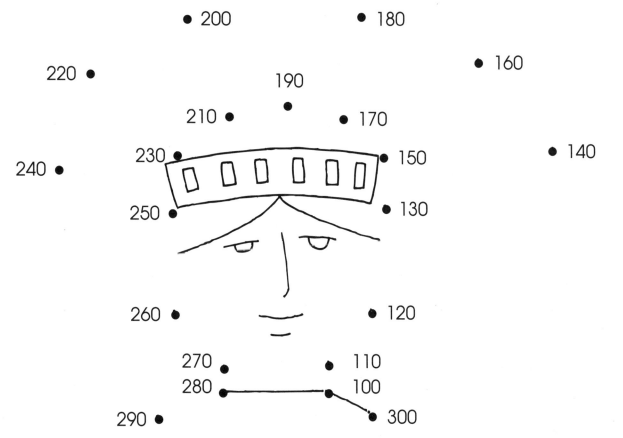

▶ Arrange the numbers in order for each word below. Write the letters that go with the numbers in the empty boxes. You should get the solution to this riddle.

What should you do if the Statue of Liberty sneezes?

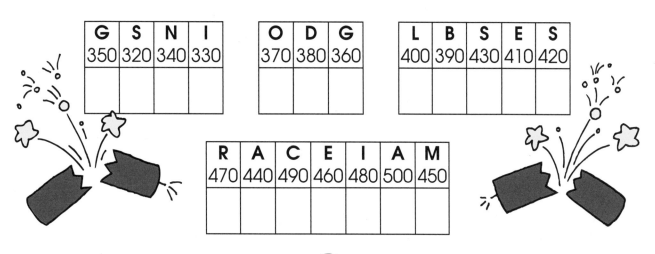

G	S	N	I
350	320	340	330

O	D	G
370	380	360

L	B	S	E	S
400	390	430	410	420

R	A	C	E	I	A	M
470	440	490	460	480	500	450

Name _____

Rocket's Red Glare

▶ Write the answers for these multiplication facts. Match the letters to the answers on the lines below. You will discover the answer to this question.

4th of July

What did one firecracker say to the other firecracker?

A 7 × 7   B 3 × 2   E 6 × 4   G 9 × 8   H 5 × 8   I 3 × 7   M 5 × 3   N 4 × 4

O 8 × 7   P 3 × 4   R 10 × 5   S 7 × 6   T 9 × 9   U 4 × 7   Y 5 × 6

___ ___   ___ ___ ___   ___ ___
15 30   12 56 12   21 42

___ ___ ___ ___ ___ ___   ___ ___ ___ ___
6   21 72 72 24 50   81 40 49 16

___ ___ ___ ___ ___!
30 56 28 50 42

268

Name _____

► Write the answers for all the problems.   4th of July

Color the space **red** if the answer is **greater than 50**.
Color the space **blue** if the answer is **between 1 and 49**.
Color or leave the space **white** if the answer is **50**.
Color the space **tan** if the answer is **0**.

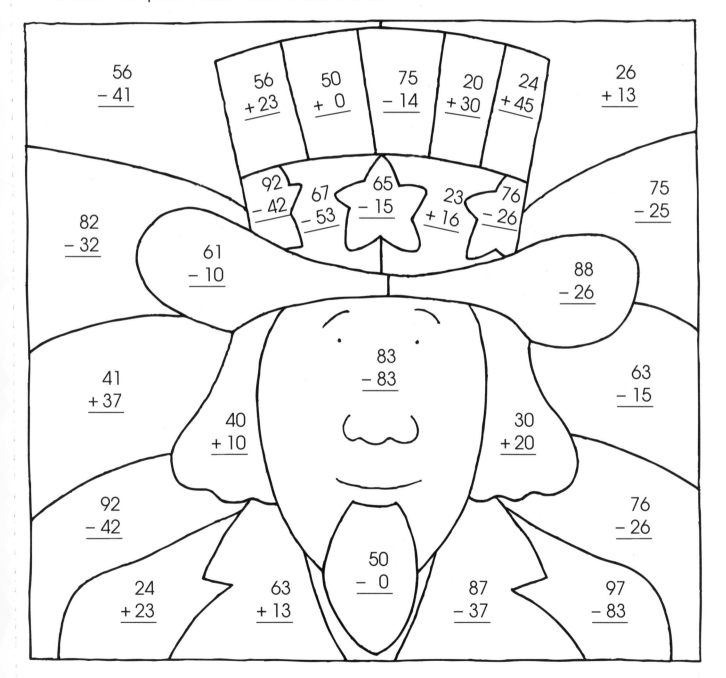

56
− 41

56
+ 23

50
+ 0

75
− 14

20
+ 30

24
+ 45

26
+ 13

92
− 42

67
− 53

65
− 15

23
+ 16

76
− 26

75
− 25

82
− 32

61
− 10

88
− 26

41
+ 37

83
− 83

63
− 15

40
+ 10

30
+ 20

92
− 42

76
− 26

24
+ 23

63
+ 13

50
− 0

87
− 37

97
− 83

Seasonal Brainteasers

My Cup of Tea

▶ Count by **3's** to rearrange the numbers in order and write the letters on the teacups. The letters will answer this riddle.

What was the American colonists' favorite tea?

E	Y	T	H
9	12	3	6

D	L	E	I	K
27	15	24	18	21

T	R	I	H	E
30	42	39	33	36

I	Y	B	L	T	E	R
48	63	51	45	60	54	57

▶ Now, count by **3's** to connect the dots.

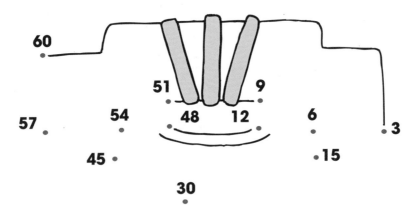

60
51   9
57   54   48   12   6   3
45   15
30
42   18
39   21
36   33   27   24

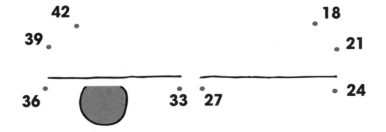

Name _____

Don't Give Up!

Labor Day

▶ Circle the lesser number in each bottle. Match that number with the one in the code at the bottom of the page to find the correct letter to write on each line. Now you know the answer to this question.

What job is very easy to stick to?

| 753 735 | 821 830 | 141 137 | 381 390 | 232 321 | 991 919 | 856 685 |

_____ _____ _____ _____ _____ _____ _____

| 322 232 | 919 920 | 106 160 | 685 692 | 871 786 | 463 436 | 216 260 |

_____ _____ _____ _____ _____ _____ _____

| 521 529 | 165 106 | 494 501 | 981 987 | 850 821 | 153 137 | 625 619 |

_____ _____ _____ _____ _____ _____ _____

Code:

106	494	216	521	685	232	381	786	919	821	137	981	436	735	619
A	C	E	F	G	I	K	L	N	O	R	T	U	W	Y

271

Seasonal Brainteasers

Taking It Easy

▶ Write the answers for these number problems. Match the letters to the answers on the lines below. You will discover the answer to this question.

Why is working in a rubber band factory one of the easiest jobs in the world?

A   56
   + 9
   ____

B   78
   − 59
   ____

C   67
   − 29
   ____

E   28
   + 67
   ____

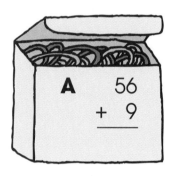   

H   45
   − 18
   ____

I   72
   + 18
   ____

N   83
   − 15
   ____

P   54
   + 16
   ____

S   66
   + 14
   ____

T   33
   − 15
   ____

U   59
   + 19
   ____

A   90
   − 25
   ____

 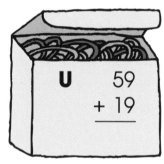 

___ ___ ___ ___ ___ ___ ___   ___ ___ ___
19   95   38   65   78   80   95   90   18   80

              ___   ___ ___ ___ ___!
              65   80   68   65   70

Name _____

Flags of the Nations

▶ Look at the flags below, then follow these directions.   United Nations Day

Color the space **orange** if the number is from **1–25**.
Color the space **red** if the number is from **26–50**.
Color the space **black** if the number is from **5–75**.
Color the space **yellow** if the number is from **76–100**.
Color the space **green** if the number is from **101–125**.
Color the space **blue** if the number is from **126–150**.
Color or leave the space **white** if the number is from **151–175**.

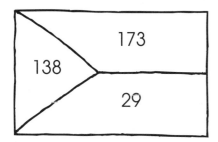

Czech Republic

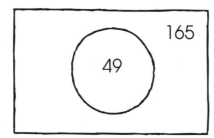

Japan

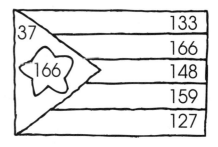

Cuba

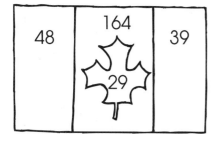

Canada

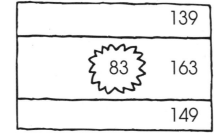

Argentina

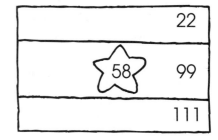

Ghana

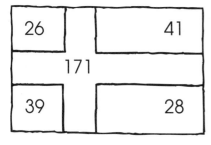

Denmark

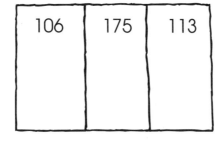

Nigeria

Somalia

Seasonal Brainteasers

Olive Branch of Peace

▶ Solve each problem. Write the answers in the boxes. Then, match the letters to the answers on the lines below to solve the riddle.

United Nations Day

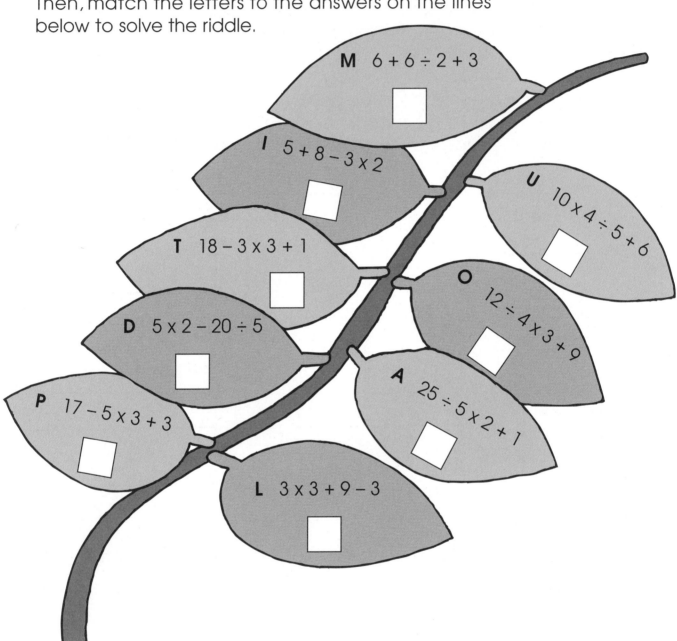

M $6 + 6 \div 2 + 3$

I $5 + 8 - 3 \times 2$

U $10 \times 4 \div 5 + 6$

T $18 - 3 \times 3 + 1$

O $12 \div 4 \times 3 + 9$

D $5 \times 2 - 20 \div 5$

A $25 \div 5 \times 2 + 1$

P $17 - 5 \times 3 + 3$

L $3 \times 3 + 9 - 3$

What animal can sometimes be seen in the United Nations building?

___   ___ ___ ___ ___ ___ - ___ ___ ___ ___
11   6   7   5   15   18   12   14   10   10

Name _____

Beastly Banquet

The dilapidated house on the corner had always appeared vacant, but when I peered into one of its windows, I got the surprise of my life. A very scary party was in full swing. Below is some of the conversation I overheard.

▶ Use the Word Bank and the bold word clues in each sentence to write the missing verbs or adverbs in the sentences.

"It's not a time to be so **wrapped up** in your problems. Let's relax and _____," said the mummy.

"I'd like **honey** in my herbal tea," said the monster _____.

"I'm on a seafood diet—I **eat whatever food I see!**" laughed the sea monster _____, "I like fish and ships."

While _____ a sandwich with his huge hands, the gorilla announced, "My favorite food is **squash**."

". . . And I devour plump and juicy **hot dogs**," said werewolf _____.

"I don't care about the type of food as long as it's served with evaporated milk," whispered the **invisible man**. His statement passed _____.

Word Bank

crushing
frankly
icily
sweetly
gluttonously
unnoticed
scrambled
unwind

"You all have poor taste. **Cold** cuts are the **coolest** around," stated the snow monster _____.

As he _____ for attention, the ghost moaned, "I like my eggs terri-**fried**."

(275)

I Need My Mummy

▶ Each mummy is wrapped in five bandages marked A, B, C, D   Halloween
and E. Write the two numbers from each bandage on the lines.
Then, add them together to find the length of each bandage.

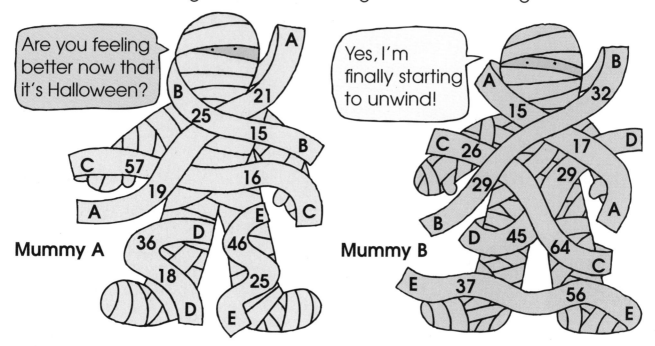

Mummy A

Mummy B

A ____ + ____ = ____ ft.   A ____ + ____ = ____ ft.

B ____ + ____ = ____ ft.   B ____ + ____ = ____ ft.

C ____ + ____ = ____ ft.   C ____ + ____ = ____ ft.

D ____ + ____ = ____ ft.   D ____ + ____ = ____ ft.

E ____ + ____ = ____ ft.   E ____ + ____ = ____ ft.

▶ Make your mummy proud! Find which mummy is wrapped in the greater
length of bandages. Add the five sums for each mummy to solve this
mystery. Circle the number that's greater.

___ + ___ + ___ + ___ + ___ = ___ ft.   ___ + ___ + ___ + ___ + ___ = ___ ft.

Name _____

A Boo-tiful Parade

▶ Follow the directions. Begin with the leader ghost on the left.

1. Color a **red number 1** on the **first** ghost.

2. Draw **silly orange hats** on the **fifth** and **seventh** ghosts.

3. Color **purple polka-dots** on the **ninth** ghost.

4. Color **green stripes** on the **third** ghost.

5. Write **"Boo!"** on the **tenth** ghost.

6. Draw a **big tooth** in the **second** ghost's mouth.

7. Draw **funny yellow hair** on the **fourth** ghost's head.

8. Draw **black beards** on the **sixth** and **eighth** ghosts.

277

Name _____

Count on Me!

▶ Help Igor and Agar get ready for Halloween by coloring some of their fingernails. Always begin on the left side.

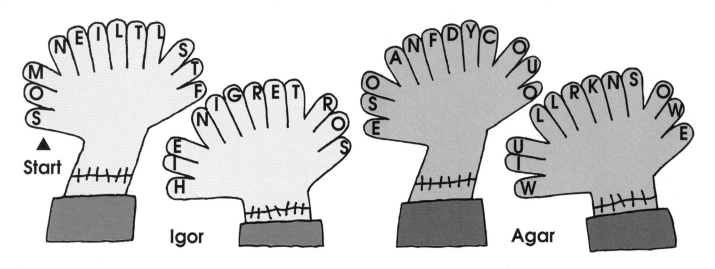

Start

Igor

Agar

1. Count by **2's** on Igor's fingers. Color those fingernails **orange**.

2. How many are orange? _____

3. How many twos are in 24? _____

1. Count by **3's** on Agar's fingers. Color those fingernails **yellow**.

2. How many are yellow? _____

3. How many threes are in 24? _____

▶ Write the letters you colored orange and yellow on the lines below, and you will answer this riddle: How does a monster count?

___ ___ ___   ___ ___ ___

___ ___ ___ ___ ___ ___ ___,

___ ___   ___ ___ ___ ___ ___!

▶ Write the remaining letters on the lines below to find out why they don't use their feet.

___ ___ ___   ___ ___ ___ ___ ___

___ ___ ___   ___ ___ ___   ___ ___ ___ ___

___ ___ ___   ___ ___ ___ ___!

Name _____

Monster Treats

Frank and Stein have sorted their Halloween treats into groups. **Halloween**
If the treats are shared equally, how many pieces of each kind
will each monster get?

▶ Circle every two treats. Write the division problem that represents this
and solve it. The first one has been done for you.

_____   _____
     $8 \div 2 = 4$

Frank and Stein will each get __**4**__   Frank and Stein will each get _____
candy bars.   pieces of licorice.

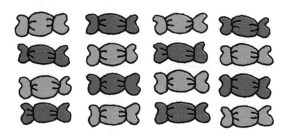   

_____   _____

Frank and Stein will each get _____   Frank and Stein will each get _____
pieces of taffy.   caramel apples.

_____   _____

Frank and Stein will each get _____   Frank and Stein will each get _____
pieces of candy corn.   lollipops.

Seasonal Brainteasers

Down to the Bones

▶ Solve the addition problems. Then, color each bone as directed.

Halloween

34 — orange   97 — red   56 — green
75 — black   48 — yellow   83 — purple

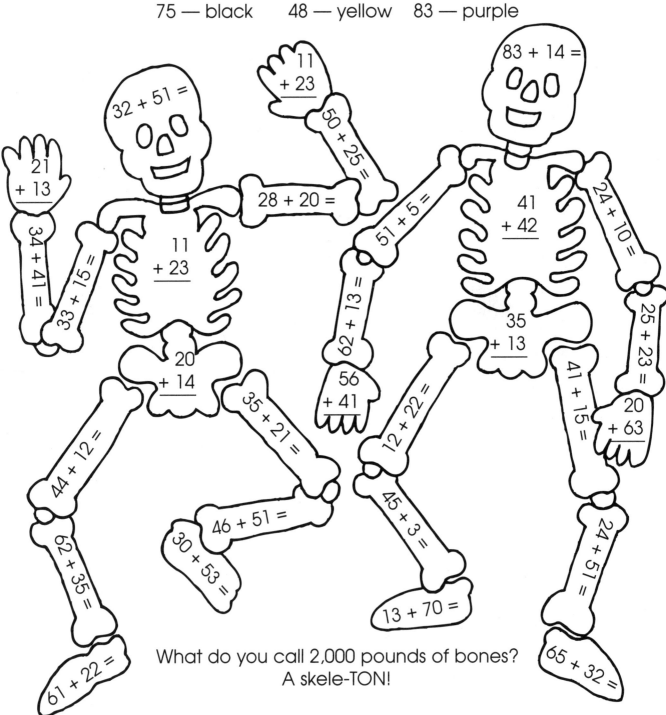

What do you call 2,000 pounds of bones?
A skele-TON!

Name _____

▶ Follow the directions to trace the path of each spider on
its web. Stay on the lines of the web.

Halloween

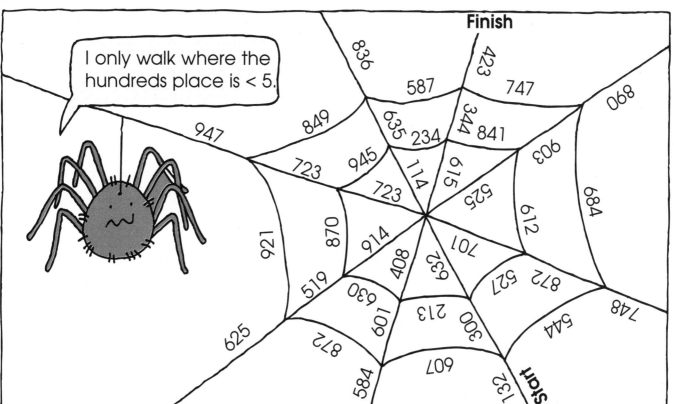

Seasonal Brainteasers

Give Me "Five"!

▶ Have you got a pencil "handy?" Begin at **55** and count by **5's** to connect the dots.

Halloween

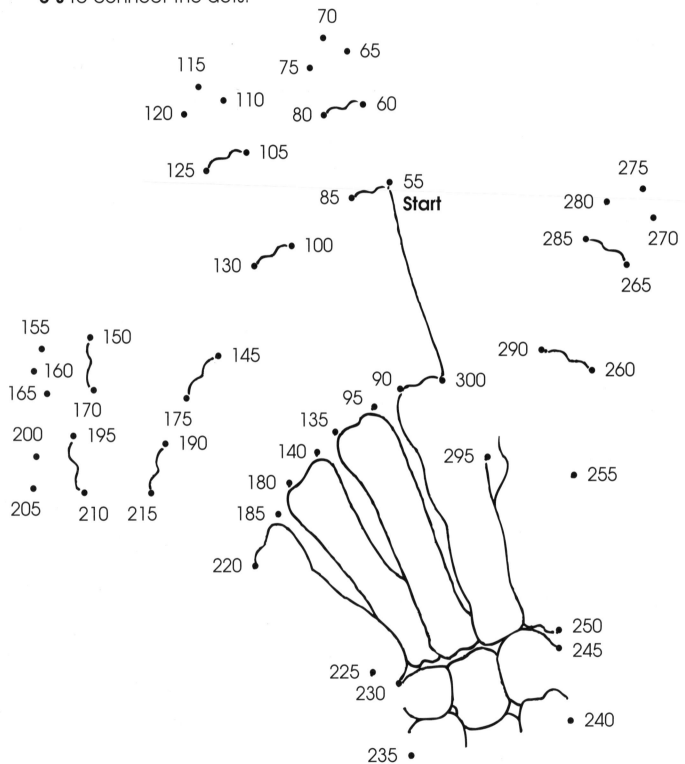

Name _____

Glowing Grins

▶ Add the three numbers in each jack-o'-lantern's eyes and nose. Write the answer in its mouth.

Color the jack-o'-lantern **orange** if the number is **even**.
Color the jack-o'-lantern **black** if the number is **odd**.

Seasonal Brainteasers

Sailing, Sailing . . .

▶ Circle the smallest number in each sail.
Draw a box around the largest number in each sail.

24	38
59	65

92	63
79	96

58	62
39	45

47	78
28	19

55	71
67	72

87	39
44	50

140	126
133	185

272	288
264	269

581	587
585	583

782	791
755	746

904	914
940	934

838	880
856	883

Nina

Pinta

36	75
146	132

328	479
236	487

792	826
787	814

527	461
809	826

401	324
398	400

940	904
887	878

Santa Maria

Name _____

Birds of a Feather

▶ Write the missing signs (+, −, =) in each feather. Use the answers and color key to color the feathers correctly.

3 — yellow   7 — orange
4 — blue   8 — green
5 — red   9 — purple

Ticklish Situation

▶ How many feathers does each turkey have?
Read the clues. Write the numbers on the lines.

Thanksgiving

This even number is between 380 and 390. If you add the 3 digits, the answer is 15.

I have _____ feathers.

This number is between 500 and 550. It has a 5 in the ones place. The sum of the digits is 13.

I have _____ feathers.

This odd number is less than 790 and more than 770. The sum of the digits is 22.

I have _____ feathers.

Just between us turkeys . . .

Question: What has feathers on its body, feathers under its head and feathers floating on top of it?

Answer: A turkey sleeping on a feather pillow, snuggling under a feather comforter.

Name _____

All Wrapped Up

▶ Solve each problem by providing the missing number.   Thanksgiving

Across

2.
$$\begin{array}{r} 2 \\ \times\ \boxed{} \\ \hline 12 \end{array}$$

4.
$$\begin{array}{r} 39 \\ -\ 31 \\ \hline \boxed{} \end{array}$$

7.
$$\begin{array}{r} 14 \\ +\ \boxed{} \\ \hline 21 \end{array}$$

8. $16 \div 4 = \boxed{}$

9.
$$\begin{array}{r} 100 \\ \times\ \boxed{} \\ \hline 100 \end{array}$$

Down

1. 256 = 2 hundred + $\boxed{}$ tens + 6 ones

3.
$$\begin{array}{r} \boxed{} \\ +\ 73 \\ \hline 83 \end{array}$$

5. $18 \div \boxed{} = 9$

6. 83 = 8 tens + $\boxed{}$ ones

10. $\boxed{} \times 9 = 81$

▶ Write the number words from 1 through 10 in this puzzle.

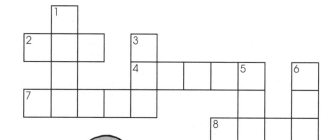

▶ Use this code for a special message.

Code:

one	two	three	four	five	six	seven	eight	nine	ten
O	A	E	G	F	L	D	I	N	S

What did the leftover turkey drumstick say?

___ ___ ___ ___ ___ ___   ___ ___ ___ ___ ___!
five one eight six three seven   two four two eight nine

Seasonal Brainteasers

Let's Get Corny

▶ Use a crayon to circle hidden division facts. Look across, up or down. Write them on the lines below. The first one has been done for you.

Thanksgiving

12 ÷ 6 = 2

_____   _____

_____   _____

_____   _____

_____   _____

_____   _____

_____   _____

Name _____

Please, Pass the Pumpkin Pie

▶ Help Grandma make six whole pumpkin pies by drawing a line to connect the pieces that go together. Then, write the letter from each piece of pie on the line above the matching fraction at the bottom.

Thanksgiving

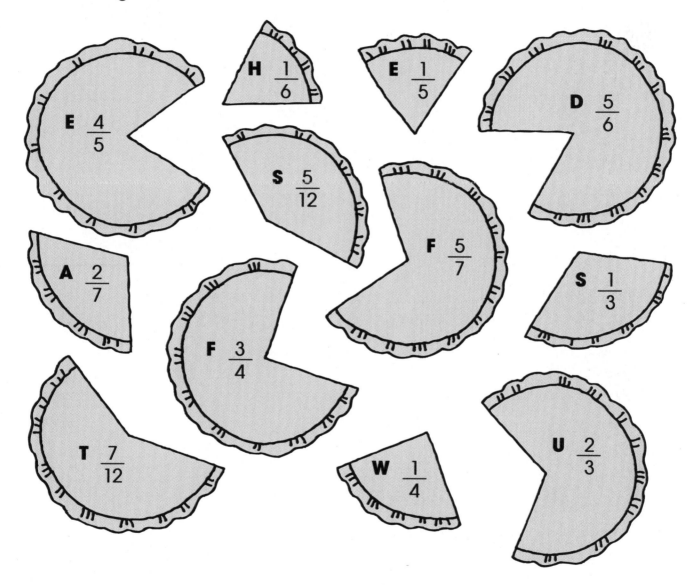

Why didn't the turkey want a piece of pumpkin pie?

____ ____   ____ ____ ____   ____ ____ ____ ____ ____ ____ ____ .

$\frac{1}{6}$ $\frac{1}{5}$ $\frac{1}{4}$ $\frac{2}{7}$ $\frac{1}{3}$ $\frac{5}{12}$ $\frac{7}{12}$ $\frac{2}{3}$ $\frac{5}{7}$ $\frac{3}{4}$ $\frac{4}{5}$ $\frac{5}{6}$

Food for Thought

Thanksgiving

▶ Solve the addition and subtraction problems by writing the missing numbers. Use the code to write the letters that match the missing numbers on the lines below. Now you know the answer to this riddle.

Why do cranberries cry each Thanksgiving?

1	2	3	4	5	6	7	8	9	10
L	O	A	H	S	E	B	N	C	M

11	12	13	14	15	16	17	18	19	20
Y	D	T	R	P	I	B	U	C	K

```
   3        18     3         4     11
 + [ ]    - 5    - 9   +[ ]   -9   +[ ]  - 5
 ------   ----   ----  -----  ---  ----- ----
   10       1    [ ]     6     9     9   [ ]


  [ ]     [ ]    [ ]    13          9    [ ]    14    [ ]
 - 10    - 7    - 8    - 8        + 6    - 9   -[ ]  - 10
 -----   ----   ----   ----       ----   ----  ----  -----
   10      9      4    [ ]        [ ]      7     5     10


  [ ]      15     [ ]    13     [ ]    13
 - 2     -[ ]    - 8    -[ ]   + 9    - 3
 -----   -----   ----   -----  ----   ----
   0       7       5      9      15   [ ]
```

___ ___ ___ ___ ___ ___ ___   ___ ___ ___ ___ ___ ___ ___ ___   ___ ___   ___ ___ ___ ___ .

Name _____

M-m-m-mmm *Good!*

▶ Help the Native Americans and Pilgrims calculate how much food they need to prepare for their feast. Write each answer on the line below the problem.

Thanksgiving

78 + 20 ÷ 10 + 15
_____ turkeys

5 x 9 + 27 – 12
_____ ears of corn-on-the-cob

75 + 55 x 2 – 100
_____ carrots

15 + 10 ÷ 5
_____ deer

99 – 52 ÷ 2
_____ loaves of bread

25 x 4 + 100 ÷ 2
_____ potatoes

100 x 10 ÷ 2 – 150
_____ beans

20 x 5 ÷ 2 + 6
_____ apples

Name _____

Stepping in the Right Direction

▶ Look at the footsteps toward the Thanksgiving feast.
Write <, > or = between the footprints in each path.
The first four have been done for you.

Thanksgiving

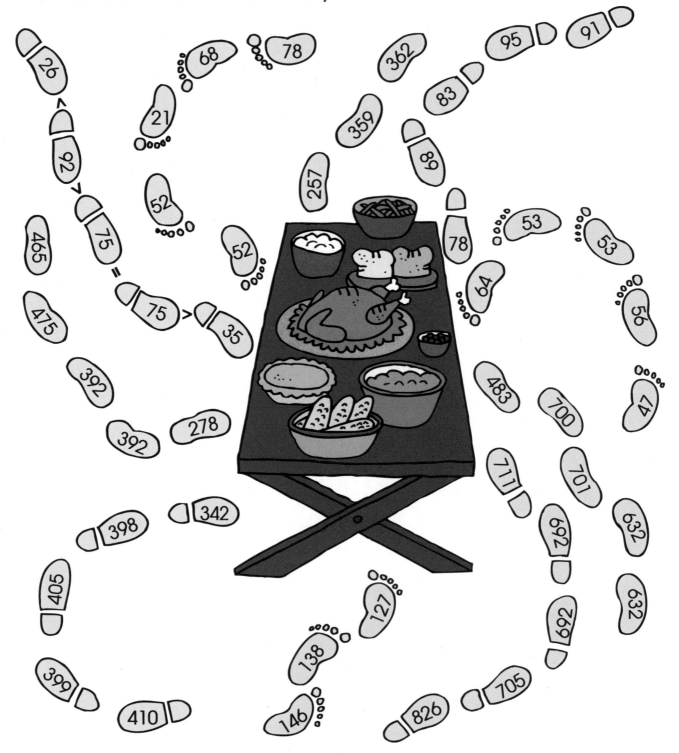

Name _____

▶ Solve the equations by writing the missing number in each box.   Kwanzaa

Color the space **black** if the missing number is from **0–2**.
Color the space **red** if the missing number is from **3–5**.
Color the space **green** if the missing number is from **6–8**.
Color the space **yellow** if the missing number is from **9–11**.
Color the space **orange** if the missing number is from **12–15**.

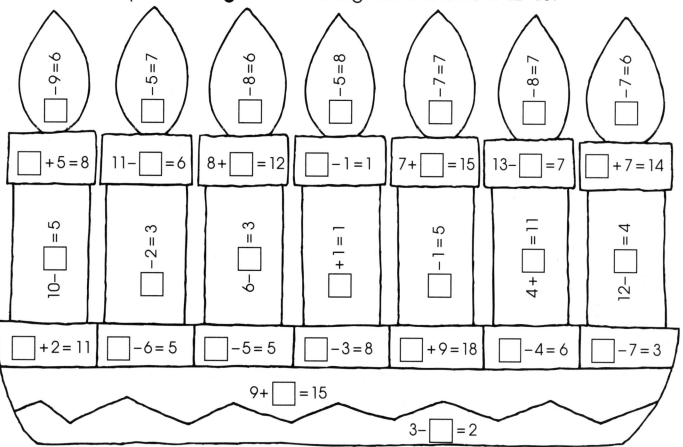

▶ Then, unscramble the words to learn more about Kwanzaa.

1. The _____ candle shows the beauty of African skin.
   (cbkal)

2. The _____ candles are a reminder of past and present struggles.
   (erd)

3. The _____ candles point to a happy future.
   (ergen)

Vibunzi

Vibunzi are dried ears of corn. They represent the children in a family who are the hope of the future.

Kwanzaa

▶ Write the missing signs (<, >, =) between the numbers.

Color the kernel **red** if the sign is <.
Color the kernel **black** if the sign is >.
Color the kernel **yellow** if the sign is =.

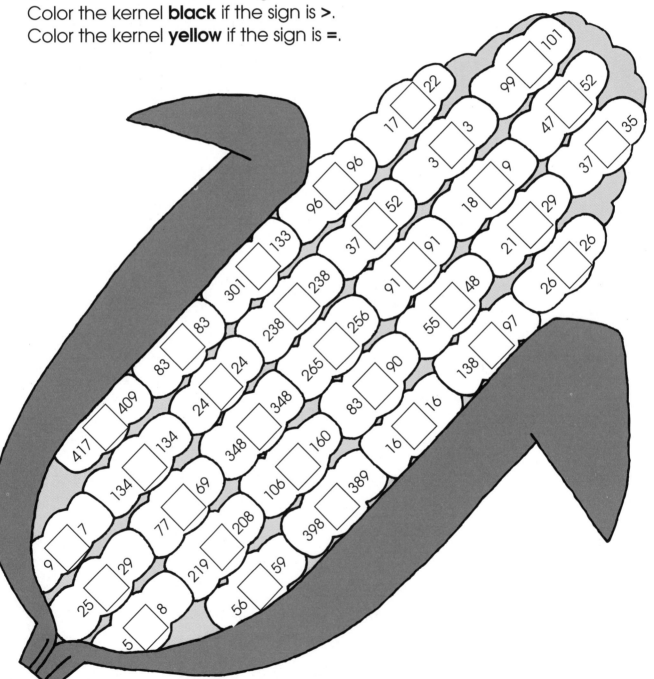

Name _____

Swahili Speech

▶ Write the answer for each multiplication fact on the line. Use the code to match numbers with letters to spell Swahili words that are used during the Kwanzaa holiday. Write the letters in the boxes below the facts.

Kwanzaa

| 9
x 3 | 9
x 4 | 4
x 4 | 4
x 9 | 6
x 6 | | 6
x 5 | 9
x 9 | 3
x 5 | 2
x 9 | 3
x 3 | 4
x 8 |

☐ ☐ ☐ ☐ ☐   ☐ ☐ ☐ ☐ ☐ ☐

(family)   (love)

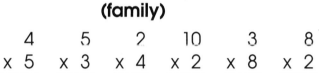

| 4
x 5 | 5
x 3 | 2
x 4 | 10
x 2 | 3
x 8 | 8
x 2 | 12
x 3 | | 6
x 8 | 9
x 4 | 7
x 7 | 6
x 4 |

☐ ☐ ☐ ☐ ☐ ☐ ☐   ☐ ☐ ☐ ☐

(pride)   (work)

| 3
x 4 | 3
x 10 | 8
x 5 | 6
x 6 | 2
x 10 | 4
x 9 | | 3
x 12 | 2
x 8 | 6
x 6 | 9
x 2 | 4
x 6 |

☐ ☐ ☐ ☐ ☐ ☐   ☐ ☐ ☐ ☐ ☐

(happiness)   (peace)

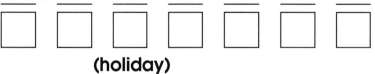

| 2
x 4 | 8
x 3 | 8
x 6 | 5
x 6 | 12
x 4 | 10
x 3 | 6
x 5 | | 4
x 4 | 12
x 2 | 2
x 5 | 9
x 4 |

☐ ☐ ☐ ☐ ☐ ☐ ☐   ☐ ☐ ☐ ☐

(holiday)   (tradition)

Code:

36	9	15	12	20	24	27	48	10	16	18	32	81	40	8	30	49
A	D	E	F	H	I	J	K	L	M	N	O	P	R	S	U	Z

Twelve Days of Christmas

▶ Complete each number sentence so that the two numbers in each picture equal the number in the song. Use **+**, **−**, **x** or **÷** between the numbers. The first number sentence has been done for you.

___**8 – 7**___ = 1 partridge in a pear tree

_____ = 2 turtledoves

_____ = 3 French hens

_____ = 4 calling birds

_____ = 5 golden rings

_____ = 6 geese a-laying

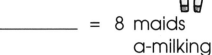

_____ = 7 swans a-swimming

_____ = 8 maids a-milking

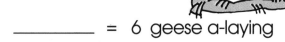

_____ = 9 ladies dancing

_____ = 10 lords a-leaping

_____ = 11 pipers piping

_____ = 12 drummers drumming

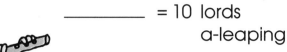

Name _____

Frosty the Snowman

▶ Frosty the Snowman and his friends need a few items.
Start at the top left and follow the directions carefully,
but don't take too long or the page may melt!

Christmas

1. Draw three coal buttons on the
   1st, 3rd, 4th and 7th snowmen.

2. Put a baseball cap on the 2nd, 5th
   and 8th snowmen.

3. Wrap a big scarf around the necks
   of the 4th, 6th and 10th snowmen.

4. Color orange carrot noses on the
   snowmen that follow the 3rd, 7th
   and 9th snowmen.

5. Draw a coal nose on the rest of the
   snowmen.

6. Place a black top hat on Frosty's
   head. (**Hint:** He already has a scarf,
   three buttons and a carrot nose.)

Season for Singing

▶ Circle the greatest number in each musical note. Use the code below to write the matching letter on the line in each note. The letters make words to solve the riddle below.

Christmas

What song does a peanut butter sandwich sing each Christmas?

Code:

66	71	49	54	83	36	51	80	74	92	75	96
A	B	E	H	I	J	L	N	O	S	T	Y

Name _____

▶ Use a calculator to solve these riddles. Remember to press the equal key after each operation. Then, turn the calculator upside down at the end to read the answer.

Christmas

Riddle: What does Santa say as he plants snow peas in his garden?

Enter: the number of pounds in 3 short tons (1 short ton = 2,000 pounds)

x	five hundred
+	40,000
+	four hundred
+	4
=	◯

Answer: _____

Riddle: What does Santa call his summer home?

Enter: the number of years in a century

+	three
÷	two hundred
−	0.4389
=	◯

Answer: _____

Seasonal Brainteasers

▶ Use a calculator to answer the questions. Remember to press the equal key after each operation. Then, turn the calculator upside down at the end to read the answer.

Riddle: How does Santa's voice change when he's getting a sore throat?

Enter: one thousand

+	656
+	0.1656
÷	four thousand
=	◯

Answer: _____

Riddle: What is Santa's least favorite thing about stockings hung on a mantel?

Enter: half of 100

+	2,400
÷	0.35
−	287
x	eight
=	◯

Answer: _____

Trip Up North

▶ Trace the safest way to the North Pole. Finish the clues and connect the dots in the order of the missing numbers. Be careful! Not all the numbers will be used.

Christmas

Clues: 1. 6 tens = _____
2. The number in the hundreds place in 849 _____
3. $900 + 50 + 6 = 9$_____6
4. 7 hundreds = _____
5. The number in the tens place in 934 _____
6. $400 + 60 + 1 = 46$_____
7. 2 ones = _____
8. 2 hundreds + 9 tens + 5 ones = $200 +$_____$+ 5$

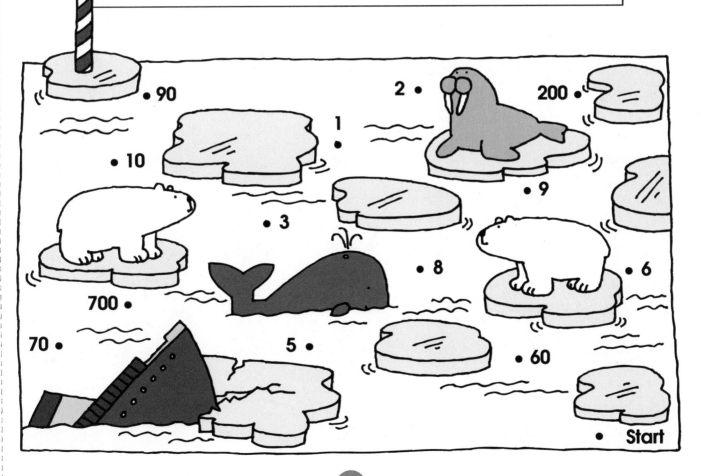

Seasonal Brainteasers

Smart Tree

▶ Solve the subtraction problems. Then, match the letters to the answers to solve the riddle.

Christmas

What is the name of the world's smartest Christmas tree?

31   424   115   202   11   321

527   67   112   202   199   321   202   67   112

A	B	E	I
156 − 125	262 − 147	325 − 123	565 − 498

L	N	P	R
878 − 454	732 − 620	655 − 128	904 − 893

S	T	E	N
395 − 196	826 − 505	468 − 266	590 − 478

While Visions of . . .

Christmas

▶ Solve the addition problems. Then, match the letters to the answers to solve the riddle.

How do the children all nestled in bed sleep on Christmas Eve?

___ ___ ___ ___   ___ ___ ___ ___
912 839 639 990   839 379 469 639

___ ___ ___ ___ ___ ___ ___
809 699 639 836 639 889 912

___ ___ ___ ___ ___ ___ !
983 699 639 379 904 836

A		D		E		H	
256 + 123		856 + 127		364 + 275		516 + 323	

M		N		P		R	
726 + 178		267 + 622		482 + 327		376 + 323	

S		T		V		Y	
706 + 130		427 + 485		275 + 194		875 + 115	

Seasonal Brainteasers

A Special Glow

▶ Find the missing part of each candle below to make it a whole candle. Color it the same color as the part shown in the candle holder.

Hanukkah

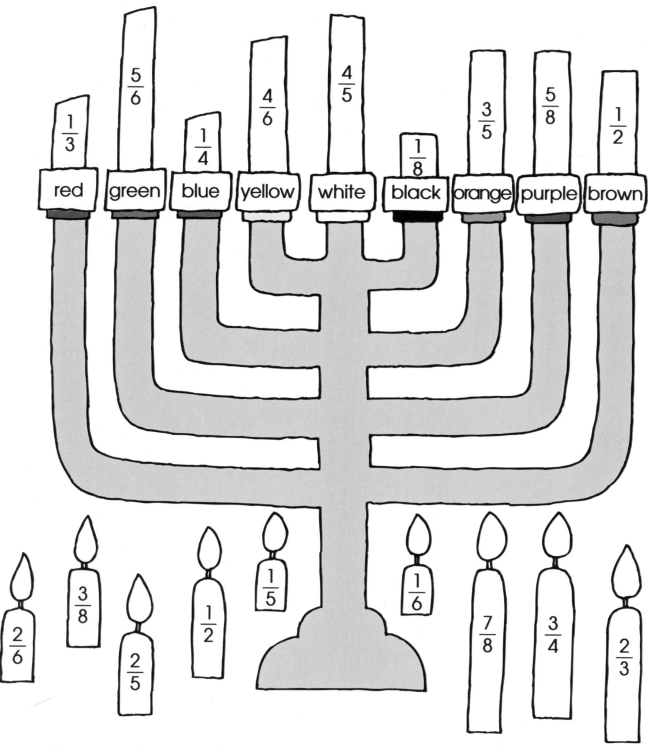

Page 8 — Mirror, Mirror, on the Door

Name _____

Mirror, mirror, on the door
Bounces words back off the floor.
A word comes up,
And it is found
With letters switched all around! pat

▶ Find the word in each sentence that can be spelled backwards to make a new word. Circle the word in the sentence. Then, write the new word on the line to complete the sentence.

Example: I can use a (net) to catch **ten** fish.

1. I will get into the **tub** (but) I don't want a bath!
2. Who put **gum** on my (mug)?
3. Please get me the (top) **pot**
4. (Now) we have finally **won** the game.
5. Losing **gas** made the balloon start to (sag)
6. The **saw** for cutting wood (was) very sharp.
7. Would you like to ride on a **sub** or a (bus)?
8. They used a **tool** to get the (loot)
9. Don't (step) on my **pets** !
10. (Pam) drew a **map** for the trip.
11. The hardest (part) is to **trap** the mouse.
12. My cat is my **pal** when it sits on my (lap)

What do you notice about the words "MIRROR RIM"? **it spells the same backward and forward.**

8

Page 9 — Stretch and Grow

Name _____

Gladys has some goofy glasses. They have springs on them which stretch out words to make room for more vowels.

▶ Add a vowel to each word below to make a new word Gladys can see through her glasses.

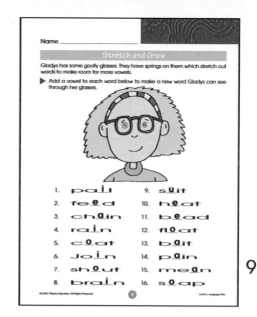

1. pa i l
2. fe e d
3. ch a in
4. ra i n
5. c o at
6. jo i n
7. sh o ut
8. br a in
9. s u it
10. h e at
11. be a d
12. fl o at
13. b a it
14. p a in
15. me a n
16. s o ap

9

Page 10 — Alphabet Soup

Name _____

Nan Cook has a special way of making alphabet soup. She mixes two boxes of soup together. Then, she adds two secret ingredients—mystery and fun. After the soup is cooked, a strange thing happens. All the vowels rise to the top of the pot.

▶ Write the consonant that can be used in both the front and back of each vowel or pair of vowels to make a word. One is done for you.

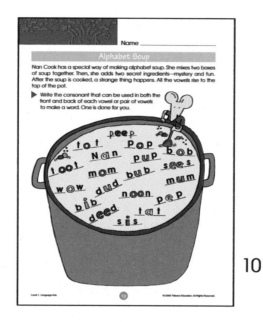

peep
tot   pop   bob
toot   Nan   pup
mom   dud   bub   sees
wow   dud   mum
bib   noon   pep
deed   tat
sis

10

Page 11 — Everything in Its Place

Name _____

Tillie likes everything to be in its place. When things are not just so, she waves her magic feather duster around the room and says five times, "You cannot beat a place that's neat!" The pictures and words below would make Tillie very unhappy. Each picture is missing something, and the word that tells what is missing has its letters jumbled.

▶ First, unscramble the letters and write the word on the line. (The first letter of each word is underlined.) Then, write the number of the word by the picture where it belongs.

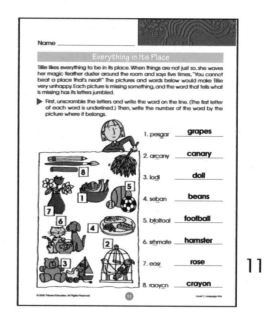

1. pesgar — **grapes**
2. arcany — **canary**
3. lodl — **doll**
4. seban — **beans**
5. bfoltoal — **football**
6. srhmate — **hamster**
7. eosr — **rose**
8. raoycn — **crayon**

11

Page 12 — Flip-Flop

Name _____

Professor Turnabout is teaching his class new vocabulary words. However, he seems to be a little mixed-up. When he gives the students a word, he actually means another word that has the same letters but in a different order.

▶ Look at the words below. Help the students figure out which words the professor really wants them to have.

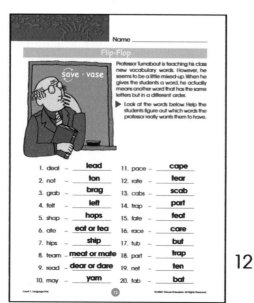

save = vase

1. deal — **lead**
2. not — **ton**
3. grab — **brag**
4. felt — **left**
5. shop — **hops**
6. ate — **eat or tea**
7. hips — **ship**
8. team — **meat or mate**
9. read — **dear or dare**
10. may — **yam**
11. pace — **cape**
12. rate — **tear**
13. cabs — **scab**
14. trap — **part**
15. fate — **feat**
16. race — **care**
17. tub — **but**
18. part — **trap**
19. net — **ten**
20. tab — **bat**

12

Page 13 — Spelling As Easy As ABC

Name _____

A boy named PT likes to take shortcuts when he has a lot to write. On this page, he will show U an EZ way to spell. B prepared to B the NV of all your friends. R U ready?

▶ Use the clues and the Word Bank to help you. Write these words like PT would.

1. A kind of tent — **TP**
2. An insect — **B**
3. A hot drink — **T**
4. A vegetable — **P**
5. A question word — **Y**
6. A banana's skin — **PL**
7. A word that means slippery — **IC**
8. A kind of meat — **VL**
9. Not difficult — **EZ**
10. To look — **C**
11. A period of time — **YL**
12. Pass cards to players — **DL**
13. Nothing in it — **MT**
14. A girl's name — **KT**
15. Pep — **NRG**
16. I am, he is, you — **R**
17. A bird that is blue — **J**
18. A water mammal — **CL**

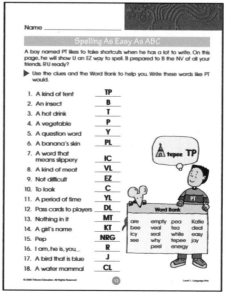

tepee TP

Word Bank

are   empty   pea   Katie
bee   veal   tea   deal
icy   seal   while easy
see   why   tepee jay
       peel   energy

13

14 — Vet to the Rescue

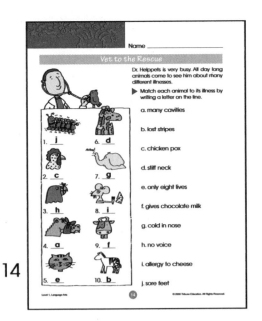

Dr. Helppets is very busy. All day long animals come to see him about many different illnesses.

▶ Match each animal to its illness by writing a letter on the line.

1. j   6. d
2. c   7. g
3. h   8. i
4. a   9. f
5. e   10. b

a. many cavities
b. lost stripes
c. chicken pox
d. stiff neck
e. only eight lives
f. gives chocolate milk
g. cold in nose
h. no voice
i. allergy to cheese
j. sore feet

15 — The Puzzling Print-Out

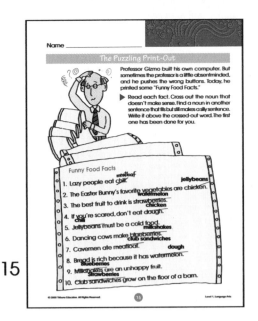

Professor Gizmo built his own computer. But sometimes the professor is a little absentminded, and he pushes the wrong buttons. Today, he printed some "Funny Food Facts."

▶ Read each fact. Cross out the noun that doesn't make sense. Find a noun in another sentence that fits but still makes a silly sentence. Write it above the crossed-out word. The first one has been done for you.

Funny Food Facts

1. Lazy people eat chili. — meatloaf
2. The Easter Bunny's favorite vegetables are chicken. — watermelon
3. The best fruit to drink is strawberries. — chicken
4. If you're scared, don't eat dough. — chili
5. Jellybeans must be a cold food. — milkshakes
6. Dancing cows make blueberries. — club sandwiches
7. Cavemen ate meatloaf. — dough
8. Bread is rich because it has watermelon. — blueberries
9. Milkshakes are an unhappy fruit. — strawberries
10. Club sandwiches grow on the floor of a barn. — jellybeans

16 — Hot Stuff

To become king, the brave, young prince had to have his picture painted with a dragon. He set out on his journey and came upon a cave in which a fire-breathing dragon lived.

The prince called in, "To become king I need to have you pose with me for a painting."

The dragon laughed and answered, "If you can solve the puzzle on the rocks around the entrance to my cave, I will do as you ask."

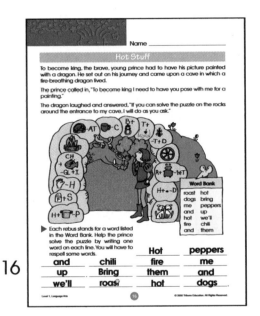

Word Bank
roast · hot · dogs · bring · me · peppers · and · up · hot · we'll · fire · chili · and · them

▶ Each rebus stands for a word listed in the Word Bank. Help the prince solve the puzzle by writing one word on each line. You will have to respell some words.

Hot	peppers
and	chili	fire	me
up	Bring	them	and
we'll	roast	hot	dogs

17 — Pucker Power

One day a princess walked in the forest. She met a bullfrog who croaked loudly, "Every time you kiss me, I will turn into something different. By the seventh kiss, I will have what I need to be your prince."

▶ On each line write the word that is pictured.

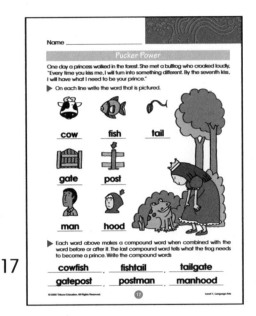

cow   fish   tail
gate   post
man   hood

▶ Each word above makes a compound word when combined with the word before or after it. The last compound word tells what the frog needs to become a prince. Write the compound words.

| cowfish | fishtail | tailgate |
| gatepost | postman | manhood |

18 — Word Magic

Maggie Magician announces, "One plus one equals one!" The audience giggles. So Maggie puts two words into a hat and waves her magic wand. When she reaches into the hat, Maggie pulls out one word and a picture. "See," says Maggie, "I was right!"

▶ Look at each picture below. Use the Word Bank to help write a compound word for each.

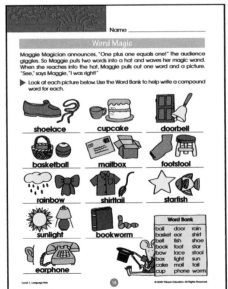

shoelace   cupcake   doorbell
basketball   mailbox   footstool
rainbow   shirttail   starfish
sunlight   bookworm   earphone

Word Bank
ball · door · rain · basket · ear · shirt · bell · fish · shoe · book · foot · star · bow · lace · stool · box · light · sun · cake · mail · tail · cup · phone · worm

19 — Alike, But So Different

Jim and Tim are twins, but they do not look alike and often don't think alike. The boys like to speak in rhymes and finish each other's sentences using words with opposite meanings.

▶ Read each sentence. Then write the missing words. The first one has been done for you. You can use the Word Bank to help find the words.

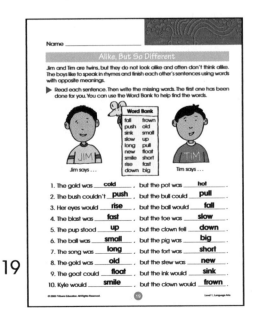

Word Bank
fall · frown · push · old · sink · small · slow · up · long · pull · new · float · smile · short · rise · fast · down · big

Jim says . . .   Tim says . . .

1. The gold was **cold**, but the pot was **hot**.
2. The bush couldn't **push**, but the bull could **pull**.
3. Her eyes would **rise**, but the ball would **fall**.
4. The blast was **fast**, but the toe was **slow**.
5. The pup stood **up**, but the clown fell **down**.
6. The ball was **small**, but the pig was **big**.
7. The song was **long**, but the fort was **short**.
8. The gold was **old**, but the stew was **new**.
9. The goat could **float**, but the ink would **sink**.
10. Kyle would **smile**, but the clown would **frown**.

Brainteaser Answer Keys

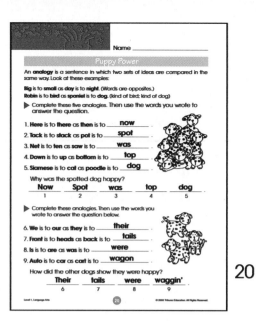

Puppy Power

An **analogy** is a sentence in which two sets of ideas are compared in the same way. Look at these examples:

Big is to **small** as **day** is to **night**. (Words are opposites.)
Robin is to **bird** as **spaniel** is to **dog**. (kind of bird; kind of dog)

▶ Complete these five analogies. Then use the words you wrote to answer the question.

1. **Here** is to **there** as **then** is to __now__
2. **Tack** is to **stack** as **pot** is to __spot__
3. **Net** is to **ten** as **saw** is to __was__
4. **Down** is to **up** as **bottom** is to __top__
5. **Siamese** is to **cat** as **poodle** is to __dog__

Why was the spotted dog happy?

Now	Spot	was	top	dog
1	2	3	4	5

▶ Complete these analogies. Then use the words you wrote to answer the question below.

6. **We** is to **our** as **they** is to __their__
7. **Front** is to **heads** as **back** is to __tails__
8. **Is** is to **are** as **was** is to __were__
9. **Auto** is to **car** as **cart** is to __wagon__

How did the other dogs show they were happy?

Their	tails	were	waggin'
6	7	8	9

Level 1, Language Arts (20)

20

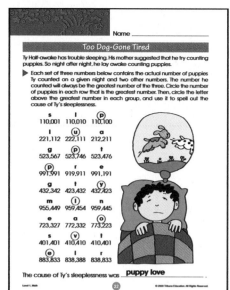

Too Dog-Gone Tired

Ty Half-awake has trouble sleeping. His mother suggested that he try counting puppies. So night after night, he lay awake counting puppies.

▶ Each set of three numbers below contains the actual number of puppies Ty counted on a given night and two other numbers. The number he counted will always be the greatest number of the three. Circle the number of puppies in each row that is the greatest number. Then, circle the letter above the greatest number in each group, and use it to spell out the cause of Ty's sleeplessness.

s   l   (p)
110,001   110,010   110,100

l   (u)   a
221,112   222,111   212,111

g   (p)   t
523,567   523,746   523,476

(p)   r   e
991,991   919,911   991,191

g   t   (y)
432,342   423,432   432,423

m   (l)   n
955,449   959,454   959,445

e   (a)   n
723,327   772,332   773,223

s   (v)   l
401,401   410,410   410,401

(e)   l   r
883,833   838,388   838,833

The cause of Ty's sleeplessness was __puppy love__

Level 1, Math (22)

22

Share and Share Alike

A certain farmer had a vegetable garden. He did not need all the lettuce and carrots that he grew, so he shared part of his crops with six friendly rabbits.

The farmer followed certain rules:
• Each rabbit would be given one bag of vegetables.
• Each bag had to have one carrot and one head of lettuce.
• All the bags had to weigh exactly the same.

(carrots: 7 oz., 10 oz., 9 oz., 12 oz., 11 oz.)
(lettuce: 1 oz., 2 oz., 3 oz., 4 oz., 5 oz., 6 oz.)

▶ Help the farmer choose which carrot and which head of lettuce to put together in each bag. Write the weight on each carrot and each head of lettuce in the bags at the bottom of the page.

4 oz.	2 oz.	6 oz.	3 oz.	5 oz.	1 oz.
9 oz.	11 oz.	7 oz.	10 oz.	8 oz.	12 oz.

Level 1, Math (23)

23

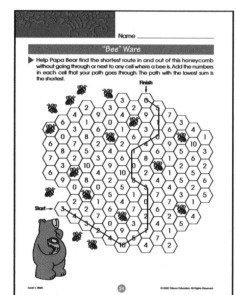

"Bee" Ware

▶ Help Papa Bear find the shortest route in and out of this honeycomb without going through or next to any cell where a bee is. Add the numbers in each cell that your path goes through. The path with the lowest sum is the shortest.

24

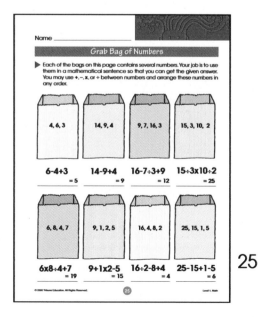

Grab Bag of Numbers

▶ Each of the bags on this page contains several numbers. Your job is to use them in a mathematical sentence so that you can get the given answer. You may use +, –, x, or ÷ between numbers and arrange these numbers in any order.

4, 6, 3	14, 9, 4	9, 7, 16, 3	15, 3, 10, 2
6–4+3 = 5	14–9+4 = 9	16–7÷3+9 = 12	15÷3x10÷2 = 25

6, 8, 4, 7	9, 1, 2, 5	16, 4, 8, 2	25, 15, 1, 5
6x8÷4+7 = 19	9+1x2–5 = 15	16÷2–8+4 = 4	25–15+1–5 = 6

Level 1, Math (25)

25

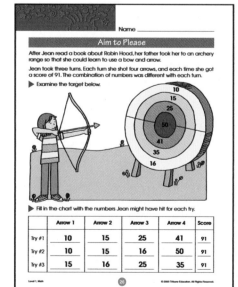

Aim to Please

After Jean read a book about Robin Hood, her father took her to an archery range so that she could learn to use a bow and arrow.

Jean took three turns. Each turn she shot four arrows, and each time she got a score of 91. The combination of numbers was different with each turn.

▶ Examine the target below.

(target values: 10, 15, 25, 50, 41, 35, 16)

▶ Fill in the chart with the numbers Jean might have hit for each try.

	Arrow 1	Arrow 2	Arrow 3	Arrow 4	Score
Try #1	10	15	25	41	91
Try #2	10	15	16	50	91
Try #3	15	16	25	35	91

Level 1, Math (26)

26

27

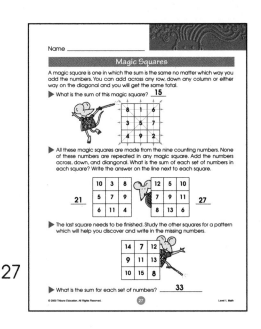

Magic Squares

A magic square is one in which the sum is the same no matter which way you add the numbers. You can add across any row, down any column or either way on the diagonal and you will get the same total.

▶ What is the sum of this magic square? __15__

8	1	6
3	5	7
4	9	2

▶ All these magic squares are made from the nine counting numbers. None of these numbers are repeated in any magic square. Add the numbers across, down, and diagonal. What is the sum of each set of numbers in each square? Write the answer on the line next to each square.

__21__

10	3	8
5	7	9
6	11	4

12	5	10
7	9	11
8	13	6

__27__

▶ The last square needs to be finished. Study the other squares for a pattern which will help you discover and write in the missing numbers.

14	7	12
9	11	13
10	15	8

▶ What is the sum for each set of numbers? __33__

© 2000 Tribune Education. All Rights Reserved. (27) Level 1, Math

---

28

This Side Up

These cubes are six-sided. The sum of the numbers on opposite sides of each cube always equals 7.

▶ Complete the mathematical sentences on the 3 sides of each cube that can be seen. Then, write and complete a mathematical sentence for the 3 sides that can't be seen. You can use addition, subtraction, multiplication or division. Remember, the answers on opposite sides must have a sum of 7.

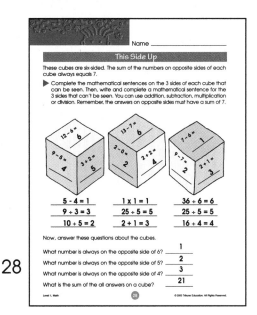

5 - 4 = 1	1 x 1 = 1	36 ÷ 6 = 6
9 ÷ 3 = 3	25 ÷ 5 = 5	25 ÷ 5 = 5
10 ÷ 5 = 2	2 + 1 = 3	16 ÷ 4 = 4

Now, answer these questions about the cubes.

What number is always on the opposite side of 6? __1__

What number is always on the opposite side of 5? __2__

What number is always on the opposite side of 4? __3__

What is the sum of the all answers on a cube? __21__

Level 1, Math (28) © 2000 Tribune Education. All Rights Reserved.

29

A Bag of Sweets

The candy store is having a sale and you decide to stock up on your favorites.

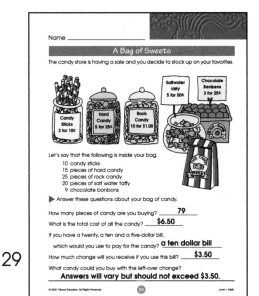

Let's say that the following is inside your bag.

10 candy sticks
15 pieces of hard candy
25 pieces of rock candy
20 pieces of salt water taffy
9 chocolate bonbons

▶ Answer these questions about your bag of candy.

How many pieces of candy are you buying? __79__

What is the total cost of all the candy? __$6.50__

If you have a twenty, a ten and a five-dollar bill,
which would you use to pay for the candy? __a ten dollar bill__

How much change will you receive if you use this bill? __$3.50__

What candy could you buy with the left-over change?
Answers will vary but should not exceed $3.50.

© 2000 Tribune Education. All Rights Reserved. (29) Level 1, Math

---

30

Feeding Time

Ken and Angie enjoy watching the animals being fed at the zoo. However, when they arrive, they are a little confused by the signs.

▶ Help them figure out the feeding time for each kind of animal, and write it below the description. Be sure to include A.M. or P.M.

Seals: Feeding time is two hours after the monkeys.
200 P.M.

Tigers: Feeding time is two hours after 9:00 A.M.
1100 A.M.

Lions: Feeding time is 1:00 P.M.
100 P.M.

Giraffes: Feeding time is one hour before the elephants.
300 P.M.

Monkeys: Feeding time is three hours before the giraffes.
1200 P.M.

Elephants: Feeding time is three hours after the lions.
400 P.M.

▶ Now, trace the path in the zoo that Ken and Angie should take, so that they can see all the animals being fed.

Paths will vary.

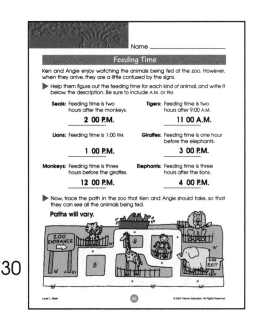

Level 1, Math (30) © 2000 Tribune Education. All Rights Reserved.

31

Fast Foods

Jamie noticed that some restaurants call their food "Fast Food." He decided to see which food is the fastest. He attached small paper plates onto three remote-controlled cars. He put one fast food on each plate. Car 1 is called "Hot Rod Dog." Car 2 is called "Cheeseburger Champion." Car 3 is called "French Fry Fury." Then, Jamie put them at the Starting Line of the track you see below.

▶ Carefully study the dark tracks and all the ways each car can go. Trace the shortest path for each car. Then, decide who the winner of the race is. Use the number of squares to help you.

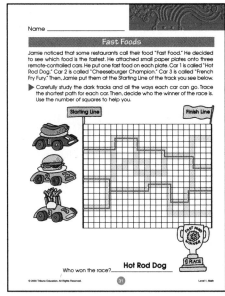

Who won the race? **Hot Rod Dog**

© 2000 Tribune Education. All Rights Reserved. (31) Level 1, Math

---

32

Plainly a Plane

A **plane figure** is a shape on a flat surface. The most common plane figures are shown below:

Triangle Circle Square Rectangle

▶ Find and label any shapes in the pictures below which remind you of any of these plane figures. Some of the pictures might suggest more than one plane figure. Label them all.

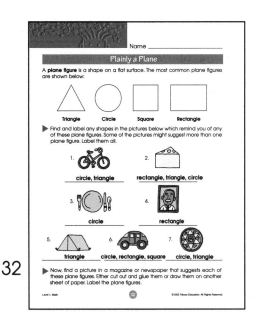

1. circle, triangle
2. rectangle, triangle, circle
3. circle
4. rectangle
5. triangle
6. circle, rectangle, square
7. circle, triangle

▶ Now, find a picture in a magazine or newspaper that suggests each of these plane figures. Either cut out and glue them or draw them on another sheet of paper. Label the plane figures.

Level 1, Math (32) © 2000 Tribune Education. All Rights Reserved.

Brainteaser Answer Keys

Page 33

Name _____

A Picture Diagram

In the diagrams on this page, the outside rectangle stands for a whole set of things. The inside circle or circles stand for part or parts of the whole set.

Example: This rectangle stands for all the dishes in your cupboard. Circle A stands for all the plates in the cupboard. Circle B stands for all the glasses there.

▶ Use this diagram to tell if these sentences are true or false. Write TRUE or FALSE on each line.

1. All the plates are in the cupboard. **True**
2. Some of the glasses belong in the set of plates. **False**
3. All of the things in the cupboard are plates. **False**
4. None of the glasses are in the cupboard. **False**

Now, look carefully at this diagram. The rectangle stands for all the children in your class. Circle C stands for all the boys in the class. Circle D stands for all the children in the class who are 10 years old or older.

▶ Use this diagram to tell if these sentences are true or false. Write TRUE or FALSE on each line.

5. All of the boys are 10 years old or older. **False**
6. All of the boys are in the class. **True**
7. Some of those who are 10 years old or older are boys. **True**
8. None of the boys are younger than 10 years. **False**
9. None of the boys are 10 years old or older. **False**

33

Page 34

Name _____

Gordon Gopher

Gordon Gopher wanted a new home. After many days of hard work, he finished a long tunnel. In the tunnel, he hid nuts for the long winter months ahead according to a particular pattern.

▶ Continue the pattern below by drawing the correct number of nuts at each spot marked with an **X**. Then, count the total number of nuts hidden by Gordon Gopher.

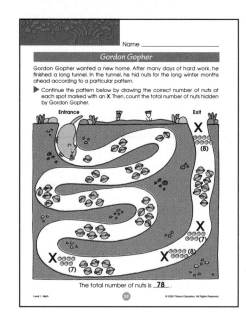

The total number of nuts is __78__.

34

Page 36

Name _____

The Adventure Begins

A good place to start to know about the world around you is to visit a museum or other place where large collections have been gathered. Imagine that one rainy Saturday morning you have the opportunity to do just that. Study these ads from the telephone book, and then decide where you will go.

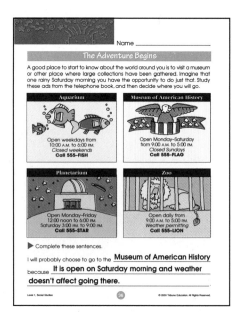

▶ Complete these sentences.

I will probably choose to go to the **Museum of American History**
because **It is open on Saturday morning and weather doesn't affect going there.**

36

Page 37

Name _____

Home Sweet Home

If you visit a museum of American history, you may see exhibits about Native Americans and their historic homes like those pictured below.

▶ Use the rebuses to discover which nation of Native Americans lived in each kind of home. After you sound out your answer find the correct spelling in the Word Bank, and use it to complete each sentence.

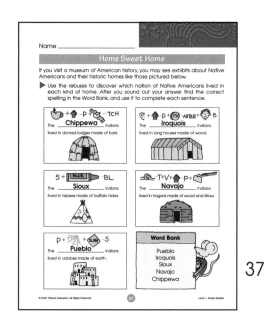

The **Chippewa** Indians lived in domed lodges made of bark.

The **Iroquois** Indians lived in long houses made of wood.

The **Sioux** Indians lived in tepees made of buffalo hides.

The **Navajo** Indians lived in hogans made of wood and straw.

The **Pueblo** Indians lived in adobes made of earth.

Word Bank
Pueblo
Iroquois
Sioux
Navajo
Chippewa

37

Page 38

Name _____

Dinner Time

Eskimos live in the cold lands of northern North America. In this region, people eat a lot of fish because fish are so plentiful. The children on this page caught many fish. Read the clues given by each Eskimo. On the line below each child, write the number of fish he or she caught.

Hint: When an Eskimo speaks of his or her right or left, it is his or her right or left, not yours. Put an L or R on their left and right arms to help you.

Speech bubbles:
- I caught twice as many fish as the person on my far left.
- I have 4 more fish than the person to my left.
- The number of fish I caught is an odd number between 7 and 10.
- I caught half as many fish as the 3rd person from my right.
- I caught 3 fewer fish than the person in the middle.

12   13   9   6   6

1. Circle the person who caught the most fish.
2. Put a check next to the two whose fish added together equal 21.

38

Page 39

Name _____

A Family of Friends

The Native Americans lived in America long before anyone else. When the Pilgrims came from England in 1620, they landed in a place called Plymouth. They survived that first hard winter because the Native Americans helped them to hunt and grow and harvest food.

▶ Read each riddle. Use the Word Bank to write the name of a food that the Native Americans helped the Pilgrims find or grow.

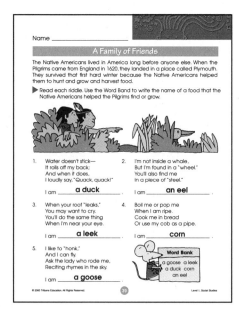

1. Water doesn't stick—
It rolls off my back;
And when it does,
I loudly say, "Quack, quack!"
I am **a duck**

2. I'm not inside a whale,
But I'm found in a "wheel."
You'll also find me
In a piece of "steel."
I am **an eel**

3. When your roof "leaks,"
You may want to cry.
You'll do the same thing
When I'm near your eye.
I am **a leek**

4. Boil me or pop me
When I am ripe.
Cook me in bread
Or use my cob as a pipe.
I am **corn**

5. I like to "honk,"
And I can fly.
Ask the lady who rode me,
Reciting rhymes in the sky.
I am **a goose**

Word Bank
a goose a leek
a duck corn
an eel

39

40

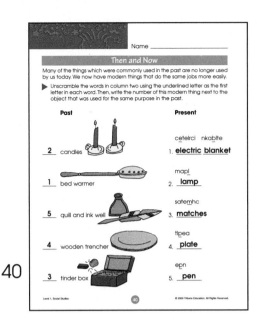

Then and Now

Many of the things which were commonly used in the past are no longer used by us today. We now have modern things that do the same jobs more easily.

▶ Unscramble the words in column two using the underlined letter as the first letter in each word. Then, write the number of this modern thing next to the object that was used for the same purpose in the past.

Past — **Present**

- 2 candles
- 1 bed warmer
- 5 quill and ink well
- 4 wooden trencher
- 3 tinder box

cetelrci nkablte
1. **electric blanket**

mapl
2. **lamp**

satemhc
3. **matches**

tlpea
4. **plate**

epn
5. **pen**

Level 1, Social Studies   © 2000 Tribune Education. All Rights Reserved.

41

Sew What?

A favorite activity of colonial women and girls was getting together for a quilting bee. The quilts, made from scraps of linen, wool and cotton, were frequently sewn together in a pattern.

▶ Look carefully at the pattern in the unfinished quilt below. Then, continue the pattern by drawing pictures in the blank sections to complete the quilt.

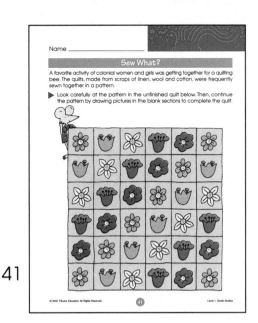

© 2000 Tribune Education. All Rights Reserved.   Level 1, Social Studies

42

Go West, Young Man!

In the first half of the nineteenth century, many pioneers moved westward across the United States. They traveled in big covered wagons called Conestoga wagons.

Some of the trails that the pioneers took in their Conestoga wagons are marked on the map below.

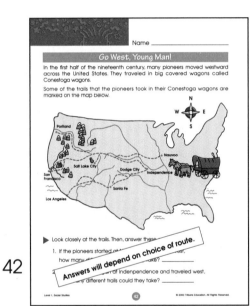

▶ Look closely at the trails. Then, answer these

1. If the pioneers started
   how many

Answers will depend on choice of route.

of Independence and traveled west, many different trails could they take?

Level 1, Social Studies   © 2000 Tribune Education. All Rights Reserved.

43

Signs of the Times

In Pennsylvania, there is an area called the Pennsylvania Dutch Country. Many of the people who live there try to live simple lives much like their ancestors did long ago. Some people still use a horse and buggy for transportation.

▶ Look carefully at the paths from the farmhouse to the barn. Count how many different ways a horse and buggy could travel.

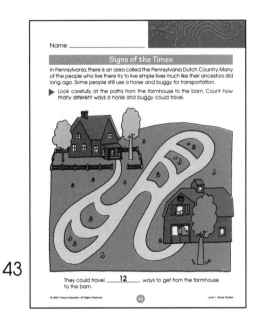

They could travel __12__ ways to get from the farmhouse to the barn.

© 2000 Tribune Education. All Rights Reserved.   Level 1, Social Studies

44

What's Your Brand?

Cowboys were very important in the development of the American West. They went on long cattle drives that lasted two or three months at a time and covered hundreds of miles. Cowboys were often in danger from rattlesnakes, stampedes, wild horses and horse thieves.

During cattle roundups in the spring and fall, cowboys branded the newborn calves to show which ranch owned them.

▶ Look at the brands below. Use the Word Bank to help you write what each brand means.

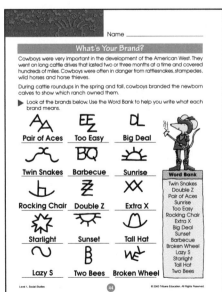

Pair of Aces   Too Easy   Big Deal

Twin Snakes   Barbecue   Sunrise

Rocking Chair   Double Z   Extra X

Starlight   Sunset   Tall Hat

Lazy S   Two Bees   Broken Wheel

Word Bank
Twin Snakes
Double Z
Pair of Aces
Sunrise
Too Easy
Rocking Chair
Extra X
Big Deal
Sunset
Barbecue
Broken Wheel
Lazy S
Starlight
Tall Hat
Two Bees

Level 1, Social Studies   © 2000 Tribune Education. All Rights Reserved.

45

R-r-r-r-r-ing!

The Liberty Bell in Philadelphia, Pennsylvania, was rung to announce important events during the early days in America. Today, we often use a telephone to tell others about events in our lives. You can also use the numbers and letters on a telephone to write a secret message.

▶ Use the numbers to decode the sentence below. Remember, for each number you have a choice of three letters.

T H E   L I B E R T Y   B E L L
8 4 3   5 4 2 3 7 8 9   2 3 5 5

S T A N D S   F O R   F R E E D O M
7 8 2 6 3 7   3 6 7   3 7 3 3 3 6 6

Use this code system to write a message of your own, and try it on a friend.

© 2000 Tribune Education. All Rights Reserved.   Level 1, Social Studies

It Was a Great Year

At the end of every year we usually like to recall the major events that took place during the past twelve months. For example, at the end of 1888 Americans might have read articles about these events.

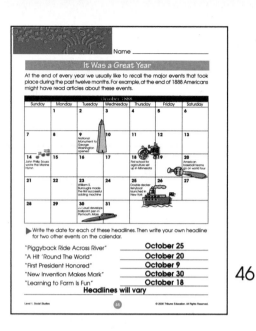

▶ Write the date for each of these headlines. Then write your own headline for two other events on the calendar.

Headline	Date
"Piggyback Ride Across River"	October 25
"A Hit 'Round The World"	October 20
"First President Honored"	October 9
"New Invention Makes Mark"	October 30
"Learning to Farm Is Fun"	October 18

Headlines will vary.

46

The American Alphabet

The United States is sometimes called a nation of immigrants because it has people from almost every country in the world.

▶ Print the letters of the alphabet in order in the boxes. Then, complete the name of each country using the suggestions listed in the Word Bank.

1. India
2. Mozambique
3. China
4. Ireland
5. Greece
6. Afghanistan
7. Egypt
8. Netherlands
9. Israel
10. Japan
11. Korea
12. Philippines
13. Germany
14. Canada
15. Poland
16. Puerto Rico
17. Iraq
18. France
19. Australia
20. Italy
21. Cuba
22. Vietnam
23. Norway
24. Mexico
25. Kenya
26. Venezuela

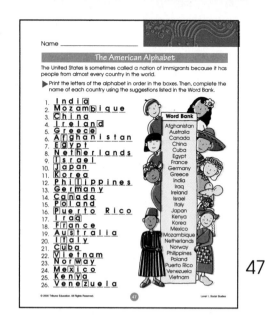

Word Bank
Afghanistan
Australia
Canada
China
Cuba
Egypt
France
Germany
Greece
India
Iraq
Ireland
Israel
Italy
Japan
Kenya
Korea
Mexico
Mozambique
Netherlands
Norway
Philippines
Poland
Puerto Rico
Venezuela
Vietnam

47

Where's Our Mummy?

▶ Many museums, like the Field Museum of Natural History in Chicago, have great exhibits of Egyptian mummies. Look carefully at the mummies pictured below. Think about word clues that could help someone identify each mummy. Then, write three words to describe or name something about each mummy that makes it different from the others.

Answers will vary.

48

Getting Better With Age

Like many inventions, the automobile, bicycle, airplane and telephone are constantly being improved to make them more useful.

▶ Show that you know how these inventions have developed by numbering each set of three pictures in the correct order.

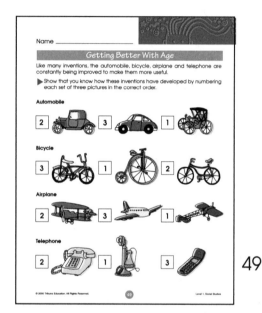

Automobile — 2, 3, 1

Bicycle — 3, 1, 2

Airplane — 2, 3, 1

Telephone — 2, 1, 3

49

Getting the Job Done

America is often called the "Land of Opportunity." This means that its people may choose from many types of work to make a living.

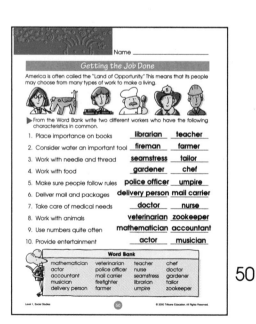

▶ From the Word Bank write two different workers who have the following characteristics in common.

1. Place importance on books — librarian, teacher
2. Consider water an important tool — fireman, farmer
3. Work with needle and thread — seamstress, tailor
4. Work with food — gardener, chef
5. Make sure people follow rules — police officer, umpire
6. Deliver mail and packages — delivery person, mail carrier
7. Take care of medical needs — doctor, nurse
8. Work with animals — veterinarian, zookeeper
9. Use numbers quite often — mathematician, accountant
10. Provide entertainment — actor, musician

Word Bank
mathematician	veterinarian	teacher	chef
actor	police officer	nurse	doctor
accountant	mail carrier	seamstress	gardener
musician	firefighter	librarian	tailor
delivery person	farmer	umpire	zookeeper

50

Inside Out

Animals whose skeletons have backbones or spines are called vertebrates.

▶ Look at each skeleton below. Read the riddle. Then decide from the Word Bank which vertebrate is pictured. Write its name to complete the sentence.

1. I am thankful to be alive at holidays. People might "gobble me up!" — I am a **turkey**

2. I have wings, but I cannot fly. I love to strut around in my "tuxedo." — I am a **penguin**

3. I am not a bird, but I can fly. I work at night and sleep all day. — I am a **bat**

4. My legs and tail are very strong. I even come with a pocket. — I am a **kangaroo**

5. I stand tall and proud. So please don't ask me to eat from the ground. — I am a **giraffe**

6. They say I have no hair, and they're right. I represent a great country. — I am a **bald eagle**

Word Bank
bald eagle	kangaroo
turkey	penguin
giraffe	bat

52

Amazing Amphibians

Amphibians are cold-blooded vertebrates (animals with backbones). They have no scales on their skin. Most amphibians hatch from eggs laid in water or on damp ground. Many amphibians grow legs as they develop into adults. Some live on land and have both lungs and gills for breathing. Frogs and toads are examples of amphibians.

Santjie, a South African sharp-nosed frog, holds the record for the longest triple jump. It jumped a total of more than 33 feet!

▶ The frogs below won 1st, 2nd and 3rd place in a recent triple-jump contest. Each succeeding jump was two feet shorter than the jump before. How many total feet did each frog jump?

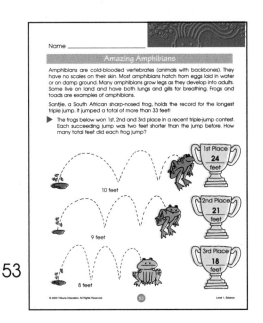

1st Place **24** feet — 10 feet

2nd Place **21** feet — 9 feet

3rd Place **18** feet — 8 feet

53

The Reptile House

There are about 6,000 different kinds of reptiles. They come in all sorts of shapes and colors. Their sizes in length range from 2 inches to almost 30 feet. Reptiles can be found on every continent except Antarctica. Even though reptiles can seem quite different, they all...
- breathe with lungs.
- are cold-blooded.
- have dry, scaly skin.
- have backbones.

▶ Look at the pictures of these five reptiles and read their descriptions. Then, use these clues to write the name of each reptile in its correct home.

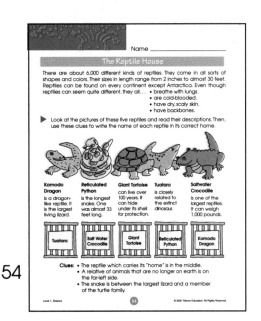

Komodo Dragon is a dragon-like reptile. It is the largest living lizard.

Reticulated Python is the longest snake. One was almost 33 feet long.

Giant Tortoise can live over 100 years. It can hide under its shell for protection.

Tuatara is closely related to the extinct dinosaur.

Saltwater Crocodile is one of the largest reptiles. It can weigh 1,000 pounds.

Homes: Tuatara | Salt Water Crocodile | Giant Tortoise | Reticulated Python | Komodo Dragon

Clues:
- The reptile which carries its "home" is in the middle.
- A relative of animals that are no longer on earth is on the far-left side.
- The snake is between the largest lizard and a member of the turtle family.

54

Interesting Invertebrates

Invertebrates are animals that have no backbone or inside skeleton. Some have soft bodies protected by shells. Others have soft bodies that are not protected. Some invertebrates are so small that they can only be seen with a microscope.

▶ Below are the names of some invertebrates. Use the rebuses to help complete each one.

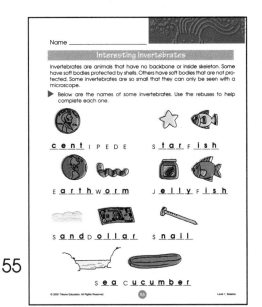

c e n t I P E D E

s t a r f i s h

E a r t h w o r m

J e l l y F i s h

s a n d D o l l a r

s n a i l

s e a c u c u m b e r

55

Dynamic Dinosaurs

Dinosaurs were reptiles that lived millions of years ago. Some of them were the biggest animals to ever live on land.

Scientists have given names to the dinosaurs that often describe their special bodies, sizes and habits.

▶ Match these dinosaurs with their names in the Word Bank. Use the objects pictured with the dinosaurs as clues to help you.

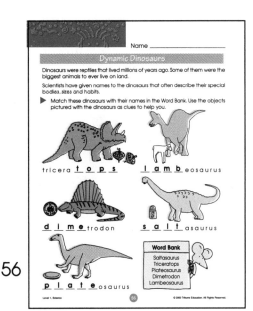

t r i c e r a t o p s

l a m b e o s a u r u s

d i m e t r o d o n

s a l t a s a u r u s

p l a t e o s a u r u s

Word Bank
Saltasaurus
Triceratops
Plateosaurus
Dimetrodon
Lambeosaurus

56

The Mighty Bear

Bears are large and powerful animals. Depending on the type of bear, they can weigh from 60 to 2,000 pounds.

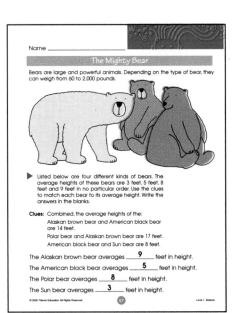

▶ Listed below are four different kinds of bears. The average heights of these bears are 3 feet, 5 feet, 8 feet and 9 feet in no particular order. Use the clues to match each bear to its average height. Write the answers in the blanks.

Clues: Combined, the average heights of the:
Alaskan brown bear and American black bear are 14 feet.
Polar bear and Alaskan brown bear are 17 feet.
American black bear and Sun bear are 8 feet.

The Alaskan brown bear averages **9** feet in height.

The American black bear averages **5** feet in height.

The Polar bear averages **8** feet in height.

The Sun bear averages **3** feet in height.

57

Butterflies and Moths

People sometimes confuse butterflies with moths, but there are some important differences.

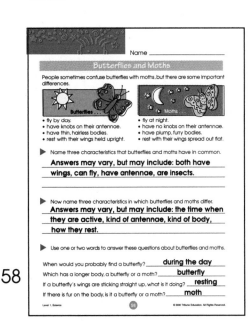

Butterflies...
- fly by day.
- have knobs on their antennae.
- have thin, hairless bodies.
- rest with their wings held upright.

Moths...
- fly at night.
- have no knobs on their antennae.
- have plump, furry bodies.
- rest with their wings spread out flat.

▶ Name three characteristics that butterflies and moths have in common.
Answers may vary, but may include: both have wings, can fly, have antennae, are insects.

▶ Now name three characteristics in which butterflies and moths differ.
Answers may vary, but may include: the time when they are active, kind of antennae, kind of body, how they rest.

▶ Use one or two words to answer these questions about butterflies and moths.

When would you probably find a butterfly? **during the day**

Which has a longer body, a butterfly or a moth? **butterfly**

If a butterfly's wings are sticking straight up, what is it doing? **resting**

If there is fur on the body, is it a butterfly or a moth? **moth**

58

The Chocolate Tree

Have you ever thought about chocolate growing on a tree? Actually, chocolate is made from the seeds of tropical trees called cacao trees. Most of these trees grow in the warm, wet climate of western Africa.

▶ Make a list of all the things which are made of chocolate that you could put in this basket. Then, draw some items from your list in the basket.

Answers may vary, but may include: bon bons, chocolate-covered cherries, cocoa, chocolate cake, chocolate chip cookies, Easter bunnies, candy bars, chocolate-covered raisins, chocolate-covered malt balls, chocolate-covered peanuts and chocolate kisses.

59

Level 1, Science

Weather Watch

Weather is the condition of the air around the earth for a period of time. A weatherman's job is to predict the weather.

▶ There were some very unusual weather patterns recorded for a recent month. Use the key to draw the correct weather symbols for each day.

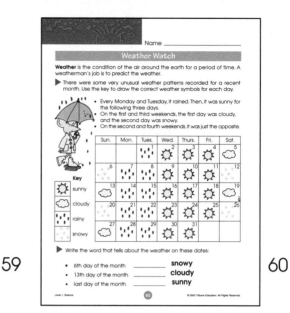

- Every Monday and Tuesday, it rained. Then, it was sunny for the following three days.
- On the first and third weekends, the first day was cloudy, and the second day was snowy.
- On the second and fourth weekends, it was just the opposite.

Key
- ☀ sunny
- ☁ cloudy
- rainy
- snowy

▶ Write the word that tells about the weather on these dates:

- 6th day of the month _____ snowy
- 13th day of the month _____ cloudy
- last day of the month _____ sunny

60

Level 1, Science

Travel Light

Earth's closest neighbor in space is the Moon. The Moon is very different from the Earth. It has no wind, no air and no water. The sky around the Moon always looks black, and stars can always be seen. Because there is a lot less gravity on the Moon, astronauts can jump much farther there than on Earth. There are large holes, called craters, on the Moon.

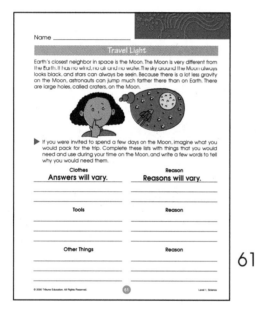

▶ If you were invited to spend a few days on the Moon, imagine what you would pack for the trip. Complete these lists with things that you would need and use during your time on the Moon, and write a few words to tell why you would need them.

Clothes	Reason
Answers will vary.	Reasons will vary.
Tools	Reason
Other Things	Reason

61

Level 1, Science

What's the Matter?

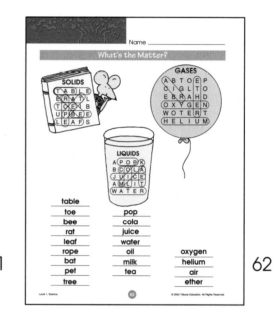

table	pop
toe	cola
bee	juice
rat	water
leaf	oil
rope	milk
bat	tea
pet	
tree	oxygen
	helium
	air
	ether

62

Level 1, Science

Magnetic Attraction

The word "magnet" begins with the same three letters as the word "magic", and sometimes magnets do seem a little magical.

Every magnet has two poles–north and south. The north pole of one magnet attracts, or pulls toward, the south pole of another magnet. Two poles that are the same (two north poles or two south poles) do not attract each other. Instead, they repel, or push away from, each other.

▶ Using the information above, continue labeling the horseshoe and bar magnets below with N (for north) and S (for south).

63

Level 1, Science

Man's Best Friend

Dogs are often called "Man's Best Friend," and there are many good reasons for this. Dogs help with hunting and herding. They help guide visually–impaired people and also help the police do detective work. Most often, they are kept as pets and provide both friendship and protection to their owners.

There are over 130 breeds of dogs in the United States. According to one source, the following were the most popular breeds:

Golden Retriever   Cocker Spaniel   Rottweiler   Poodle   Labrador Retriever

▶ Use the clues below to discover the order of the dogs' popularity. Then, write each dog's name on the correct ribbon.

Clues:
- This dog is the third most popular. His name sounds like something that forms during a rainstorm.
- This dog's name includes one of man's most precious metals. It ranks fourth.
- This dog has the most vowels of all the names. It ranks second.
- This dog doesn't consider it a rotten deal to be last.
- This dog ranks first. It is as proud as a peacock.

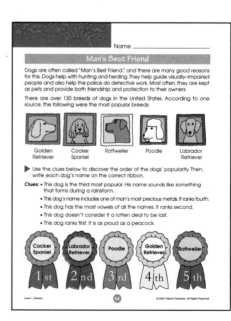

1st	2nd	3rd	4th	5th
Cocker Spaniel	Labrador Retriever	Poodle	Golden Retriever	Rottweiler

64

Level 1, Science

Page 65 — Earth's Eruptions

Name _____

Earth's Eruptions

Hot solids, liquids and gases sometimes erupt from the Earth in places called volcanoes.

▶ Use the clues below to locate six volcanoes in North America which erupted in the last century. Write the name of each volcano by the flag which indicates the year of its last eruption.

Clues:
- El Chichón erupted a year before the volcano called Pavlof.
- Colima is not in the United States.
- Shishaldin last erupted 2 years before El Chichón did.
- Iliamna last erupted 3 years before one of the volcanoes and 8 years before another.
- Mount St. Helens erupted the same year as the one in Mexico.

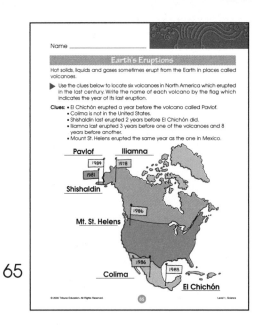

Pavlof 1984 / 1981
Iliamna 1978
Shishaldin
Mt. St. Helens 1986
Colima 1986
El Chichón 1983

© 2000 Tribune Education. All Rights Reserved.

Level 1, Science

65

Page 66 — Plant, Animal or Mineral?

Name _____

Plant, Animal or Mineral?

▶ Things on the Earth can be sorted into three categories—plants, animals or minerals. Read the description of each of them and sort the things listed into their correct category. Then, list other things that belong in each category.

Plants: It includes all living things that can't move on their own, like trees, plants, vines, bushes and herbs.

Animals: It includes all living things that can move on their own, animals big or small, alive or dead, simple or complex.

Minerals: It includes all non-living things on the Earth that are neither plants or animals.

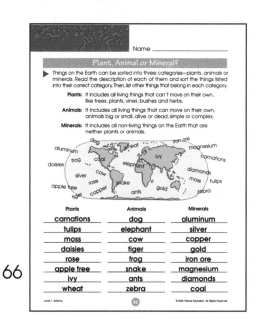

Plants	Animals	Minerals
carnations	dog	aluminum
tulips	elephant	silver
moss	cow	copper
daisies	tiger	gold
rose	frog	iron ore
apple tree	snake	magnesium
ivy	ants	diamonds
wheat	zebra	coal

Level 1, Science

© 2000 Tribune Education. All Rights Reserved.

66

Page 68 — Art That Moves

Name _____

Art That Moves

Below are examples of mobiles that could hang from the ceiling in your room. Something is missing from each mobile.

▶ Select things from the Picture Bank at the bottom of the page and draw them to finish each mobile.

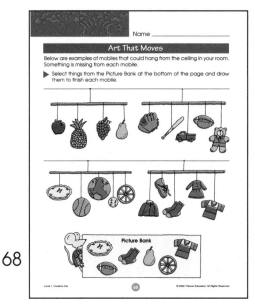

Picture Bank

Level 1, Creative Arts

© 2000 Tribune Education. All Rights Reserved.

68

Page 69 — A Funny Message

Name _____

A Funny Message

A cartoon is a drawing whose purpose is to make you laugh. This cartoon also has a message. There is a hidden letter in each picture below. Find each letter and write it on the line under the picture.

▶ When you have all the letters in place, you will know what the artist is trying to say.

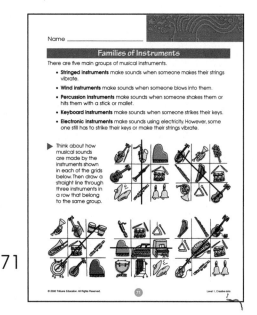

T U R N
O N T H E
R A D I O

© 2000 Tribune Education. All Rights Reserved.

Level 1, Creative Arts

69

Page 70 — A Rainbow of Colors

Name _____

A Rainbow of Colors

The three primary colors are red, yellow and blue. If an artist mixes two of these colors together, the result will be a secondary color.

Examples: Red + Yellow = Orange
Red + Blue = Purple
Blue + Yellow = Green

▶ See how the artist has mixed the paints on the palette pictured below. Label the new secondary colors that have been made. Then, use crayons to show how this happens.

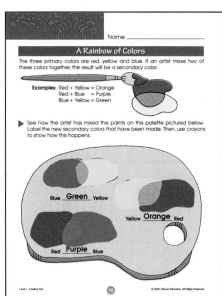

Blue **Green** Yellow
Yellow **Orange** Red
Red **Purple** Blue

Level 1, Creative Arts

© 2000 Tribune Education. All Rights Reserved.

70

Page 71 — Families of Instruments

Name _____

Families of Instruments

There are five main groups of musical instruments.

- **Stringed instruments** make sounds when someone makes their strings vibrate.
- **Wind instruments** make sounds when someone blows into them.
- **Percussion instruments** make sounds when someone shakes them or hits them with a stick or mallet.
- **Keyboard instruments** make sounds when someone strikes their keys.
- **Electronic instruments** make sounds using electricity. However, some one still has to strike their keys or make their strings vibrate.

▶ Think about how musical sounds are made by the instruments shown in each of the grids below. Then draw a straight line through three instruments in a row that belong to the same group.

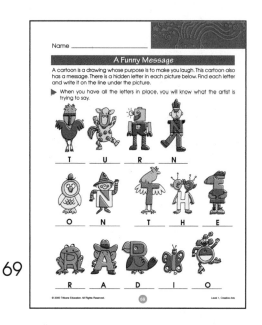

© 2000 Tribune Education. All Rights Reserved.

Level 1, Creative Arts

71

315

Brainteaser Answer Keys

Instrument Chatter

Name _____

▶ Use the Word Bank to help solve each riddle about musical instruments.

1. Grab the sticks
   And take a seat
   Hit my head
   You'll make a beat!

   I am a(n) **drum**

2. In my triangle-shaped body
   Many strings have I.
   The notes I play
   Are from low to high.

   I am a(n) **harp**

3. I'm the biggest horn
   With a deep, deep voice.
   You must be strong
   If I'm your choice.

   I am a(n) **tuba**

4. High sounds you'll hear
   When you play me.
   A long tube with holes
   Is what you'll see.

   I am a(n) **flute**

5. Strum my strings
   And sing in a band.
   I play rock and roll
   In a way so grand!

   I am a(n) **electric guitar**

6. You'll hear a clang
   When you hit my top.
   Once you shake me,
   It's hard to stop.

   I am a(n) **tambourine**

7. Different sizes
   Are my bars of wood.
   From low to high
   My tones sound good.

   I am a(n) **xylophone**

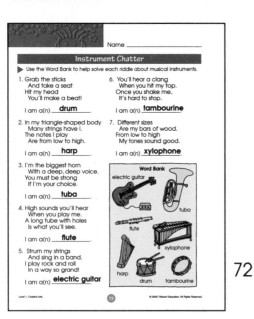

Word Bank: electric guitar, tuba, flute, xylophone, harp, drum, tambourine

72

Keys to Spelling

Name _____

A piano has 88 keys. Fifty-two keys are white, and 36 are black. Each white key has a letter name from A through G. This A–G pattern keeps repeating.

The picture below shows only part of a piano's keyboard. The white C key near the middle is for key number 40.

28	30	32	33	35	37	39	40	42	44	45	47	49	51	52	54	56	57
C	D	E	F	G	A	B	C	D	E	F	G	A	B	C	D	E	F

▶ Number the rest of the keys on the keyboard, but don't forget to count the black keys. Now, use these numbers to spell out some simple words. The last word includes some keys not shown on this part of the keyboard, but you can still find the letters if you use the A–G pattern.

39 49 47 **B A G**

40 37 51 **C A B**

39 49 54 **B A D**

51 44 54 **B E D**

45 49 52 56 **F A C E**

30 44 37 57 **D E A F**

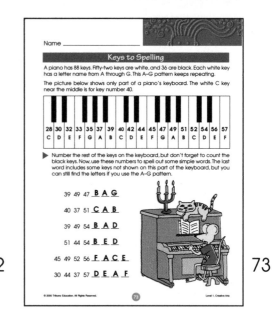

73

Let Us Entertain You!

Name _____

Puppets are dolls. People use strings, wires, rods or their hands to make them move.

▶ Below are five animal hand-puppets. Match each puppet to its job description by writing the puppet's name on the line

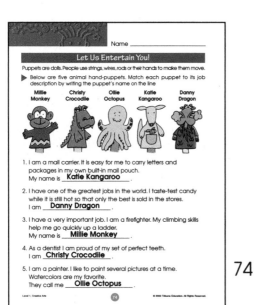

Millie Monkey   Christy Crocodile   Ollie Octopus   Katie Kangaroo   Danny Dragon

1. I am a mail carrier. It is easy for me to carry letters and packages in my own built-in mail pouch.
   My name is **Katie Kangaroo**

2. I have one of the greatest jobs in the world. I taste-test candy while it is still hot so that only the best is sold in the stores.
   I am **Danny Dragon**

3. I have a very important job. I am a firefighter. My climbing skills help me go quickly up a ladder.
   My name is **Millie Monkey**

4. As a dentist I am proud of my set of perfect teeth.
   I am **Christy Crocodile**

5. I am a painter. I like to paint several pictures at a time. Watercolors are my favorite.
   They call me **Ollie Octopus**

74

Playing the Part

Name _____

You are starring in a play about nursery rhymes. The director has given you a list of props, one for each nursery rhyme.

▶ Match each prop to the correct nursery rhyme title by writing its number in the star.

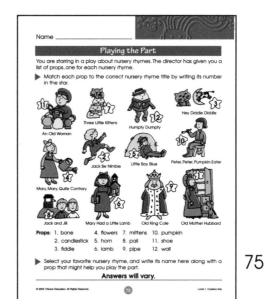

An Old Woman — Three Little Kittens — Humpty Dumpty — Hey Diddle Diddle — Jack Be Nimble — Little Boy Blue — Peter, Peter, Pumpkin-Eater — Mary, Mary, Quite Contrary — Jack and Jill — Mary Had a Little Lamb — Old King Cole — Old Mother Hubbard

Props:
1. bone
2. candlestick
3. fiddle
4. flowers
5. horn
6. lamb
7. mittens
8. pail
9. pipe
10. pumpkin
11. shoe
12. wall

▶ Select your favorite nursery rhyme, and write its name here along with a prop that might help you play the part.
   Answers will vary.

75

Dressing the Part

Name _____

People who act in plays are called actors. For each play, costumes and masks are chosen that make the characters in the story seem more realistic.

Below is the inside of a costume closet.

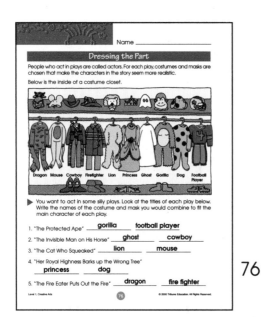

Dragon Mouse Cowboy Firefighter Lion Princess Ghost Gorilla Dog Football Player

▶ You want to act in some silly plays. Look at the titles of each play below. Write the names of the costume and mask you would combine to fit the main character of each play.

1. "The Protected Ape"   **gorilla**   **football player**

2. "The Invisible Man on His Horse"   **ghost**   **cowboy**

3. "The Cat Who Squeaked"   **lion**   **mouse**

4. "Her Royal Highness Barks up the Wrong Tree"
   princess   **dog**

5. "The Fire Eater Puts Out the Fire"   **dragon**   **fire fighter**

76

A Sweet Dream

Name _____

The Nutcracker is a popular ballet. It is the story of a little girl named Clara who is given a wooden nutcracker for Christmas. The nutcracker looks like a soldier. While everyone is sleeping, it comes to life. It takes Clara to many wonderful places. One special place they go is called the "Kingdom of Sweets."

▶ Choose from the Word Bank names of treats that Clara might enjoy in the "Kingdom of Sweets," and write them on the sign in front of the kingdom. Cross out the six foods listed in the Word Bank that she probably wouldn't find in the kingdom.

Kingdom of Sweets	
pie	candy canes
sugar cubes	ice cream
cotton candy	chocolates
gum drops	sherbert
cake	licorice
lollipops	cookies

Word Bank
pie
sugar cubes
~~dill pickles~~
cotton candy
~~spinach~~
gum drops
~~chicken soup~~
cake
~~beets~~
lollipops
candy canes
ice cream
~~potatoes~~
chocolates
sherbet
licorice
~~turkey~~
cookies

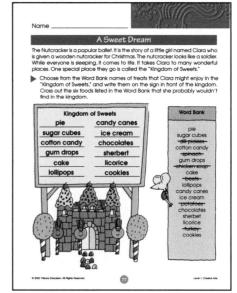

77

Brainteaser Answer Keys

Page 78 — Classy Clay

Name _____

Classy Clay

A potter is an artist who makes plates, vases, jars, bowls and even cooking utensils as works of art.

▶ Carefully examine the pattern blocks on each of these two pieces of pottery. Then, decide which of the blocks continues the pattern. Draw that pattern in the empty box.

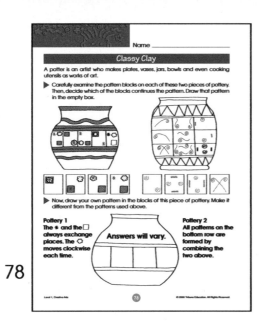

▶ Now, draw your own pattern in the blocks of this piece of pottery. Make it different from the patterns used above.

Answers will vary.

Pottery 1
The ✱ and the ☐ always exchange places. The ◯ moves clockwise each time.

Pottery 2
All patterns on the bottom row are formed by combining the two above.

78

Page 79 — A Rhyme at a Time

Name _____

A Rhyme at a Time

Some poetry rhymes. Each set of two lines ends with words that rhyme.

Example: Goodness, I would like to be
Nobody else, but just me.

▶ Finish each of these short poems by selecting and writing a word from the Word Bank that makes sense and also continues the rhyme.

1. I can't decide what to say,
And yet I talk all the **day** .

2. One, two, three, four,
Please, may I have some **more** ?

3. I can't swim outside in the winter;
I can't go sledding in spring;
But when autumn comes in September,
I can hear the school bells **ring** .

4. The wind is blowing through the tree,
Waving its branches for all to **see** .
The leaves are dragging one by one
Playing in them in fall can be **fun** .

Word Bank

toe	see
kite	sing
more	day
best	may
tore	ring
nest	we
me	run
son	

▶ Now, try to create your own 2- or 4-line rhyme.

Poems will vary.

79

Page 82 — Presto Chango!

Name _____

Presto Chango!

Marvo the Magician likes to do word tricks. He takes two word cards and drops them into his magic hat. When he pulls the cards out, a letter from one word has traded places with a letter from the other word and two new words appear.

▶ Become as clever as Marvo! Exchange one letter from each pair of words to make two new words. **Example:** lost — pace becomes post — lace.
Hint: the letter will not always be the first letter of each word.

1. hat — point	**hot**	—	**paint**
2. meat — nail	**neat**	—	**mail**
3. brain — get	**grain**	—	**bet**
4. like — bat	**lake**	—	**bit**
5. dear — way	**wear**	—	**day**
6. reach — pail	**peach**	—	**rail**
7. tray — rage	**gray**	—	**rate**
8. brown — cat	**crown**	—	**bat**
9. cake — book	**bake**	—	**cook**
10. robe — dear	**rode**	—	**bear**
11. hide — creep	**ride**	—	**cheep**
12. lamb — cop	**lamp**	—	**cob**
13. fin — master	**fan**	—	**mister**
14. letter — gab	**better**	—	**gal**

82

Page 83 — Fascination with Nations

Name _____

Fascination with Nations

When most people think of "nations," they probably think of countries like Canada, the United States and Mexico. However, on this page you are asked to name another kind of "nation."

▶ Use the clues to help select the correct "nations" from the Word Bank and write them on the lines.

Nation that uses creatively **imagination**	Nation that rids itself of pesky critters **extermination**	Nation that gives reasons **explanation**
Nation that tries very hard **determination**	Nation that's very bright **illumination**	Nation that gives tests **examination**
Nation that pretends to be somebody else **impersonation**	Nation that ends **termination**	Nation that's going places **destination**

Word Bank

destination · explanation · imagination
determination · extermination · impersonation
examination · illumination · termination

▶ **Challenge!** See how many other "nations" you can add to this list.

83

Page 84 — Word Building

Name _____

Word Building

A **compound word** is made up of two or more small words. Together, these small words make a new word with its own meaning.

▶ Some of the words in the figure below can be combined with other words next to them to form compound words. There are 18 possible combinations. Can you find and write them all?

down	hard	sportsman	book	note
stairs	sun	ship	cook	work	foot
up	fish	mate	room	ball

upstairs	**sunup**	**sundown**
downstairs	**sunfish**	**sportsmanship**
hardship	**shipmate**	**workbook**
cookbook	**workroom**	**footnote**
football	**notebook**	**sunroom**
roommate	**ballroom**	**hardball**

▶ Some of the words in each circle below can be combined with those in a circle next to it to form compound words. There are at least 10 possibilities.

bandstand	**manhole**
pinhole	**pinball**
milkshake	**milkman**
handshake	**handball**
handstand	**kickstand**
sundown	**standdown**

84

Page 85 — An Amazon Adventure

Name _____

An Amazon Adventure

▶ Trace a path through this Amazon jungle by stepping from one stone to another so that each two words make a compound word.

Example: base → ball
room → mate

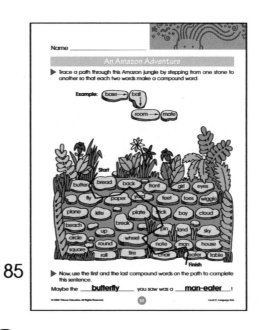

▶ Now, use the first and the last compound words on the path to complete this sentence.

Maybe the **butterfly** you saw was a **man-eater** !

85

317

Brainteaser Answer Keys

Wheel of Nouns

▶ Try your hand at creating "Wheels of Nouns." Here are the rules.

1. Begin with the first word in each circle.
2. Continue clockwise around each circle by adding a word that is spelled like the previous word except for one letter.
3. Make sure that the last word you choose can again turn into the first word with a one-letter change.

The first wheel has picture clues to help you. The other wheels contain no clues. Remember, all the words must be nouns.

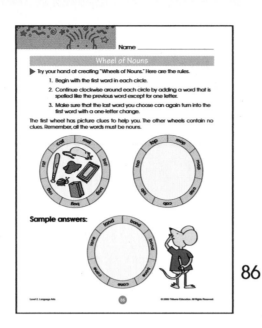

Sample answers:

86

Quick and EZ

I was so tired last night I took some shortcuts with my homework. Today, I have to do it all over again the right way.

▶ Can you help me rewrite each sentence as it should be?

1. The homework assignment was EZ for a Y's person.
   The homework assignment was easy for a wise person.

2. Although KT, LN and LC XL in 10S, they were B10 in the final round.
   Although, Katie, Alan and Elsie excel in tennis, they were beaten in the final round.

3. The BD eyes of the blue J stared at the MT nest.
   The beady eyes of the blue jay stared at the empty nest.

4. The DK in the K9's teeth was XSive.
   The decay in the canine's teeth was excessive.

5. Did NE1 T's the new boy in R classroom?
   Did anyone tease the new boy in our classroom?

6. His XLNC, the king, did not XQ's the conduct of his NME.
   His excellency, the king, did not excuse the conduct of his enemy.

7. 4T pounds of honE had the B's in XTC.
   Forty pounds of honey had the bees in ecstasy.

8. Y do U NV the NRG of an electric EL?
   Why do you envy the energy of an electric eel?

9. The AV8R flew the jet in XS of 4T5 hundred mph.
   The aviator flew the jet in excess of forty-five hundred miles per hour.

10. I threw salt on the IC sidewalk.
    I threw salt on the icy sidewalk.

87

Using a Magnifying Glass

Palindromes are words that are spelled exactly the same, forward and backward, like "mom" and "dad."

▶ Read this story. The clues will suggest palindromes that can be found in the story. Circle each palindrome in the story. Then, write it on the line next to the clue. The first one has been done for you.

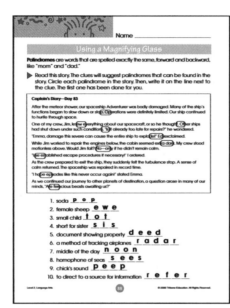

1. soda **p o p**
2. female sheep **e w e**
3. small child **t o t**
4. short for sister **s i s**
5. document showing property **d e e d**
6. a method of tracking airplanes **r a d a r**
7. middle of the day **n o o n**
8. homophone of seas **s e e s**
9. chick's sound **p e e p**
10. to direct to a source for information **r e f e r**

88

Not What It Seems

The most important thing to a person in a desert is water. Travelers tell stories of how they have seen ponds of beautiful clear water only to find, upon getting closer, that what they saw was a mirage. A **mirage** is an optical illusion caused by the bending of the sun's rays as they pass through different temperatures in the air.

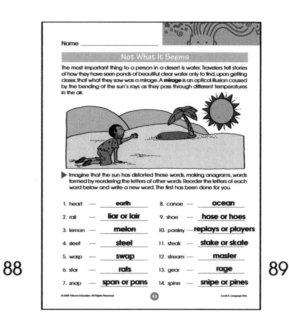

▶ Imagine that the sun has distorted these words, making anagrams, words formed by reordering the letters of other words. Reorder the letters of each word below and write a new word. The first has been done for you.

1. heart — **earth**
2. rail — **liar or lair**
3. lemon — **melon**
4. sleet — **steel**
5. wasp — **swap**
6. star — **rats**
7. snap — **span or pans**
8. canoe — **ocean**
9. shoe — **hose or hoes**
10. parsley — **replays or players**
11. steak — **stake or skate**
12. stream — **master**
13. gear — **rage**
14. spine — **snipe or pines**

89

Making Comparisons

▶ An **analogy** is a sentence in which two sets of things are compared. The relationship of the first thing to the second is the same as the relationship of the third thing to the fourth. To solve an analogy, study how the first two parts are related. Then, write a word for the missing part so that the second set is related in the same way. The first one has been done for you.

1. Any is to anyone as **what** is to whatever.
2. Come is to came as do is to **did**
3. Her is to she as their is to **they**
4. Sang is to sing as got is to **get**
5. T is to then as W is to **when**
6. N is to M as B is to **A**
7. Adult is to coffee as baby is to **milk**
8. Convertible is to car as pickup is to **truck**
9. Bad is to fad as bell is to **fell**
10. In front of is to behind as out of is to **in**
11. Skin is to ski as they is to **the**
12. Stream is to river as pond is to **lake**
13. Drop is to crop as dream is to **cream**
14. In is to if as on is to **of**
15. Scientist is to robot as Dr. Frankenstein is to **monster**
16. Greed is to seed as group is to **soup**

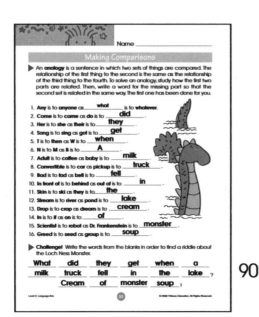

▶ **Challenge!** Write the words from the blanks in order to find a riddle about the Loch Ness Monster.

What did they get when a milk truck fell in the lake ? Cream of monster soup .

90

And the Opposite Is...

▶ **Antonyms** are words that are directly opposite in meaning. Choose from the pot the antonym of each of the words listed below. Then, write it on the line.

false	**true**
joined	**apart**
light	**heavy**
frown	**smile**
fact	**opinion**
give	**take**
weak	**strong**
easy	**difficult**
open	**closed**
empty	**full**
poor	**rich**
cool	**warm**
sorrow	**happiness**
gone	**here**
frequently	**seldom**

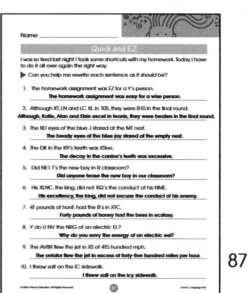

▶ **Challenge!** Think of several more pairs of antonyms that are not listed here and write them below.

Antonyms will vary.

91

Brainteaser Answer Keys

92 — The Case of the Missing Capitals

The Case of the Missing Capitals

Captain Smith got this note in the mail. He noticed that the writer used no capital letters.

▶ Help Captain Smith interpret the letter by circling the words that need to start with a capital letter. Then, write each word correctly on the lines below. Try to find all twenty-six words.

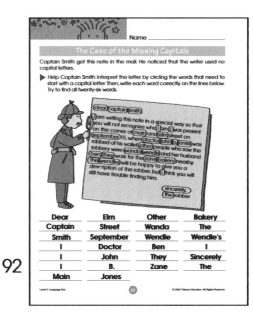

Dear	Elm	Other	Bakery
Captain	Street	Wanda	The
Smith	September	Wendle	Wendle's
I	Doctor	Ben	I
I	John	They	Sincerely
I	B.	Zane	The
Main	Jones		

Level 2, Language Arts — 92 — © 2000 Tribune Education. All Rights Reserved.

---

93 — In Other Words

In Other Words

An **idiom** is a way of expressing an idea with a group of words. Usually the words themselves in an idiom have different meanings, but when they are put together, their meaning becomes something else.

For example, "It's raining cats and dogs!" is an idiom. You know what rain is. You also know what cats and dogs are, but put together in an idiom, the words become a way of saying that it is raining hard. It has nothing to do with actual cats and dogs.

▶ Match the idioms below with their meanings by writing the letter of the meaning next to the idiom.

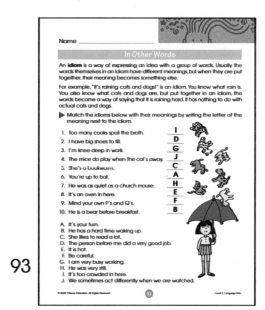

1. Too many cooks spoil the broth. — I
2. I have big shoes to fill. — D
3. I'm knee-deep in work. — G
4. The mice do play when the cat's away. — J
5. She's a bookworm. — C
6. You're up to bat. — A
7. He was as quiet as a church mouse. — H
8. It's an oven in here. — E
9. Mind your own P's and Q's. — F
10. He is a bear before breakfast. — B

A. It's your turn.
B. He has a hard time waking up.
C. She likes to read a lot.
D. The person before me did a very good job.
E. It is hot.
F. Be careful.
G. I am very busy working.
H. He was very still.
I. It's too crowded in here.
J. We sometimes act differently when we are watched.

© 2000 Tribune Education. All Rights Reserved. — 93 — Level 2, Language Arts

---

94 — I Smell an Onion!

I Smell an Onion!

Once there was a king who loved to eat! In fact, he ate anything that was edible-anything, that is, except onions. He absolutely hated onions!

One day, he sat down at his table to eat his lunch-a large red apple, a batch of golden French fries and a burger with the works (except onions, of course). He took a large bite from the apple and then nibbled on a few fries. Finally, he lifted the burger, bit down and screamed, "Who put onions on my burger?"

Immediately he called for the three royal cooks, Silly Nilly, Dipsey Doodle and Noodle Head. The cooks knew that trouble lay ahead. When they entered the royal dining room, each cook had a sign hanging around his neck.

▶ The cooks admitted that two signs were true and one sign was false. They hoped to confuse the king.

Look at the information and decide who put the onions on the king's burger.

The guilty cook was **Noodle Head**

Level 2, Language Arts — 94 — © 2000 Tribune Education. All Rights Reserved.

---

96 — Video Venture

Video Venture

Vincent likes to play games at the Video Adventure Arcade.

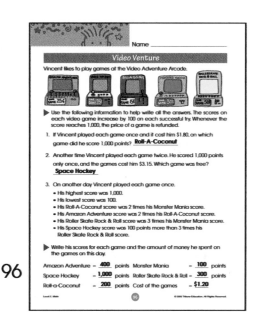

▶ Use the following information to help write all the answers. The scores on each video game increase by 100 on each successful try. Whenever the score reaches 1,000, the price of a game is refunded.

1. If Vincent played each game once and it cost him $1.80, on which game did he score 1,000 points? **Roll-A-Coconut**

2. Another time Vincent played each game twice. He scored 1,000 points only once, and the games cost him $3.15. Which game was free? **Space Hockey**

3. On another day Vincent played each game once.
   - His highest score was 1,000.
   - His lowest score was 100.
   - His Roll-A-Coconut score was 2 times his Monster Mania score.
   - His Amazon Adventure score was 2 times his Roll-A-Coconut score.
   - His Roller Skate Rock & Roll score was 3 times his Monster Mania score.
   - His Space Hockey score was 100 points more than 3 times his Roller Skate Rock & Roll score.

▶ Write his scores for each game and the amount of money he spent on the games on this day.

Amazon Adventure = **400** points   Monster Mania = **100** points

Space Hockey = **1,000** points   Roller Skate Rock & Roll = **300** points

Roll-a-Coconut = **200** points   Cost of the games = **$1.20**

Level 2, Math — 96 — © 2000 Tribune Education. All Rights Reserved.

---

97 — Set Your Watches

Set Your Watches

Dawn and Meagan were at the entrance of the amusement park with their parents. The girls wanted to go on some rides by themselves. Dad said the present time was 11:30 A.M. and they were to meet back at the entrance by 1:00.

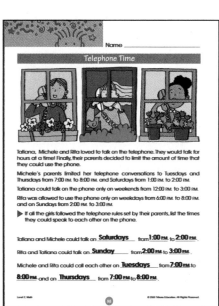

▶ List four different combinations of rides the girls could go on and still be back between 12:45 and 1:00 P.M. Allow a 5-minute walk between each ride and from the entrance to a ride.

The girls could ride on **Sample answers: merry-go-round, roller coaster, train, octopus** and return at **12:55**

The girls could ride on **roller coaster, fun house, spinning top, merry-go-round** and return at **12:45**

The girls could ride on **octopus, spinning top, merry-go-round, race cars** and return at **12:55**

The girls could ride on **merry-go-round, train, roller coaster, fun house** and return at **1:00**

© 2000 Tribune Education. All Rights Reserved. — 97 — Level 2, Math

---

98 — Telephone Time

Telephone Time

Tatiana, Michele and Rita loved to talk on the telephone. They would talk for hours at a time! Finally, their parents decided to limit the amount of time that they could use the phone.

Michele's parents limited her telephone conversations to Tuesdays and Thursdays from 7:00 P.M. to 8:00 P.M. and Saturdays from 1:00 P.M. to 2:00 P.M.

Tatiana could talk on the phone only on weekends from 12:00 P.M. to 3:00 P.M.

Rita was allowed to use the phone only on weekdays from 6:00 P.M. to 8:00 P.M. and on Sundays from 2:00 P.M. to 3:00 P.M.

▶ If all the girls followed the telephone rules set by their parents, list the times they could speak to each other on the phone.

Tatiana and Michele could talk on **Saturdays** from **1:00** P.M. to **2:00** P.M.

Rita and Tatiana could talk on **Sunday** from **2:00** P.M. to **3:00** P.M.

Michele and Rita could call each other on **Tuesdays** from **7:00** P.M. to **8:00** P.M. and on **Thursdays** from **7:00** P.M. to **8:00** P.M.

Level 2, Math — 98 — © 2000 Tribune Education. All Rights Reserved.

Brainteaser Answer Keys

Hard Work Pays Off

The little ant wanted to help the other ants make tunnels in the sand. A big ant came by and laughed, "You're too little to dig a tunnel!" The little ant did not listen. She started digging, lifting out one grain of sand each minute.

The big ant was strong, but lazy. He could lift two grains of sand at the same time, but he took 5 minutes to do this.

▶ Determine how many grains of sand each ant had removed after one hour. Finish drawing each ant hill below with the correct number of grains of sand, and complete the sentences below.

Little Ant's Hill   **Big Ant's Hill**

The __Little Ant__ made the larger hill. It contained __36__ more grains of sand than the smaller hill.

99

Age-Old Questions

The Taylor family went to a carnival. A man in a straw hat yelled out, "I bet I can tell you the correct ages of all five of your children!"

Mr. Taylor thought for a moment and decided to accept the man's challenge. He knew that the children's sizes were deceiving and felt this would help stump the challenger.

The man's five guesses were all incorrect. "What are their actual ages?" he inquired.

"If you can solve this puzzle, you will know their ages," Mr. Taylor answered.

1. Each was born one year apart. One is 6 years old. The product of their ages is 6,720. The ages are __4__ __5__ __6__ __7__ and __8__.

2. Match each child with his/her correct age by closely examining each name and using these clues:
   - Every letter in their names represents a different number from 0 to 9.
   - Find the value of each letter by using the following information.

$a = 3$	$t - o = a$	$v + r = 9$
$a + e = a$	$m + h = a$	$r > v$
$a + a = o$	$m < h$	$s = $ odd number

a = __3__   h = __2__   m = __1__   r = __5__   t = __9__
e = __0__   i = __8__   o = __6__   s = __7__   v = __4__

   - Now, exchange the letters in each child's name for numbers. Add the numbers. Write the sums before the names. The largest sum is the oldest child, the second largest sum is the second oldest child, and so on. Combine this knowledge with the ages you found above. Now, you know each child's age and name!

Sum: 28 Thomas is __6__ years old. **29** Trevor is __7__ years old.
36 Travis is __8__ years old. **26** Theresa is __5__ years old.
24 Tamara is __4__ years old.

100

Spinning a Web

▶ The spider has woven its web according to number patterns. Can you discover them? Fill in the missing numbers. Then, explain the pattern on the lines below.

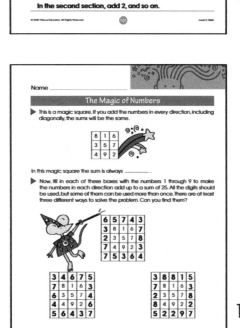

The inner circle contains the odd numbers from 1 to 15.

In the first section, add 1 to each number to get the next.

In the second section, add 2, and so on.

101

It All Adds Up

Think carefully before you answer Mrs. Integer's question about these stacks of cubes. Remember that the sum of opposite sides of any cube always equals 7.

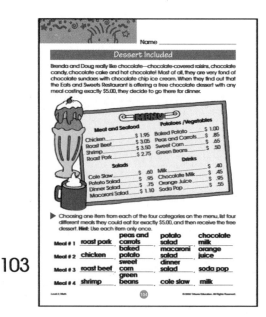

"What is the sum of all the sides you CAN'T see?"

The total number of dots that you cannot see is __181__

102

The Magic of Numbers

▶ This is a magic square. If you add the numbers in every direction, including diagonally, the sums will be the same.

8	1	6
3	5	7
4	9	2

In this magic square the sum is always _____.

▶ Now, fill in each of these boxes with the numbers 1 through 9 to make the numbers in each direction add up to a sum of 25. All the digits should be used, but some of them can be used more than once. There are at least three different ways to solve the problem. Can you find them?

6	5	7	4	3
3	8	1	6	7
2	3	5	7	8
7	4	9	2	3
7	5	3	6	4

3	4	6	7	5
7	8	1	6	3
6	3	5	7	4
4	4	9	2	6
5	6	4	3	7

3	8	8	1	5
7	8	1	6	3
5	3	5	7	5
8	4	9	2	2
5	2	2	9	7

103

Dessert Included

Brenda and Doug really like chocolate—chocolate-covered raisins, chocolate candy, chocolate cake and hot chocolate! Most of all, they are very fond of chocolate sundaes with chocolate chip ice cream. When they find out that the Eats and Sweets Restaurant is offering a free chocolate dessert with any meal costing exactly $5.00, they decide to go there for dinner.

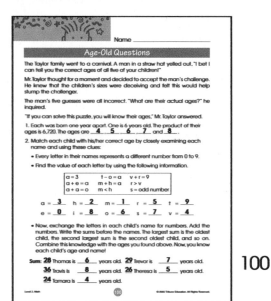

MENU

Meal and Seafood		Potatoes/Vegetables	
Chicken	$1.95	Baked Potato	$1.00
Roast Beef	$3.05	Peas and Carrots	$.85
Shrimp	$3.50	Sweet Corn	$.65
Roast Pork	$2.75	Green Beans	$.50
Salads		**Drinks**	
Cole Slaw	$.60	Milk	$.40
Potato Salad	$.95	Chocolate Milk	$.45
Dinner Salad	$.75	Orange Juice	$.95
Macaroni Salad	$1.10	Soda Pop	$.55

▶ Choosing one item from each of the four categories on the menu, list four different meals they could eat for exactly $5.00, and then receive the free dessert. **Hint:** Use each item only once.

Meal #1	roast pork	peas and carrots	potato salad	chocolate milk
Meal #2	chicken	baked potato	macaroni salad	orange juice
Meal #3	roast beef	sweet corn	dinner salad	soda pop
Meal #4	shrimp	green beans	cole slaw	milk

104

105

Piggy-Bank Countdown

Tomorrow is Mitzi's mom's birthday, so Mitzi empties her piggy bank and finds that she has just enough to buy a special locket that costs $7.43.

She has one 5-dollar bill, one 1-dollar bill and 15 coins. There is at least one quarter, one dime, one nickel and one penny.

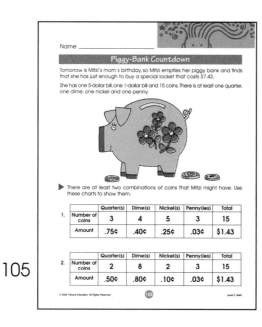

▶ There are at least two combinations of coins that Mitzi might have. Use these charts to show them.

		Quarter(s)	Dime(s)	Nickel(s)	Penny(ies)	Total
1.	Number of coins	3	4	5	3	15
	Amount	.75¢	.40¢	.25¢	.03¢	$1.43

		Quarter(s)	Dime(s)	Nickel(s)	Penny(ies)	Total
2.	Number of coins	2	8	2	3	15
	Amount	.50¢	.80¢	.10¢	.03¢	$1.43

Level 2, Math

106

Big Discount

The Terrific Toy Company is celebrating its 50th anniversary. All of the toys are discounted.

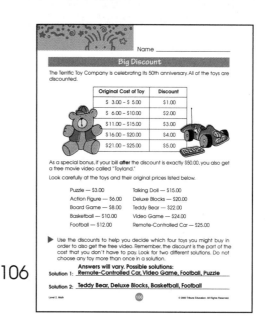

Original Cost of Toy	Discount
$ 3.00 – $ 5.00	$1.00
$ 6.00 – $10.00	$2.00
$11.00 – $15.00	$3.00
$16.00 – $20.00	$4.00
$21.00 – $25.00	$5.00

As a special bonus, if your bill **after** the discount is exactly $50.00, you also get a free movie video called "Toyland."

Look carefully at the toys and their original prices listed below.

Puzzle — $3.00
Action Figure — $6.00
Board Game — $8.00
Basketball — $10.00
Football — $12.00
Talking Doll — $15.00
Deluxe Blocks — $20.00
Teddy Bear — $22.00
Video Game — $24.00
Remote-Controlled Car — $25.00

▶ Use the discounts to help you decide which four toys you might buy in order to also get the free video. Remember, the discount is the part of the cost that you don't have to pay. Look for two different solutions. Do not choose any toy more than once in a solution.

Answers will vary. Possible solutions:

Solution 1: Remote-Controlled Car, Video Game, Football, Puzzle

Solution 2: Teddy Bear, Deluxe Blocks, Basketball, Football

107

"Cow"nting a New Way

Three children were trying to impress one another with their knowledge of numbers.

"I can count to ten," said Megan. "One, two, three . . ."

"That's really good, Megan, but I can count to one hundred," added Tamara, and she proceeded to count to one hundred.

"Big deal," shrugged Matt. "I can 'cow'nt to one hundred by using only 7 of the numbers from 1 to 10."

All of Matt's friends looked puzzled because they didn't understand what he meant.

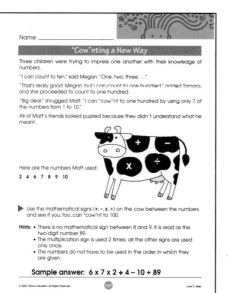

Here are the numbers Matt used:
2 4 6 7 8 9 10

▶ Use the mathematical signs (+, –, x, ÷) on the cow between the numbers and see if you, too, can "cow"nt to 100.

Hints: • There is no mathematical sign between 8 and 9. It is read as the two-digit number 89.
• The multiplication sign is used 2 times; all the other signs are used only once.
• The numbers do not have to be used in the order in which they are given.

Sample answer: 6 x 7 x 2 + 4 – 10 + 89

Level 2, Math

108

Thought Diagrams

▶ It's time to exercise your mental muscles. Each rectangle represents an exercise class. Each circle represents a special part of that class. Notice the way the circles are arranged. Then, decide if the following statements are true or false. Write TRUE or FALSE on each line.

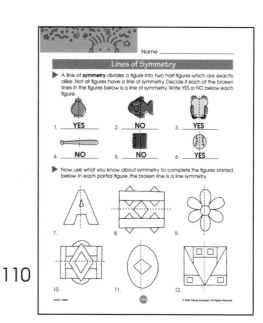

A = All girls in the class
B = All in class who are swimmers

1. All the girls in the class are swimmers. **False**
2. All the swimmers are girls. **False**
3. None of the girls are swimmers. **False**
4. Some of the girls are swimmers. **True**

A = All the boys in the class
B = All the boys in the class who are swimmers
C = All in the class who are runners

5. Some of the boys are runners. **True**
6. None of the boys are swimmers. **False**
7. All of the boys are runners and swimmers. **False**
8. Some of the boys who are swimmers are not runners. **True**
9. Some of the boys are both runners and swimmers. **True**

109

Life Is Full of Patterns

▶ Each of these series of numbers follows a different pattern. Study each one to help you determine what that pattern is. Then, write the next three numbers according to that pattern.

#							
1.	2	4	8	16	32	64	128
2.	6	8	16	18	36	38	76
3.	5	4	10	9	15	14	20
4.	3	7	15	31	63	127	255
5.	4	12	9	27	24	72	69
6.	7	7	8	16	18	54	57
7.	25	24	22	19	15	10	4
8.	3	6	8	16	18	36	38
9.	18	15	30	27	54	51	102
10.	9	7	10	6	11	5	12

Level 2, Math

110

Lines of Symmetry

▶ A line of **symmetry** divides a figure into two half-figures which are exactly alike. Not all figures have a line of symmetry. Decide if each of the broken lines in the figures below is a line of symmetry. Write YES or NO below each figure.

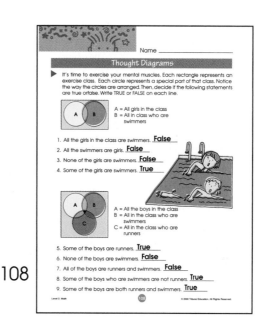

1. YES
2. NO
3. YES
4. NO
5. NO
6. YES

▶ Now, use what you know about symmetry to complete the figures started below. In each partial figure, the broken line is a line of symmetry.

7.
8.
9.
10.
11.
12.

Brainteaser Answer Keys

A Family Tree

The Cruise family visited Ellis Island, an old immigration station located in the New York Harbor. Mom and Dad reminded the children that America is a land of immigrants. Immigrants are individuals and families from other countries who have decided to live in America.

The visit prompted the children to be interested in their own ancestry, so Sally, Lee and Jim Cruise decided to create a family tree. It included their names; the names of their parents, Bob and Anita; both sets of grandparents, Tom and Sally Cruise and Sam and Mary Flyer; their dad's sister, Alice; her husband, John Jones; and their two children, Molly and Mark.

▶ Complete the family tree, starting with the grandparents and writing each person's name on the correct branch. Be sure to label each branch of the family.

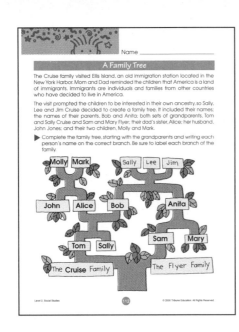

Molly Mark Sally Lee Jim
John Alice Bob Anita
Tom Sally Sam Mary
The **Cruise** Family The **Flyer** Family

112

Salute to Freedom

The Statue of Liberty has stood in New York Harbor since 1886. It was a gift from the French people to celebrate friendship with the people of the United States and the spirit of freedom for all people.

▶ Work with the clues below to discover some interesting facts about the Statue of Liberty.

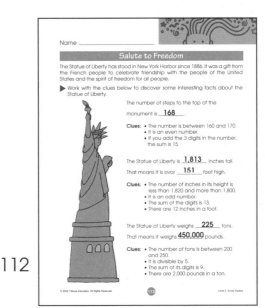

The number of steps to the top of the monument is **168**.

Clues: • The number is between 160 and 170.
• It is an even number.
• If you add the 3 digits in the number, the sum is 15.

The Statue of Liberty is **1,813** inches tall.
That means it is over **151** foot high.

Clues: • The number of inches in its height is less than 1,820 and more than 1,800.
• It is an odd number.
• The sum of the digits is 13.
• There are 12 inches in a foot.

The Statue of Liberty weighs **225** tons.
That means it weighs **450,000** pounds.

Clues: • The number of tons is between 200 and 250.
• It is divisible by 5.
• The sum of its digits is 9.
• There are 2,000 pounds in a ton.

113

The Age of Lincoln

One of the most visited sites in Washington, D.C. is the Lincoln Memorial. It is a monument that celebrates the life and work of Abraham Lincoln, the sixteenth president of the United States, who served in that job from 1861–1865.

▶ Look at the events and their dates listed below. Put a **check** after those you think could be closely related to the life and work of this great president. Write **B** on the answer line if you think an event took place before Lincoln became president and write **A** on the line if you think the event took place after he served.

World War II (1941–1945)	A
The signing of the Declaration of Independence (1776)	B
The Civil War (1861–1865)	✔
World War I (1914–1919)	A
The landing of the Pilgrims (1620)	B
The discovery of America (1492)	B
Freedom granted to slaves (1863)	✔
Man landing on the moon (1969)	A
The American Revolution (1776–1781)	B
The Gettysburg Address (1863)	✔

List any other facts or events that you connect with Abraham Lincoln.

Answers will vary.

114

Totem Poles

Totem poles were created by Native Americans with images of different birds, fish, animals, plants and other natural objects. They carved them into tree trunks.

▶ Shown below are three different totem poles. The objects carved into them follow a pattern. First, discover the pattern. Next, cut out the objects at the bottom of the page. Then, glue them correctly to form Totem Pole 4.

Totem Pole 1 Totem Pole 2 Totem Pole 3 Totem Pole 4

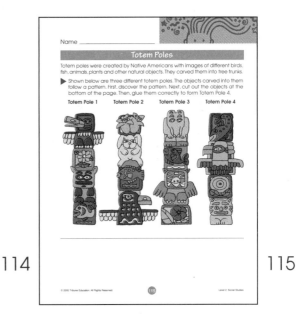

115

Viewed From Afar

Jules Verne wrote a book called *Around the World in Eighty Days*. It is the story of a man who traveled for 80 days all over the world in a hot air balloon. Some of the countries he flew over are listed below, but they are written in rebus.

▶ Match each country from the Word Bank to the correct rebus clues. Write the country on the line.

1. M + 🐝 – T + 🎨 – AT — **Mexico**
2. 🔑 – T + 🌮 – C + 🐐 – G — **Bahamas**
3. 🐝 – NCH + Z + 👁 – L — **Brazil**
4. 🏠 – NEL + 🍨 – MS — **Kenya**
5. 🍳 – G + 🎁 – R — **Egypt**
6. 🥔 – N + 🐭 – I — **Greece**
7. 🎽 – S + AL + 🥧 – B — **Italy**
8. 🌭 – K + S — **France**
9. 🐟 – M + 🍵 – 🥧 — **Japan**
10. ✈ – S + S + 🐛 – MS — **Australia**

Word Bank
Brazil   France
Japan   Mexico
Italy   Egypt
Kenya   Greece
Australia   Bahamas

117

Down Mexico Way

Not far from Mexico City is the famous Pyramid of Quetzalcóatl. It was built over 2,200 years ago and can still be seen today.

▶ Decide if each statement below states a fact or an opinion about this pyramid. Write **F** for fact or **O** for opinion on the line in front of each statement. Then, for the opinion statements, explain why you chose that answer.

F 1. The largest pyramid ever built is the Quetzalcóatl at Cholula de Rivadabia.

F 2. Ancient pyramids and temples attract many visitors to Mexico.

O 3. The pyramids in Mexico are more interesting than those in Egypt.
Some people might find the pyramids of Egypt more interesting.

F 4. The Mexican pyramids are flat on the top.

O 5. Building the pyramids took great skill and knowledge of architecture.
No records have been left behind to show how they were built.

F 6. The base of the largest Mexican pyramid covers an area of nearly 45 acres.

O 7. The people who built the pyramids were happy about their accomplishment. Some of them might not have been happy. They might have been forced to work on the pyramids.

O 8. The artists for the Mexican pyramids and temples painted more attractive murals than the Egyptian artists.
What is attractive to some is not necessarily attractive to others.

118

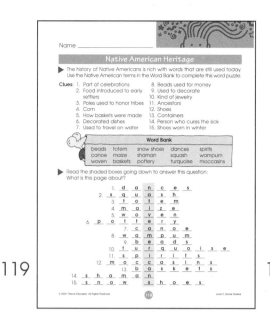
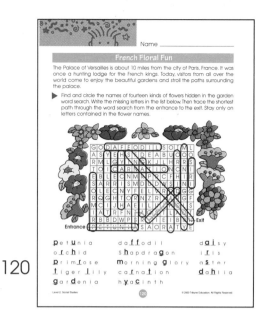

Page 119 — Native American Heritage

Name _____

The history of Native Americans is rich with words that are still used today. Use the Native American terms in the Word Bank to complete this word puzzle.

Clues:
1. Part of celebrations
2. Food introduced to early settlers
3. Poles used to honor tribes
4. Corn
5. How baskets were made
6. Decorated dishes
7. Used to travel on water
8. Beads used for money
9. Used to decorate
10. Kind of jewelry
11. Ancestors
12. Shoes
13. Containers
14. Person who cures the sick
15. Shoes worn in winter

Word Bank

beads	totem	snow shoes	dances	spirits
canoe	maize	shaman	squash	wampum
woven	baskets	pottery	turquoise	moccasins

Read the shaded boxes going down to answer this question: What is this page about?

1. d a n c e s
2. s q u a s h
3. t o t e m
4. m a i z e
5. w o v e n
6. p o t t e r y
7. c a n o e
8. w a m p u m
9. b e a d s
10. t u r q u o i s e
11. s p i r i t s
12. m o c c a s i n s
13. b a s k e t s
14. s h a m a n
15. s n o w s h o e s

Page 120 — French Floral Fun

Name _____

The Palace of Versailles is about 10 miles from the city of Paris, France. It was once a hunting lodge for the French kings. Today, visitors from all over the world come to enjoy the beautiful gardens and stroll the paths surrounding the palace.

Find and circle the names of fourteen kinds of flowers hidden in the garden word search. Write the missing letters in the list below. Then trace the shortest path through the word search from the entrance to the exit. Stay only on letters contained in the flower names.

petunia   daffodil   daisy
orchid   snapdragon   iris
primrose   morning glory   aster
tiger lily   carnation   dahlia
gardenia   hyacinth

Page 121 — Look at the Time

Name _____

The world is divided into 24 time zones. Beginning at the International Date Line, each zone is one hour ahead of the zone to the west. For example, at 12:00 A.M. at the International Date Line, it is 10:00 P.M. in Sydney, Australia because Sidney is two time zones to the west.

Study the time zone map above and decide what time it is in the listed cities when it is 12:00 A.M at the International Date Line. Draw the hands on the clocks for each city to show its time. Then, write the times including A.M. and P.M. below the clock faces.

New York U.S.A. — 7:00 A.M.
Rio de Janeiro Brazil — 9:00 A.M.
Zurich Switzerland — 1:00 P.M.
Bombay India — 5:00 P.M.
London England — 12:00 P.M.

Page 122 — Great Americans

Name _____

The history of America is filled with tales about the accomplishments of its citizens. On this page, read each achievement and then decide which famous American really did it. Fill in the small circle next to that person's name.

1. I helped lead Lewis and Clark to explore the Northwest.
   ○ Pocahontas
   ○ Susan B. Anthony
   ● Sacajawea
   ○ Eleanor Roosevelt

2. I rode to warn the people near Boston that the British were coming.
   ○ Thomas Jefferson
   ○ George Washington
   ○ Sam Adams
   ● Paul Revere

3. In 1984, I was the first woman to run for vice-president of the United States.
   ● Geraldine Ferraro
   ○ Sandra Day O'Connor
   ○ Madeline Albright
   ○ Martha Washington

4. I led a march on Washington to gain equal rights and freedom for all people.
   ○ John F. Kennedy
   ● Martin Luther King, Jr.
   ○ Sam Adams
   ○ Jesse Jackson

5. I was the commander-in-chief of all allied forces for D Day, June 6, 1944.
   ○ John F. Kennedy
   ● Dwight D. Eisenhower
   ○ Richard Nixon
   ○ Robert E. Lee

6. I was the first American to orbit the Earth.
   ● John Glenn
   ○ Paul Revere
   ○ Neil Armstrong
   ○ Sally Ride

7. I invented the phonograph and the first successful electric light bulb.
   ● Thomas Edison
   ○ Alexander Graham Bell
   ○ Wilber Wright
   ○ Albert Einstein

8. I was the first American woman to travel in space.
   ○ Betsy Ross
   ● Sally Ride
   ○ Amelia Earhart
   ○ Clara Bart

Page 123 — Down Under

Name _____

Americans and Australians usually speak the same language—English. However, there are times when it is difficult for Americans to understand Australians because of the different words that they use.

Read the sentences below. Use the Word Bank to find and write the words Americans might use for the Australian expressions in bold.

Word Bank

blanket roll	gasoline	ranches
bucking bronco	herds	elevator
hood	trunk	faucets
interior	wild horses	ranch owners

1. Many **squatters** ranch owners raise mobs herds of sheep on their **stations** ranches in Australia.

2. Others prefer taming **brumbies** wild horses and buckjumpers bucking broncos

3. If a buckjumper has a **matilda** blanket roll on its back, it is tame.

4. The **outback** interior of Australia has a variety of animals.

5. We need to add **petrol** gasoline to the automobile.

6. The attendant checked under the **bonnet** hood as I arranged things in the **boot** trunk of the car.

7. Sidney is located near the mouth of a river to provide water for the **taps** faucets

8. We will ride in the **lift** elevator up the side of one of the skyscrapers to look over the city.

Page 124 — Visitors Welcome

Name _____

The United States has many national parks, monuments and historical sites. The main purpose of these is to protect the sites and the natural beauty so that all Americans can enjoy them for years to come.

Match the national sites listed below with the natural wonders to be found in them or the events that took place in them. Write the number on the correct line in the second column. If you need help, check an encyclopedia or the Internet.

National Parks and Sites		Natural Wonders and Events
1. Mesa Verde	5	Old Faithful and other geysers
2. Grand Canyon	8	Highest waterfall
3. Rocky Mountains	6	Mauna Loa
4. Kitty Hawk, NC	7	Faces of four presidents
5. Yellowstone National Park	2	Colorado River
6. Hawaii Volcanoes	3	The Continental Divide
7. Mount Rushmore	1	Indian cliff dwellings
8. Yosemite	4	Site of the first airplane ride

Write the name of a national park you may want to visit and tell why.

Answers will vary.

Presidential Disguises

The names of ten of America's best-known presidents have been scrambled below. Each name also has a clue to help you identify the president.

▶ Write the name on the line. Try not to use the Word Bank unless you have to.

1. REGGEO GSWOAHNITN __George Washington__
   The father of our country
2. HOJN SMAAD __John Adams__
   The first president to live in the White House
3. SAMHOT FESNOJFRE __Thomas Jefferson__
   Sent Lewis and Clark to explore the West
4. WARDEN ACJONSK __Andrew Jackson__
   The first Westerner to be president
5. MABRAAH CNILLON __Abraham Lincoln__
   Freed the slaves
6. EDRETOHO VOTESOERL __Theodore Roosevelt__
   Called a "Rough Rider"
7. KNIRFALN SERVOTLOE __Franklin Roosevelt__
   Served four times as president
8. YRARH MNRATU __Harry Truman__
   Ordered the White House to be completely rebuilt
9. NJOH YDENNKE __John Kennedy__
   Assassinated after 1000 days in office
10. LANROD GRANEA __Ronald Reagan__
    Had been a movie star

Word Bank

Harry Truman	Thomas Jefferson	Abraham Lincoln
Andrew Jackson	John Adams	Franklin Roosevelt
Ronald Reagan	John Kennedy	Theodore Roosevelt
	George Washington	

125

Everything Has Its Place

A time line is a way to show the order of events as they happened. It also helps you to see the relative space of time between events. On the time lines below, beginning and ending dates are given. Your job is to make a mark on the correct line about where you think each event happened and write its name. When you are finished, all the events should be in their places and in order as they happened.

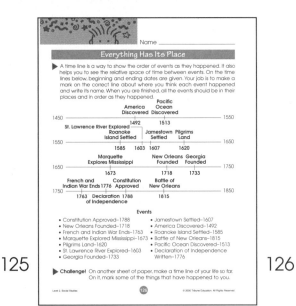

Events

- Constitution Approved—1788
- New Orleans Founded—1718
- French and Indian War Ends—1763
- Marquette Explored Mississippi—1673
- Pilgrims Land—1620
- St. Lawrence River Explored—1603
- Georgia Founded—1733
- Jamestown Settled—1607
- America Discovered—1492
- Roanoke Island Settled—1585
- Battle of New Orleans—1815
- Pacific Ocean Discovered—1513
- Declaration of Independence Written—1776

▶ **Challenge!** On another sheet of paper, make a time line of your life so far. On it, mark some of the things that have happened to you.

126

A Sampling of Snakes

The Snake House is a very popular place to visit at the zoo. There are many different types and sizes of snakes. Some snakes are poisonous while others are not. Some snakes are harmless to most creatures, and some are very dangerous.

The five snakes described here are usually held in the cages below.

▶ Decide which snake belongs in each cage by using the descriptions and clues. Then, write each snake name below the correct cage.

The King Cobra is the longest poisonous snake in the world. One of these snakes measured almost 19 feet long. It is found in southeast Asia and the Philippines.

The Gaboon Viper, a very poisonous snake, has the longest fangs of all snakes (nearly 2 inches). It is found in tropical Africa.

The Reticulated Python is the longest snake of all. One specimen measured over 32 feet in length. It is found in southeast Asia, Indonesia and the Philippines.

The Black Mamba, the fastest-moving land snake, can move at speeds of 10 to 12 miles per hour. It lives in the eastern part of tropical Africa.

The Anaconda is almost twice as heavy as a reticulated python of the same length. One anaconda that was almost 28 feet long weighed nearly 500 pounds.

Clues:
- The snake in cage 5 moves the fastest on land.
- The longest snake of all is between the snake that comes from tropical Africa and the longest poisonous snake.
- The very heavy snake is to the left of the longest poisonous snake.

1	2	3	4	5
Anaconda	King Cobra	Reticulated Python	Gaboon Viper	Black Mamba

128

Sun Power

Scientists are attempting to efficiently harness the energy produced by the sun. This energy is called solar energy. Every 40 minutes the sun sends enough energy to the earth's surface to equal what the people of the world ordinarily use in one year. We have so far only harnessed a fraction of this solar energy. Scientists are continually trying to discover new means of capturing it and putting it to use.

Listed below are some examples of how scientists so far have used solar energy.

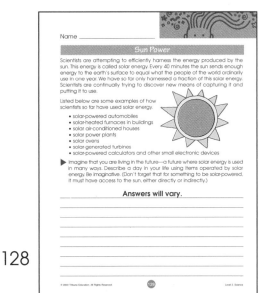

- solar-powered automobiles
- solar-heated furnaces in buildings
- solar air-conditioned houses
- solar power plants
- solar ovens
- solar-generated turbines
- solar-powered calculators and other small electronic devices

▶ Imagine that you are living in the future—a future where solar energy is used in many ways. Describe a day in your life using items operated by solar energy. Be imaginative. (Don't forget that for something to be solar-powered, it must have access to the sun, either directly or indirectly.)

Answers will vary.

129

Fabulous Feathered Friends

Most animals do not talk—at least not in a way that humans can understand. However, some birds can talk quite well. In England, there once was an African gray parrot that won a talking contest twelve years in a row. It knew almost 800 words!

▶ Imagine you are teaching your parrot to talk. Each month your parrot learns a certain number of words. The number of words listed is the total number of words known at that time. Follow the pattern to determine how many months it would take for your parrot to learn as many words as the African gray parrot mentioned above.

First Month — 50 words
Second Month — 75 words
Third Month — 125 words
Fourth Month — 150 words
Fifth Month — 200 words

It would take __21__ months to match the African gray parrot.

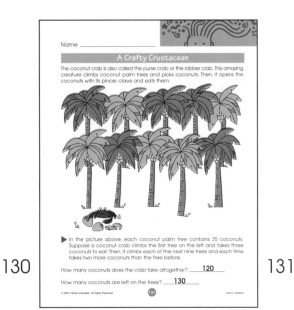

▶ Suppose you are teaching words to a very young parrot. This parrot learns slowly. It masters words according to the schedule below. The numbers refer to the total words known at any given time.

First Week — 4 words
Second Week — 5 words
Third Week — 8 words
Fourth Week — 9 words
Fifth Week — 12 words

How many weeks will it take for the parrot to learn the following? "Polly doesn't want a cracker. That's for the birds. Give me fruit, nuts and seeds." __7 weeks__

130

A Crafty Crustacean

The coconut crab is also called the purse crab or the robber crab. This amazing creature climbs coconut palm trees and picks coconuts. Then, it opens the coconuts with its pincer claws and eats them.

▶ In the picture above, each coconut palm tree contains 25 coconuts. Suppose a coconut crab climbs the first tree on the left and takes three coconuts to eat. Then, it climbs each of the next nine trees and each time takes two more coconuts than the tree before.

How many coconuts does the crab take altogether? __120__

How many coconuts are left on the trees? __130__

131

132

Name

Dino Data

Do you like to read about dinosaurs? Some people devour every dinosaur book, movie and article they can find. However, everything they read is not fact. Some things that people write about dinosaurs are opinions.

Read each statement below and write **F** for fact or **O** for opinion on the line.

F	1. The first dinosaur fossils were discovered in 1822.
F	2. A paleontologist is a scientist who studies animals and plants from the past.
F	3. Different sizes and shapes of uncovered dinosaur skeletons show that dinosaurs were not all the same.
O	4. A paleontologist knows more about dinosaurs than anyone else.
O	5. The Brachiosaurus was the most interesting dinosaur of all.
F	6. Dinosaur fossils are often found in solid rock.
O	7. The Hypsilophodon was the weirdest-looking dinosaur.
F	8. Scientists learn a lot about dinosaurs by studying their bones.
O	9. Being a paleontologist is one of the most difficult jobs in science.
F	10. Scientists can make copies of dinosaur skeletons using fiberglass so that museums may display and study them.
O	11. Everyone in the fourth grade should study dinosaur fossils.
O	12. It is more interesting to study about dinosaurs than studying about any other subject.

133

Name

Picturing Sound

Can you recognize the sounds of a flute? How about the sounds of a violin? Different instruments make different sounds. The sound wave from each instrument makes certain pressure changes in the air. The pressure changes can be illustrated with jagged and curved lines called waveforms.

For example, here's a jagged waveform that shows the sound made by a violin.

Here's a curved waveform that illustrates the smooth sound made by a flute.

Look at the waveforms below. Each contains a pattern that makes it special. Continue drawing each pattern at least once.

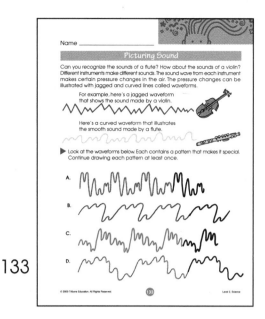

A.
B.
C.
D.

134

Name

Earth-Shaking News

One morning, Sy Z. Mograff was awakened by pictures falling off the walls. The floor shook as he stood to get out of bed. Later, Sy saw this diagram in the newspaper. It showed what had happened.

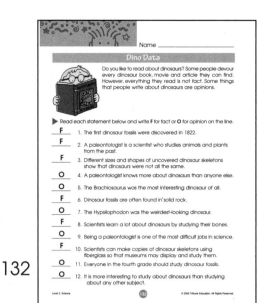

Follow the directions below to see what question Sy wanted answered.

Directions: 1. Cross out all words in the picture containing 3 or more vowels.
2. Cross out all words beginning with st, br, pl, fr or cr.
3. Cross out all remaining two-syllable words.
4. Write the remaining words on the lines to find out what Mr. Sy Z. Mograff asked.

Mr. Sy Z. Mograff asked, " **Whose** **fault** **is** **it** **anyway** ?"

To answer Sy's question, solve this riddle: "I am your parent, but not your father. Treat me with respect. Look carefully and you'll find me in your heart."

Mother Earth caused the earthquake.

135

Name

Beginnings

Gestation is the time during which a mother animal carries a baby within her body before giving birth. The length of animal gestation periods varies greatly from species to species.

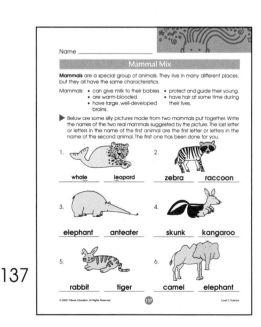

Use the clues below to determine the approximate gestation period for each animal. Write the answers on the correct lines.

Clues: • A giraffe's gestation period = 2 x a deer's gestation period.
• 3 x a deer's gestation period + 2 months = an elephant's gestation period.
• A whale's gestation period = 5 x a beaver's gestation period, or 3 x a sheep's gestation period.
• An elephant's gestation period > a whale's gestation period.
• A whale's gestation period > a giraffe's gestation period.

Possible Answers		
3 months	7 months	15 months
5 months	14 months	23 months

Animal Gestation Periods

deer	= **7** months		giraffe	= **14** months
beaver	= **3** months		sheep	= **5** months
elephant	= **23** months		whale	= **15** months

136

Name

A Balanced Meal

The foods you eat help you grow and stay healthy. All foods are divided into four main groups: dairy, meat/fish, bread/cereal and vegetables/fruit.

Let's discover the contents of the sandwiches below. Use the Word Bank to write the name of a food that completes each riddle. Not all words will be used. **Hint:** All four food groups will be represented in each sandwich.

Word Bank
bacon butter
pickle hot dog
roll peanut
bun tomatoes
milk orange
bread cheese

Sandwich 1
• A baker uses **bread** sticks to play the drums.
• The mouse said, " **cheese** ," to everyone—not just the photographer.
• A funny **pickle** could be called a "silly dilly."
• When the cow ate peanuts he made **peanut** butter.

Sandwich 2
• The pig said he was so hot he was " **bacon** ."
• The rabbit said to his sweet girl friend, "You're my honey **bun** ."
• The unusual farmer planted toes. He harvested **tomatoes** .
• One goat bragged to another goat, "I'm a better **butter** than you!"

137

Name

Mammal Mix

Mammals are a special group of animals. They live in many different places, but they all have the same characteristics.

Mammals: • can give milk to their babies. • protect and guide their young.
• are warm-blooded. • have hair at some time during
• have large, well-developed their lives.
brains.

Below are some silly pictures made from two mammals put together. Write the names of the two real mammals suggested by the picture. The last letter or letters in the name of the first animal are the first letter or letters in the name of the second animal. The first one has been done for you.

1. **whale** **leopard**
2. **zebra** **raccoon**
3. **elephant** **anteater**
4. **skunk** **kangaroo**
5. **rabbit** **tiger**
6. **camel** **elephant**

Brainteaser Answer Keys

Animal Analogies

Animals have distinguishing features and inherited characteristics. These traits can be discovered in quite interesting and unusual ways.

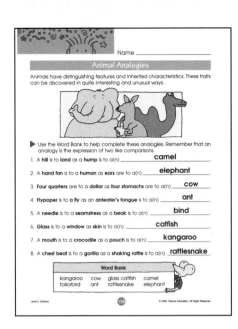

▶ Use the Word Bank to help complete these analogies. Remember that an analogy is the expression of two like comparisons.

1. A **hill** is to **land** as a **hump** is to a(n) **camel**.
2. A **hand fan** is to **a human** as **ears** are to a(n) **elephant**.
3. **Four quarters** are to **a dollar** as **four stomachs** are to a(n) **cow**.
4. **Flypaper** is to **a fly** as an **anteater's tongue** is to a(n) **ant**.
5. A **needle** is to **a seamstress** as a **beak** is to a(n) **bird**.
6. **Glass** is to **a window** as **skin** is to a(n) **catfish**.
7. A **mouth** is to **a crocodile** as a **pouch** is to a(n) **kangaroo**.
8. A **chest beat** is to **a gorilla** as a **shaking rattle** is to a(n) **rattlesnake**.

Word Bank

kangaroo	cow	glass catfish	camel
tailorbird	ant	rattlesnake	elephant

138

From Egg to Tadpole to Frog

▶ The poem below tells about the changes that occur in frogs during their life cycles. In every line, there is one word that doesn't make sense. Cross it out. Find the correct word in the Word Bank and write it in the puzzle.
Hint: The correct word rhymes with the one you cross out.

The Life Cycle of a Frog

There is jelly on the ~~logs~~ (13 across)
To protect the entire ~~match~~ (11 across)
It takes ~~tile~~ to twenty-five days (7 down)
Until they're ready to ~~catch~~ (5 down)

Out comes a ~~pollyfrog~~ (18 across)
When the time is just ~~bright~~ (8 across)
It breathes using ~~fills~~ (14 down)
And its size is very ~~tight~~ (14 across)

It loses its long ~~sail~~ (9 down)
After ~~pegs~~ begin to grow. (1 down)
Digestion and breathing ~~strange~~ (12 down)
In a process fast, yet ~~glow~~. (2 down)

What helps a frog to see ~~life~~ (3 down)
Is this thin and moist ~~skit~~ (6 down)
It also uses ~~rungs~~ (15 down)
To let the ~~hair~~ in. (10 across)

Some frogs can swim like a duck. (6 across)
And some can ~~romp~~ like a rabbit. (16 down)
Others climb ~~bees~~ like a squirrel (7 across)
Which may seem a ~~bunny~~ habit. (17 across)

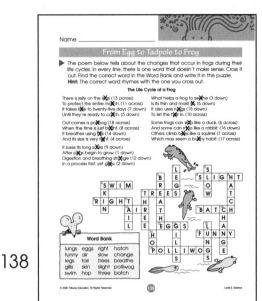

Puzzle answers include: SWIM, RIGHT, TREES, SLIGHT, SLOW, HATCH, BATCH, EGGS, FUNNY, POLLIWOGS

Word Bank

lungs	eggs	right	hatch
funny	air	slow	change
legs	tail	trees	breathe
gills	skin	slight	polliwog
swim	hop	three	batch

139

Weather Watching

Weather describes the condition of the air for a period of time. Weather maps contain symbols that describe the weather.

▶ Below is a calendar for one month. Beside it is a key for some weather symbols. Read carefully each of the clues listed below the calendar. Then, in the correct boxes, draw the symbols that tell what weather was experienced.

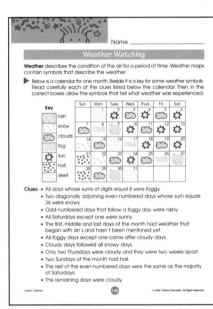

Key: rain, snow, clouds, fog, sun, hail, sleet

Clues:
- All days whose sums of digits equal 8 were foggy.
- Two diagonally adjoining even-numbered days whose sum equals 36 were snowy.
- Odd-numbered days that follow a foggy day were rainy.
- All Saturdays except one were sunny.
- The first, middle and last days of the month had weather that began with an s and hasn't been mentioned yet.
- All foggy days except one came after cloudy days.
- Cloudy days followed all snowy days.
- Only two Thursdays were cloudy, and they were two weeks apart.
- Two Sundays of the month had hail.
- The rest of the even-numbered days were the same as the majority of Saturdays.
- The remaining days were cloudy.

140

Feeling Buggy

▶ One the largest of the animal kingdoms is commonly called insects. See how many insect names you can find in the word search. List their names on the lines below.

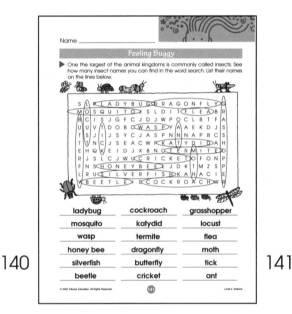

ladybug	**cockroach**	**grasshopper**
mosquito	**katydid**	**locust**
wasp	**termite**	**flea**
honey bee	**dragonfly**	**moth**
silverfish	**butterfly**	**tick**
beetle	**cricket**	**ant**

141

Fishy Cartoons

Fish live almost anywhere there is water. Although fish come in many different shapes, colors and sizes, they are alike in many ways.

- All fish have backbones.
- Fish breathe with gills.
- Most fish are cold-blooded.
- Most fish have fins.
- Many fish have scales and fairly tough skin.

▶ Some fish have names that remind us of other animals. Use the clues to unscramble these fish names. Write each name correctly on the line. Then, use your imagination to draw each fish in a cartoon.

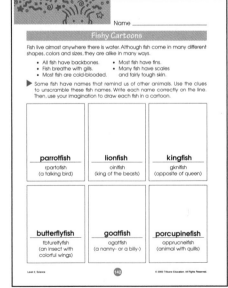

parrotfish
rpartotfish
(a talking bird)

lionfish
oinlfish
(king of the beasts)

kingfish
gknifish
(opposite of queen)

butterflyfish
tbturelyfish
(an insect with colorful wings)

goatfish
ogatfish
(a nanny- or a billy-)

porcupinefish
opprucneifish
(animal with quills)

142

Name That Key

A piano has 88 keys—52 white keys and 36 black keys. The keys are arranged according to a pattern. After every 7th white key, the pattern is repeated. Each white key is given a letter name from A to G. When you start counting all the keys from the left side of the piano, the 40th key is called "Middle C." Middle C is used as a starting point when positioning your hands on a piano.

The picture below shows part of a piano's keyboard with Middle C labeled.

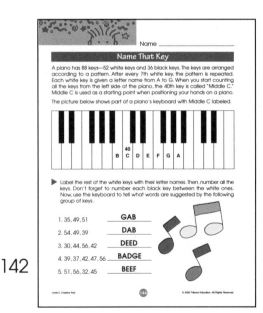

B C D E F G A
     40

▶ Label the rest of the white keys with their letter names. Then, number all the keys. Don't forget to number each black key between the white ones. Now, use the keyboard to tell what words are suggested by the following group of keys.

1. 35, 49, 51 — **GAB**
2. 54, 49, 39 — **DAB**
3. 30, 44, 56, 42 — **DEED**
4. 39, 37, 42, 47, 56 — **BADGE**
5. 51, 56, 32, 45 — **BEEF**

144

145

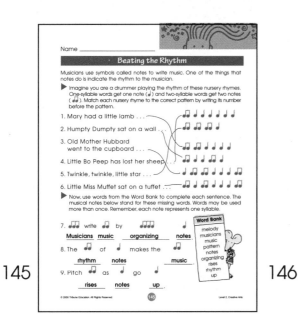

Name _____

Beating the Rhythm

Musicians use symbols called notes to write music. One of the things that notes do is indicate the rhythm to the musician.

▶ Imagine you are a drummer playing the rhythm of these nursery rhymes. One-syllable words get one note (♩) and two-syllable words get two notes (♫). Match each nursery rhyme to the correct pattern by writing its number before the pattern.

1. Mary had a little lamb . . .
2. Humpty Dumpty sat on a wall . . .
3. Old Mother Hubbard went to the cupboard . . .
4. Little Bo Peep has lost her sheep . . .
5. Twinkle, twinkle, little star . . .
6. Little Miss Muffet sat on a tuffet . . .

▶ Now, use words from the Word Bank to complete each sentence. The musical notes below stand for these missing words. Words may be used more than once. Remember, each note represents one syllable.

7. **Musicians** write **music** by **organizing** **notes**

8. The **rhythm** of **notes** makes the **music**

9. Pitch **rises** as **notes** go **up**

Word Bank
melody
musicians
music
pattern
notes
organizing
rises
rhythm
up

146

Name _____

Take a Seat!

To achieve a perfect blend of sounds for a symphony orchestra, the conductor decides the seating arrangement for each section of instruments.

- **stringed section** (violin, viola, cello, harp, bass, piano)
- **woodwind section** (flute, oboe, clarinet, bassoon)
- **brass section** (trumpet, French horn, trombone, tuba)
- **percussion section** (kettle drum, bells and cymbals, bass drum, gong, snare drum, triangle, xylophone)

▶ The conductor has the unfinished seating arrangement below. Use the clues to write in the names of the missing sections.

Clues: • The **percussion** section is directly in front of the **conductor** but as far back as possible.
- The **French horns** are directly in front of the **trombones** and behind the **oboes**.
- The remaining **woodwinds** are between the **oboes** and the **violas** with the **flutes** closest to the conductor.
- The **violins** occupy the largest section in the orchestra.
- The largest **stringed instruments** are in a back corner.
- The remaining **brass instruments** occupy the last section.

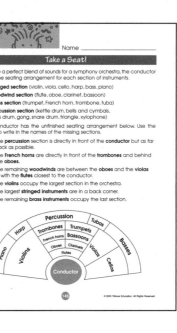

147

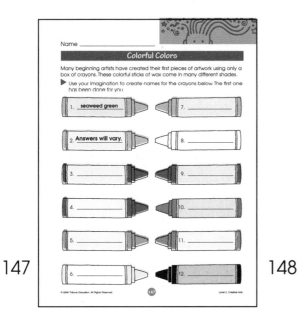

Name _____

Colorful Colors

Many beginning artists have created their first pieces of artwork using only a box of crayons. These colorful sticks of wax come in many different shades.

▶ Use your imagination to create names for the crayons below. The first one has been done for you.

1. seaweed green
2. Answers will vary.
3.
4.
5.
6.
7.
8.
9.
10.
11.
12.

148

Name _____

Who or What Am I?

A creative person is not afraid to try things that are new, original and different.

▶ Read each riddle below. Use the Word Bank to identify each creative person or product. Write the answer on the line. Each word is used only once.

1. My lips may move,
But no sound comes out.
My whole body tells the story.
It's my movements that shout!
I am a/a(n) **mime**

2. I see the world
Containing colors so vast.
With a stroke I preserve
The future, present and past.
I am a/a(n) **painter**

3. My words have tones
From high to low.
They may be uttered
Fast or slow.
I am a/a(n) **song**

4. I tell a story
From beginning to end.
Actors and actions
Wonderfully blend.
I am a/a(n) **play**

5. The words I use
May last a long time.
Depending on my talents
They may be prose or rhyme.
I am a/a(n) **writer**

6. A tear trickles down
My face, but it's dry.
I have no feelings
Though I appear to cry.
I am a/a(n) **painting**

7. I'm frozen in time,
But I'm not very cold.
I often reflect history
In a pose so bold.
I am a/a(n) **statue**

8. I can read,
But I don't see letters.
Because of me
The world sounds better.
I am a/a(n) **musician**

Word Bank
statue   painter   painting   play
musician   song   mime   writer

149

Name _____

Pottery Styles

Before beginning a project, an artist who makes pottery must think about how the piece will be used, what type of clay to use and what color and patterns to use. Every artist develops a unique style that can be recognized in the products he or she produces.

The first set of pottery pieces below were created by one talented artist and the second set by another. The third set contains two pieces created by artist number 1 and two by artist number 2.

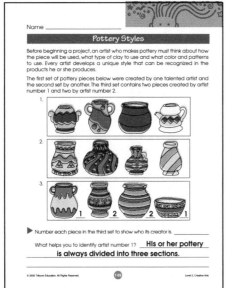

▶ Number each piece in the third set to show who its creator is.

What helps you to identify artist number 1? **His or her pottery is always divided into three sections.**

150

Name _____

Pretty As a Picture

Still life pictures are drawings or paintings of objects. These objects have no movement or life. They are simply arranged and painted.

▶ Below are three sets of still life pictures. Carefully examine each set. Then, use the lines under each set to write what all three still life pictures have in common.

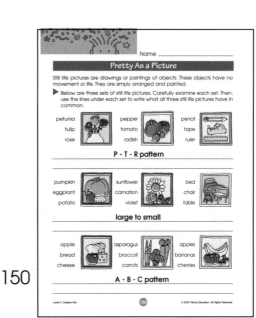

petunia   pepper   pencil
tulip   tomato   tape
rose   radish   ruler

P - T - R pattern

pumpkin   sunflower   bed
eggplant   carnation   chair
potato   violet   table

large to small

apple   asparagus   apples
bread   broccoli   bananas
cheese   carrots   cherries

A - B - C pattern

Cakes for All Occasions

You may be surprised to learn that pastry chefs are creative people, too. One of their jobs is to create decorations on cakes made for special occasions.

▶ Look at these three cakes and decide the occasion for which each was made. Write that event on the line below the cake.

football season   child's birthday   graduation

▶ Now, it's your turn. Decorate each of these cakes to be used for the indicated celebration. Be as creative as you can, but be sure that the connection between the decorations and the celebration is clear.

Decorations will vary.

Thanksgiving   4th of July   Welcome Home

© 2000 Tribune Education. All Rights Reserved.   (151)   Level 2, Creative Arts

151

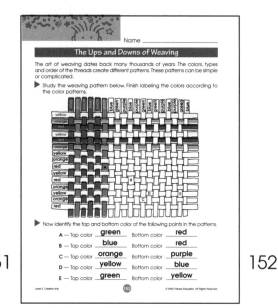

The Ups and Downs of Weaving

The art of weaving dates back many thousands of years. The colors, types and order of the threads create different patterns. These patterns can be simple or complicated.

▶ Study the weaving pattern below. Finish labeling the colors according to the color patterns.

▶ Now identify the top and bottom color of the following points in the patterns.

A — Top color **green**   Bottom color **red**
B — Top color **blue**   Bottom color **red**
C — Top color **orange**   Bottom color **purple**
D — Top color **yellow**   Bottom color **blue**
E — Top color **green**   Bottom color **yellow**

Level 2, Creative Arts   (152)   © 2000 Tribune Education. All Rights Reserved.

152

Positions, Everyone!

A ballet dancer tells a story with his or her body by using music, dance and mime. All ballet movements begin and end with the feet in one of the positions shown here.

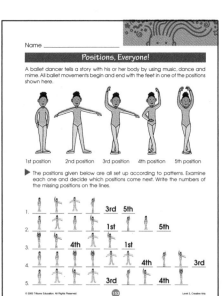

1st position   2nd position   3rd position   4th position   5th position

▶ The positions given below are all set up according to patterns. Examine each one and decide which positions come next. Write the numbers of the missing positions on the lines.

1. **3rd** **5th**
2. **1st** **5th**
3. **4th** **1st**
4. **4th** **3rd**
5. **3rd** **4th**

© 2000 Tribune Education. All Rights Reserved.   (153)   Level 2, Creative Arts

153

Clowning Around

Clowns entertain audiences through their "large" actions, bright make-up and colorful costumes. Some clowns look happy, while others appear sad. Because the costume is so important to the act, the clown must choose it very carefully. Here is a closet containing some costume items a clown might choose.

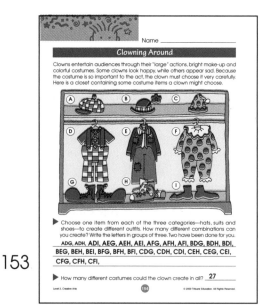

▶ Choose one item from each of the three categories—hats, suits and shoes—to create different outfits. How many different combinations can you create? Write the letters in groups of three. Two have been done for you.

ADG, ADH, ADI, AEG, AEH, AEI, AFG, AFH, AFI, BDG, BDH, BDI, BEG, BEH, BEI, BFG, BFH, BFI, CDG, CDH, CDI, CEG, CEH, CEI, CFG, CFH, CFI,

▶ How many different costumes could the clown create in all? **27**

Level 2, Creative Arts   (154)   © 2000 Tribune Education. All Rights Reserved.

154

Silence Is Golden

The first movies were silent. Dialogue between the actors was not heard until 1927. Before this, actors had to exaggerate their facial expressions and movements so that the audience could understand the plots. To help tell the stories to the audience, captions were used.

▶ The pictures tell a story. Each caption below contains an incorrect word. Underline the incorrect word and unscramble its letters to find the correct word. Write it on the line. Then, match each caption with the correct picture by writing its number in the circle.

And they slimed lovingly as they gazed into each other's eyes!
(6) **smiled**

"You will be safe in my arms forever, volley Nell!"
(4) **lovely**

"You will never least from the poor again. Dishonest John!"
(5) **steal**

"Alas, I am so poor that I even had to sell the family livers!"
(2) **silver**

"I madden your money! Give it to me or you will be very sorry!"
(1) **demand**

"Help me! Help me! The speeding train is caring down the track!"
(3) **racing**

© 2000 Tribune Education. All Rights Reserved.   (155)   Level 2, Creative Arts

155

Top Speller

▶ In each group of words on this page there is one which is not spelled correctly. Cross it out and write the word correctly on the line.

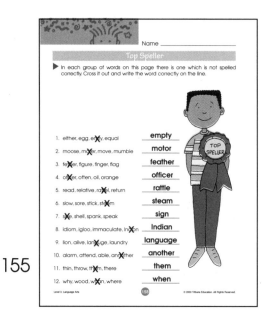

1. either, egg, ~~emty~~, equal — **empty**
2. moose, ~~mtor~~, move, mumble — **motor**
3. ~~fether~~, figure, finger, flag — **feather**
4. ~~ofcer~~, often, oil, orange — **officer**
5. read, relative, ~~ratel~~, return — **rattle**
6. slow, sore, stick, ~~steim~~ — **steam**
7. ~~sien~~, shell, spank, speak — **sign**
8. idiom, igloo, immaculate, ~~Indin~~ — **Indian**
9. lion, alive, ~~languge~~, laundry — **language**
10. alarm, attend, able, ~~anther~~ — **another**
11. thin, throw, ~~thm~~, there — **them**
12. why, wood, ~~wen~~, where — **when**

Level 3, Language Arts   (158)   © 2000 Tribune Education. All Rights Reserved.

158

Brainteaser Answer Keys

328

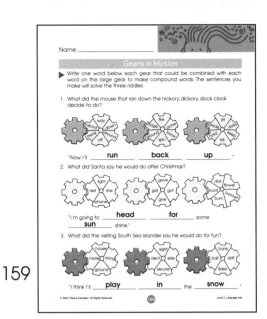

Gears in Motion

Write one word below each gear that could be combined with each word on the large gear to make compound words. The sentences you make will solve the three riddles.

1. What did the mouse that ran down the hickory, dickory, dock clock decide to do?

"Now I'll **run** **back** **up** ."

2. What did Santa say he would do after Christmas?

"I'm going to **head** **for** some **sun** shine."

3. What did the visiting South Sea islander say he would do for fun?

"I think I'll **play** **in** the **snow** ."

159

Level 3, Language Arts

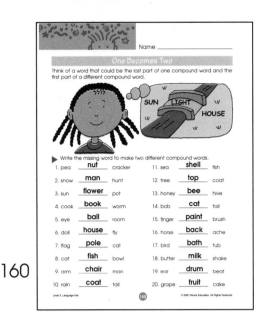

One Becomes Two

Think of a word that could be the last part of one compound word and the first part of a different compound word.

SUN LIGHT HOUSE

Write the missing word to make two different compound words.

1. pea **nut** cracker
2. snow **man** hunt
3. sun **flower** pot
4. cook **book** worm
5. eye **ball** room
6. doll **house** fly
7. flag **pole** cat
8. cat **fish** bowl
9. arm **chair** man
10. rain **coat** tail
11. sea **shell** fish
12. tree **top** coat
13. honey **bee** hive
14. bob **cat** tail
15. finger **paint** brush
16. horse **back** ache
17. bird **bath** tub
18. butter **milk** shake
19. ear **drum** beat
20. grape **fruit** cake

160

Level 3, Language Arts

Unusual Plurals

Most **plurals** are formed by adding "s" or "es" to their singular forms. But some nouns change other letters to make a plural. There are even some nouns that stay the same in both singular and plural forms. Write the plurals for the nouns listed below. You can use a dictionary if necessary.

singular

PLURAL

1. goose — **geese**
2. ox — **oxen**
3. fish — **fish**
4. tooth — **teeth**
5. spy — **spies**
6. quiz — **quizzes**
7. factory — **factories**
8. mouse — **mice**
9. foot — **feet**
10. moose — **moose**
11. deer — **deer**
12. brother-in-law — **brothers-in-law**
13. glass — **glasses**
14. sheep — **sheep**
15. person — **people**

161

Level 3, Language Arts

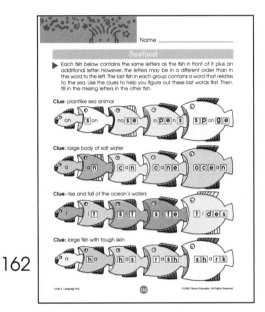

Seafood

Each fish below contains the same letters as the fish in front of it plus an additional letter. However, the letters may be in a different order than in the word to the left. The last fish in each group contains a word that relates to the sea. Use the clues to help you figure out these last words first. Then, fill in the missing letters in the other fish.

Clue: plantlike sea animal

on / son / nose / opens / sponge

Clue: large body of salt water

a / an / can / cane / ocean

Clue: rise and fall of the ocean's waters

i / it / sit / site / tides

Clue: large fish with tough skin

a / ha / has / rash / shark

162

Level 3, Language Arts

Taking a Shortcut

An **abbreviation** is the short form of a word. It is usually formed by:
   a. the first two or three letters of the word followed by a period (Avenue = Ave.).
   b. the first and last letters of the word followed by a period (Mister = Mr.).
   c. the first, middle and last letters of a word followed by a period (Boulevard = Blvd.).

Here is a story about a ghost. It contains imaginary abbreviations. Periods at the end of sentences will look like this: ☐ See if you can figure out what the paragraph says. Rewrite the story without any abbreviations.

Onc. upn. a time there ws. a sml. gst. ☐ He frgt. to lok. whr. he ws. ging., and he gt. lst. ☐ He thot. he knw. whr. he ws., so he trd. to take a shrtct. home ☐ He said. ovr. the tres. and undr. a brdge. ☐ Wen. he cam. to his nbrhd.. he thot. he wd. qlkly. fl. thrgh. ech. hse. ☐ At the first hse.. he brezd. pst. a napng. dg. who opned. hs. eys. and bgn. brkng. ☐ At the nxt. hse.. the gst. pausd. to wtch. sml. chldrn. plang. a game ☐ Wen. he entrd. the third hse.. the gst. lkd. arnd. and sw. brkn. wndws.. a crakd. strcase. and mny. cbwbs. ☐ Thn. he hrd. a gstly. voice sy.. "Yr. lat. !" ☐ The sml. gst. rcognzd. hs. mthr. ☐ "Thr's. no pl. like. hom.," he thght. ☐

Once upon a time there was a small ghost. He forgot to look where he was going, and he got lost. He thought he knew where he was, so he tried to take a shortcut home. He sailed over the trees and under a bridge. When he came to his neighborhood, he thought he would quickly fly through each house. At the first house, he breezed past a napping dog that opened his eyes and began barking. At the next house, the ghost paused to watch small children playing a game. When he entered the third house, the ghost looked around and saw broken windows, a crooked staircase and many cobwebs. Then he heard a ghostly voice say, "You're late!" The small ghost recognized his mother. "There's no place like home," he thought.

163

Level 3, Language Arts

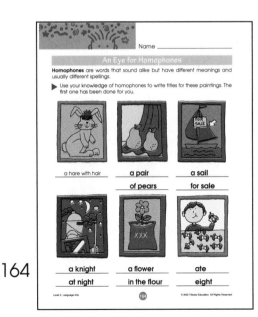

An Eye for Homophones

Homophones are words that sound alike but have different meanings and usually different spellings.

Use your knowledge of homophones to write titles for these paintings. The first one has been done for you.

a hare with hair

a pair of pears

a sail for sale

a knight at night

a flower in the flour

ate eight

164

Level 3, Language Arts

Brainteaser Answer Keys

Page 165

Double Duty

Homographs are words that have the same spellings but have different meanings and often different pronunciations.

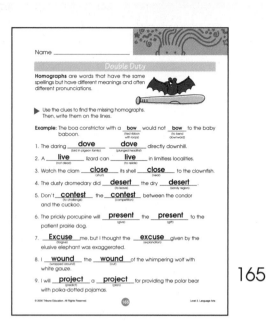

Use the clues to find the missing homographs. Then, write them on the lines.

Example: The boa constrictor with a __bow__ (tied ribbon with loops) would not __bow__ (to bend downwards) to the baby baboon.

1. The daring __dove__ (bird in pigeon family) __dove__ (plunged headfirst) directly downhill.
2. A __live__ (not dead) lizard can __live__ (to reside) in limitless localities.
3. Watch the clam __close__ (shut) its shell __close__ (near) to the clownfish.
4. The dusty dromedary did __desert__ (to leave) the dry __desert__ (sandy region).
5. Don't __contest__ (to challenge) the __contest__ (competition) between the condor and the cuckoo.
6. The prickly porcupine will __present__ (give) the __present__ (gift) to the patient prairie dog.
7. __Excuse__ (forgive) me, but I thought the __excuse__ (explanation) given by the elusive elephant was exaggerated.
8. I __wound__ (wrapped around) the __wound__ (cut) of the whimpering wolf with white gauze.
9. I will __project__ (predict) a __project__ (plan) for providing the polar bear with polka-dotted pajamas.

165

Page 166

We Don't Have the Foggiest . .

An **idiom** is a group of words that have a special meaning when they are used together. The cartoons on this page each suggest an idiom.

Write each idiom in a sentence. Then, tell its meaning in your own words.

Idiom: __There's a fork in the road.__
Meaning: __The road divides into two roads.__

Idiom: __He knows how stretch a dollar.__
Meaning: __He gets the most for his money.__

Idiom: __He has a frog in his throat.__
Meaning: __His voice sounds raspy.__

Idiom: __He is so hungry, he could eat a horse.__
Meaning: __He is very hungry.__

Idiom: __He held up a bank.__
Meaning: __He robbed the bank.__

Idiom: __It's raining cats and dogs.__
Meaning: __It's raining very hard.__

166

Page 167

Alien Visitors

An **analogy** is made of two sets of ideas that are compared in the same way. Think how the first set is compared, and compare the second the same way.

Fill in the lines to complete these analogies.

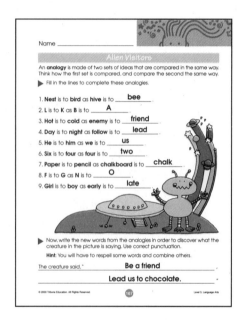

1. **Nest** is to **bird** as **hive** is to __bee__
2. **L** is to **K** as **B** is to __A__
3. **Hot** is to **cold** as **enemy** is to __friend__
4. **Day** is to **night** as **follow** is to __lead__
5. **He** is to **him** as **we** is to __us__
6. **Six** is to **four** as **four** is to __two__
7. **Paper** is to **pencil** as **chalkboard** is to __chalk__
8. **F** is to **G** as **N** is to __O__
9. **Girl** is to **boy** as **early** is to __late__

Now, write the new words from the analogies in order to discover what the creature in the picture is saying. Use correct punctuation.

Hint: You will have to respell some words and combine others.

The creature said, " __Be a friend__ __Lead us to chocolate.__ "

167

Page 168

Missing Letters in a Letter

When you receive a gift, you usually want to thank the giver right away. One way to do this is to write a thank-you note.

First, fill in the missing letters for certain words. Then, select the correct labels from the Word Bank to name each part of this thank-you note. Write the labels on the correct lines.

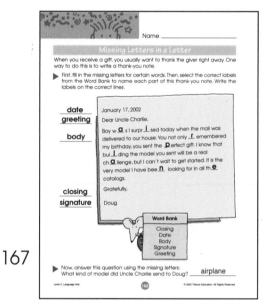

date
greeting
body

January 17, 2002
Dear Uncle Charlie,
Boy w__a__s I surpr__i__sed today when the mail was delivered to our house. You not only __r__emembered my birthday, you sent the __p__erfect gift. I know that bui__l__ding the model you sent will be a real ch__a__llenge, but I can't wait to get started. It is the very model I have bee__n__ looking for in all th__e__ catalogs.
Gratefully,
Doug

closing
signature

Word Bank
Closing
Date
Body
Signature
Greeting

Now, answer this question using the missing letters: What kind of model did Uncle Charlie send to Doug? __airplane__

168

Page 169

Nursery Rhyme Gifts

Each of the gift boxes below contains a useful thing for one of the characters in the listed nursery rhymes.

Unscramble the letters in each box. Then, write the name of each present next to the name of the character to whom you would give it. If a box in divided, it contains two words. The number on each box matches the number of the character who receives the gift.

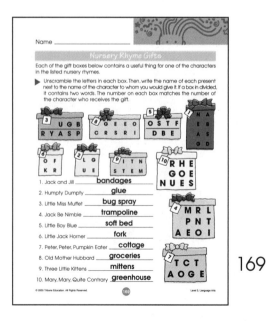

1. Jack and Jill __bandages__
2. Humpty Dumpty __glue__
3. Little Miss Muffet __bug spray__
4. Jack Be Nimble __trampoline__
5. Little Boy Blue __soft bed__
6. Little Jack Horner __fork__
7. Peter, Peter, Pumpkin Eater __cottage__
8. Old Mother Hubbard __groceries__
9. Three Little Kittens __mittens__
10. Mary, Mary, Quite Contrary __greenhouse__

169

Page 170

Be Wise!

Proverbs are folk sayings that have been used for so long that it is difficult to know who first said them. They are wise sayings whose meanings teach lessons that help people to learn.

Example: "Big oaks from little acorns grow." is a proverb. It means that even great things have small beginnings.

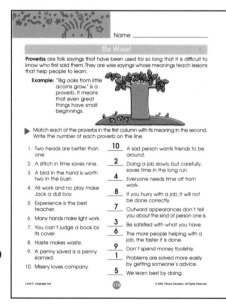

Match each of the proverbs in the first column with its meaning in the second. Write the number of each proverb on the line.

1. Two heads are better than one.
2. A stitch in time saves nine.
3. A bird in the hand is worth two in the bush.
4. All work and no play make Jack a dull boy.
5. Experience is the best teacher.
6. Many hands make light work.
7. You can't judge a book by its cover.
8. Haste makes waste.
9. A penny saved is a penny earned.
10. Misery loves company.

__10__ A sad person wants friends to be around.
__2__ Doing a job slowly, but carefully, saves time in the long run.
__4__ Everyone needs time off from work.
__8__ If you hurry with a job, it will not be done correctly.
__7__ Outward appearances don't tell you about the kind of person one is.
__3__ Be satisfied with what you have.
__6__ The more people helping with a job, the faster it is done.
__9__ Don't spend money foolishly.
__1__ Problems are solved more easily by getting someone's advice.
__5__ We learn best by doing.

170

Brainteaser Answer Keys

330

Leaping Frogs

Two large bullfrogs named Lefty and Righty are having a contest. These are the rules for their race.

➤ As each bullfrog passes a square on a domino, he must add the value if it is 5 or more and subtract the value from his total if it is 4 or less. The bullfrog with the greater number at the finish line is the winner.

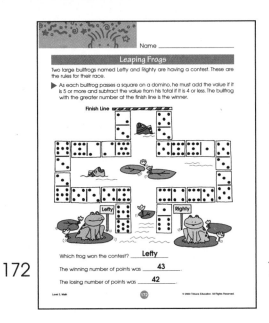

Which frog won the contest? **Lefty**

The winning number of points was **43**.

The losing number of points was **42**.

172

The Alligator and the Fish

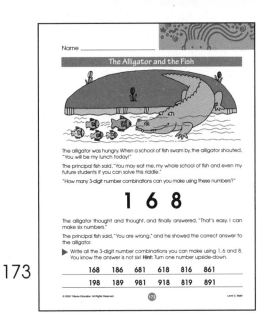

The alligator was hungry. When a school of fish swam by, the alligator shouted, "You will be my lunch today!"

The principal fish said, "You may eat me, my whole school of fish and even my future students if you can solve this riddle."

"How many 3-digit number combinations can you make using these numbers?"

1 6 8

The alligator thought and thought, and finally answered, "That's easy. I can make six numbers."

The principal fish said, "You are wrong," and he showed the correct answer to the alligator.

➤ Write all the 3-digit number combinations you can make using 1, 6 and 8. You know the answer is not six! **Hint:** Turn one number upside-down.

168	186	681	618	816	861
198	189	981	918	819	891

173

Count Your Marbles

Shawn was preparing for the big marble tournament. He opened his marble bag and dumped out the marbles to count them. There were at least 30, but no more than 50, marbles. One-third of the marbles were cats' eyes, one-fourth were aggies, one-sixth were pearlies and one-eighth were steelies. The rest of the marbles were his favorites—the shooters.

➤ How many of each type of marble did Shawn have?
Hint: To find the total number, find a common denominator first.

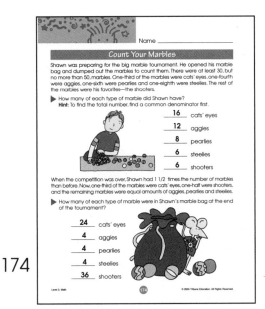

16 cats' eyes

12 aggies

8 pearlies

6 steelies

6 shooters

When the competition was over, Shawn had 1 1/2 times the number of marbles than before. Now, one-third of the marbles were cats' eyes, one-half were shooters, and the remaining marbles were equal amounts of aggies, pearlies and steelies.

➤ How many of each type of marble were in Shawn's marble bag at the end of the tournament?

24 cats' eyes

4 aggies

4 pearlies

4 steelies

36 shooters

174

Buy 1, Get 1 Free!

Sparky's Sports Cards Center is offering an unbelievable deal! If you buy one pack of any set of sports cards, you receive a second pack absolutely free!

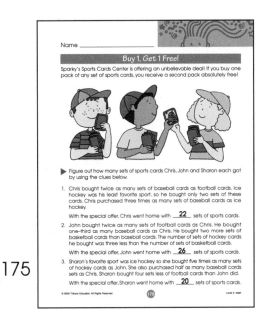

➤ Figure out how many sets of sports cards Chris, John and Sharon each got by using the clues below.

1. Chris bought twice as many sets of baseball cards as football cards. Ice hockey was his least favorite sport, so he bought only two sets of these cards. Chris purchased three times as many sets of baseball cards as ice hockey.

   With the special offer, Chris went home with **22** sets of sports cards.

2. John bought twice as many sets of football cards as Chris. He bought one-third as many baseball cards as Chris. He bought two more sets of basketball cards than baseball cards. The number of sets of hockey cards he bought was three less than the number of sets of basketball cards.

   With the special offer, John went home with **26** sets of sports cards.

3. Sharon's favorite sport was ice hockey so she bought five times as many sets of hockey cards as John. She also purchased half as many baseball cards sets as Chris. Sharon bought four sets less of football cards than John did.

   With the special offer, Sharon went home with **20** sets of sports cards.

175

Mixed Breeds

Twenty-five puppies lined up next to their masters to march in the "Perkiest Puppy Parade." Five breeds of dogs were represented.

➤ Read the clues to find out how many of each breed were in the parade.

Clues: • The German shepherds outnumbered the Old English sheep dogs by 5 to 1.
• There were twice as many cocker spaniels as German shepherds.
• The number of Dalmatians compared to toy poodles was a ratio of 2 to 1.
• The number of Dalmatians and toy poodles and Old English sheep dogs was the same as the number of cocker spaniels.

5 German shepherds

1 Old English sheepdogs

10 Cocker spaniels

3 Toy poodles

6 Dalmatians

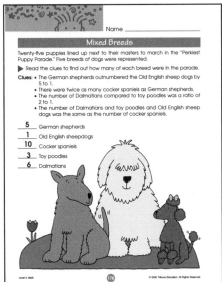

176

What a Deal!

The five magician's cards below are arranged according to a pattern.

➤ Write the four missing numbers on the last card in the series.

2 5	3 4	4 3	5 2	6 1
6 3	5 4	4 5	3 6	2 7

➤ Now, complete this set of cards by writing the three missing numbers on the last card in the series.

1		3	2	0
6	9	8	7	5
16	10	12	14	18

177

Getting Things in Order

When numbers are arranged in a pattern, you can continue it once you have identified the rule of the pattern. For example, in the pattern 1, 3, 4, 6, 7, you add 2 to the first number and 1 to the second and then keep repeating this as far as you want to go. The rule is + 2 + 1. The next three numbers in this pattern are 9, 10, and 12.

▶ Identify the rule that was used to form each of these patterns below. Write the next three numbers and the rule you used to find them.

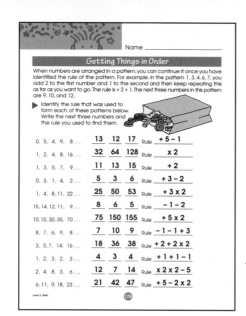

Pattern				Rule
0, 5, 4, 9, 8 ...	13	12	17	Rule + 5 − 1
1, 2, 4, 8, 16 ...	32	64	128	Rule x 2
1, 3, 5, 7, 9 ...	11	13	15	Rule + 2
0, 3, 1, 4, 2 ...	5	3	6	Rule + 3 − 2
1, 4, 8, 11, 22 ...	25	50	53	Rule + 3 x 2
15, 14, 12, 11, 9 ...	8	6	5	Rule − 1 − 2
10, 15, 30, 35, 70 ...	75	150	155	Rule + 5 x 2
8, 7, 6, 9, 8 ...	7	10	9	Rule − 1 − 1 + 3
3, 5, 7, 14, 16 ...	18	36	38	Rule + 2 + 2 x 2
1, 2, 3, 2, 3 ...	4	3	4	Rule + 1 + 1 − 1
2, 4, 8, 3, 6 ...	12	7	14	Rule x 2 x 2 − 5
6, 11, 9, 18, 23 ...	21	42	47	Rule + 5 − 2 x 2

178

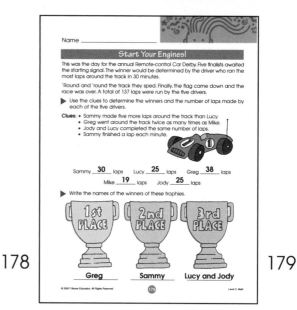

Start Your Engines!

This was the day for the annual Remote-control Car Derby. Five finalists awaited the starting signal. The winner would be determined by the driver who ran the most laps around the track in 30 minutes.

'Round and 'round the track they sped. Finally, the flag came down and the race was over. A total of 137 laps were run by the five drivers.

▶ Use the clues to determine the winners and the number of laps made by each of the five drivers.

Clues: • Sammy made five more laps around the track than Lucy.
• Greg went around the track twice as many times as Mike.
• Jody and Lucy completed the same number of laps.
• Sammy finished a lap each minute.

Sammy __30__ laps   Lucy __25__ laps   Greg __38__ laps

Mike __19__ laps   Jody __25__ laps

▶ Write the names of the winners of these trophies.

1st PLACE — Greg

2nd PLACE — Sammy

3rd PLACE — Lucy and Jody

179

Racing Chimps

One chimpanzee always liked to brag that it could get more fruit than any other animal in the forest. So, an older and wiser chimpanzee decided to challenge him to a race.

"Let us see who can bring back more bananas in one hour," said the older chimp. And so the race began.

Quickly, the younger chimp picked a bunch of five bananas and carried it back. He continued doing this once every five minutes.

The older chimp was not quite as fast. Every ten minutes he carried back eight bananas.

After 45 minutes, the young chimp decided to stop and eat one of his bananas before continuing. By the time he finished, the hour was over and the older chimp called out, "The race is over. Let's see who the winner is."

▶ Use the information above to figure out how many bananas were in each pile, and which chimp won the race.

The younger chimp had __44__ bananas in his pile.

The older chimp had __48__ bananas in his pile.

The winner was the __older__ chimp!

180

Try, Try Again

A young mountain goat was learning how to climb. Unfortunately, he fell down a lot. An adult goat saw him and laughed. "You will never be able to climb mountains."

First, the little goat's feelings were hurt. Then, he became angry. "I will show that old mountain goat. I will learn to climb mountains," he said.

The young goat approached the bottom of the mountain and began climbing over the rocks. But, every time he climbed over three rocks, he slipped and fell back one rock. Finally, he made it to the top. "I knew I could do it!" he said proudly.

▶ How many times did the mountain goat have to start to climb to reach the peak? __8__ times

181

Venn Diagrams

A **Venn diagram** is a picture that represents a collection. The rectangle always stands for the whole collection. Any circle inside the rectangle stands for a part of it.

This Venn diagram represents all the trucks manufactured by a certain company. Circle R stands for all the red trucks, circle B for all the blue trucks and circle F for all the four-wheel-drive trucks the company made.

▶ Read each statement about this Venn diagram and identify it as either TRUE or FALSE.

1. All the trucks have four-wheel drive. __False__

2. Some of the red trucks have four-wheel drive. __True__

3. Some of the four-wheel-drive trucks are blue. __True__

4. All of the blue trucks have four-wheel drive. __False__

5. None of the red trucks have four-wheel drive. __False__

6. All of the four-wheel-drive trucks are either red or blue. __False__

7. None of the trucks with four-wheel drive are either red or blue. __False__

182

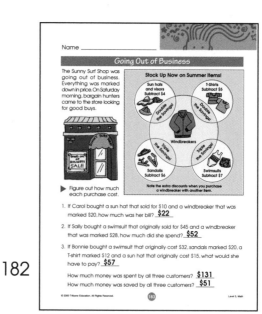

Going Out of Business

The Sunny Surf Shop was going out of business. Everything was marked down in price. On Saturday morning, bargain hunters came to the store looking for good buys.

Stock Up Now on Summer Items!

- Sun hats and visors — Subtract $4
- T-Shirts — Subtract $5
- Windbreakers — Double the savings!
- Sandals — Subtract $6
- Swimsuits — Subtract $7

Note the extra discounts when you purchase a windbreaker with another item.

▶ Figure out how much each purchase cost.

1. If Carol bought a sun hat that sold for $10 and a windbreaker that was marked $20, how much was her bill? __$22__

2. If Sally bought a swimsuit that originally sold for $45 and a windbreaker that was marked $28, how much did she spend? __$52__

3. If Bonnie bought a swimsuit that originally cost $32, sandals marked $20, a T-shirt marked $12 and a sun hat that originally cost $15, what would she have to pay? __$57__

How much money was spent by all three customers? __$131__

How much money was saved by all three customers? __$51__

183

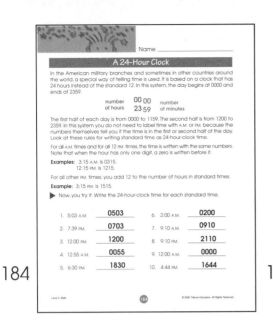

184

A 24-Hour Clock

In the American military branches and sometimes in other countries around the world, a special way of telling time is used. It is based on a clock that has 24 hours instead of the standard 12. In this system, the day begins at 0000 and ends at 2359.

number of hours	00 00 23 59	number of minutes

The first half of each day is from 0000 to 1159. The second half is from 1200 to 2359. In this system you do not need to label time with A.M. or P.M. because the numbers themselves tell you if the time is in the first or second half of the day. Look at these rules for writing standard time as 24-hour-clock time.

For all A.M. times and for all 12 P.M. times, the time is written with the same numbers. Note that when the hour has only one digit, a zero is written before it.

Examples: 3:15 A.M. is 0315.
12:15 P.M. is 1215.

For all other P.M. times, you add 12 to the number of hours in standard times.

Example: 3:15 P.M. is 1515.

▶ Now, you try it. Write the 24-hour-clock time for each standard time.

1. 5:03 A.M.   **0503**
2. 7:39 P.M.   **0703**
3. 12:00 P.M.   **1200**
4. 12:55 A.M.   **0055**
5. 6:30 P.M.   **1830**
6. 2:00 A.M.   **0200**
7. 9:10 A.M.   **0910**
8. 9:10 P.M.   **2110**
9. 12:00 A.M.   **0000**
10. 4:44 P.M.   **1644**

185

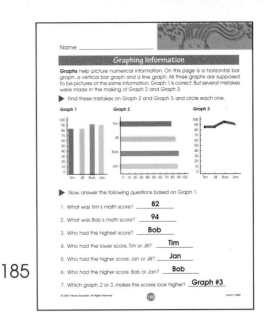

Graphing Information

Graphs help picture numerical information. On this page is a horizontal bar graph, a vertical bar graph and a line graph. All three graphs are supposed to be pictures of the same information. Graph 1 is correct. But several mistakes were made in the making of Graph 2 and Graph 3.

▶ Find these mistakes on Graph 2 and Graph 3, and circle each one.

Graph 1   **Graph 2**   **Graph 3**

▶ Now, answer the following questions based on Graph 1.

1. What was Tim's math score?   **82**
2. What was Bob's math score?   **94**
3. Who had the highest score?   **Bob**
4. Who had the lower score, Tim or Jill?   **Tim**
5. Who had the higher score, Jan or Jill?   **Jan**
6. Who had the higher score, Bob or Jan?   **Bob**
7. Which graph, 2 or 3, makes the scores look higher?   **Graph #3**

186

Don't Be Fooled

▶ There are four answers given for each mathematical question on this page, but only one is correct. Fill in the circle in front of the correct answer.

1. If a mile measures 5,280 feet, how many feet are there in 3 miles?
   ○ a. 10,560   ○ b. 5,280
   ○ c. 5,283   ● d. 15,840

2. If a farmer has 7 goats and he sells all but 4, how many are left?
   ● a. 4   ○ b. 3
   ○ c. 7   ○ d. 0

3. If some months have 31 days and others 30, how many months have 28 days?
   ○ a. 2   ○ b. 1
   ● c. 12   ○ d. 3

4. If a yard contains 36 inches, how many inches are there in half of a yard?
   ● a. 18   ○ b. 12
   ○ c. 72   ○ d. 46

5. How many 6-cent candies are there in a dozen?
   ○ a. 6   ○ b. 24
   ○ c. 2   ● d. 12

6. If there are 2 pints in a quart and 4 quarts in a gallon, how many pints are there in a gallon?
   ● a. 8   ○ b. 6
   ○ c. 16   ○ d. 2

7. If there are 10 pieces of paper and you take away 6 of them how many pieces do you have?
   ● a. 4   ○ b. 10
   ○ c. 6   ○ d. 5

8. If you drink a glass of water every half-hour beginning at 9:00, when will you have drunk 4 glasses of water?
   ○ a. 10:00   ● b. 10:30
   ○ c. 11:00   ○ d. 11:30

9. If February has 29 days in 2000, when were the last two leap years?
   ● a. 1992 and 1996   ○ b. 1995 and 1999
   ○ c. 1994 and 1998   ○ d. 1980 and 1990

10. If two 2-inch thick books are standing next to each other on a shelf, how many inches are there between the last page of the first book and the first page of the last?
    ○ a. 2   ○ b. 4
    ● c. less than 1   ○ d. more than 1

188

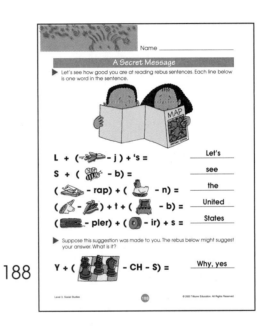

A Secret Message

▶ Let's see how good you are at reading rebus sentences. Each line below is one word in the sentence.

L + (🐝 – j) + 's =   **Let's**
S + (🐝 – b) =   **see**
(🖼 – rap) + (🎩 – n) =   **the**
(🦄 – 🎩) + t + (🚗 – b) =   **United**
(🖼 – pler) + (⭕ – ir) + s =   **States**

▶ Suppose this suggestion was made to you. The rebus below might suggest your answer. What is it?

Y + (♟♟ – CH – S) =   **Why, yes**

189

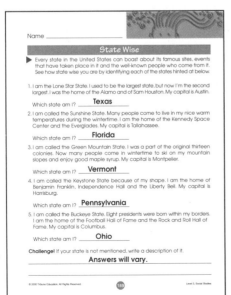

State Wise

▶ Every state in the United States can boast about its famous sites, events that have taken place in it and the well-known people who come from it. See how state wise you are by identifying each of the states hinted at below.

1. I am the Lone Star State. I used to be the largest state, but now I'm the second largest. I was the home of the Alamo and of Sam Houston. My capital is Austin.
   Which state am I?   **Texas**

2. I am called the Sunshine State. Many people come to live in my nice warm temperatures during the wintertime. I am the home of the Kennedy Space Center and the Everglades. My capital is Tallahassee.
   Which state am I?   **Florida**

3. I am called the Green Mountain State. I was a part of the original thirteen colonies. Now many people come in wintertime to ski on my mountain slopes and enjoy good maple syrup. My capital is Montpelier.
   Which state am I?   **Vermont**

4. I am called the Keystone State because of my shape. I am the home of Benjamin Franklin, Independence Hall and the Liberty Bell. My capital is Harrisburg.
   Which state am I?   **Pennsylvania**

5. I am called the Buckeye State. Eight presidents were born within my borders. I am the home of the Football Hall of Fame and the Rock and Roll Hall of Fame. My capital is Columbus.
   Which state am I?   **Ohio**

Challenge! If your state is not mentioned, write a description of it.
Answers will vary.

190

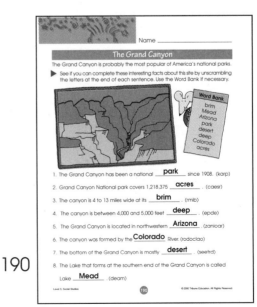

The Grand Canyon

The Grand Canyon is probably the most popular of America's national parks.

▶ See if you can complete these interesting facts about this site by unscrambling the letters at the end of each sentence. Use the Word Bank if necessary.

Word Bank
brim
Mead
Arizona
park
desert
deep
Colorado
acres

1. The Grand Canyon has been a national **park** since 1908. (karp)
2. Grand Canyon National park covers 1,218,375 **acres**. (caesr)
3. The canyon is 4 to 13 miles wide at its **brim**. (rmib)
4. The canyon is between 4,000 and 5,000 feet **deep**. (epde)
5. The Grand Canyon is located in northwestern **Arizona**. (zanioar)
6. The canyon was formed by the **Colorado** River. (rodoclao)
7. The bottom of the Grand Canyon is mostly **desert**. (seetrd)
8. The Lake that forms at the southern end of the Grand Canyon is called Lake **Mead**. (deam)

Brainteaser Answer Keys

Page 191 — Plymouth Rock

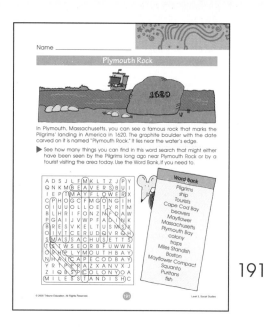

Name _____

Plymouth Rock

1620

In Plymouth, Massachusetts, you can see a famous rock that marks the Pilgrims' landing in America in 1620. The graphite boulder with the date carved on it is named "Plymouth Rock." It lies near the water's edge.

▶ See how many things you can find in this word search that might either have been seen by the Pilgrims long ago near Plymouth Rock or by a tourist visiting the area today. Use the Word Bank, if you need to.

```
A D S J L F M K L T Z J P Y
Q N K M B E A V E R S B U I
I E P T M A Y F L O W E R B
C P H O G C F M G O N G I H
O I U U O L L O E T Y R T M
B L H R I F O N Z N F O A W
P G A I J V W P F A D I N K
B R E S V K E L T U S M S X
O I V T C E R U D Q V R Q H
S M A S S A C H U S E T T S
T S T W S E O R B F U W W N
O P H L Y M O U T H B A Y I
N H A C A P E C O D B A Y J
Y R T H Q Z X A N V X J
Z I Q S C O L O N Y O A
M I L E S S T A N D I S H C
```

Word Bank
Pilgrims
ship
Tourists
Cape Cod Bay
beavers
Mayflower
Massachusetts
Plymouth Bay
colony
traps
Miles Standish
Boston
Mayflower Compact
Squanto
Puritans
fish

191

Page 192 — Our National Anthem

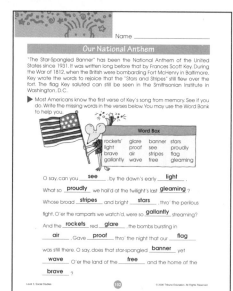

Name _____

Our National Anthem

"The Star-Spangled Banner" has been the National Anthem of the United States since 1931. It was written long before that by Frances Scott Key. During the war of 1812, when the British were bombarding Fort McHenry in Baltimore, Key wrote the words to rejoice that the "Stars and Stripes" still flew over the fort. The flag Key saluted can still be seen in the Smithsonian Institute in Washington, D.C.

▶ Most Americans know the first verse of Key's song from memory. See if you do. Write the missing words in the verses below. You may use the Word Bank to help you.

Word Box
rockets' glare banner stars
light proof see proudly
brave air stripes flag
gallantly wave free gleaming

O say, can you **see** , by the dawn's early **light** ,

What so **proudly** we hail'd at the twilight's last **gleaming** ?

Whose broad **stripes** and bright **stars** , thro' the perilous

fight, O'er the ramparts we watch'd, were so **gallantly** streaming?

And the **rockets'** red **glare** , the bombs bursting in

air , Gave **proof** thro' the night that our **flag**

was still there. O say, does that star-spangled **banner** yet

wave O'er the land of the **free** and the home of the

brave ?

192

Page 193 — Down on the Farm

Name _____

Down on the Farm

The colonists were the people who were the first Europeans to come and live in what is now the United States. They needed much help and hard work just to get by in those early days. One of the things they did was to learn how to grow corn. Look at the rows of corn below. Each stalk is numbered from 1 to 24. Notice that the first number has a circle around it, the second a square and the third a triangle.

▶ Continue the pattern of shapes for all the corn.

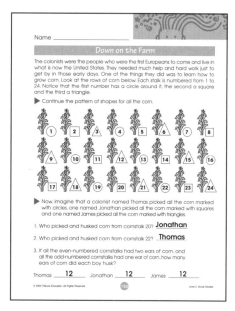

▶ Now, imagine that a colonist named Thomas picked all the corn marked with circles, one named Jonathan picked all the corn marked with squares and one named James picked all the corn marked with triangles.

1. Who picked and husked corn from cornstalk 20? **Jonathan**

2. Who picked and husked corn from cornstalk 22? **Thomas**

3. If all the even-numbered cornstalks had two ears of corn, and all the odd-numbered cornstalks had one ear of corn, how many ears of corn did each boy husk?

Thomas **12**   Jonathan **12**   James **12**

193

Page 194 — Inventions and Inventors

Name _____

Inventions and Inventors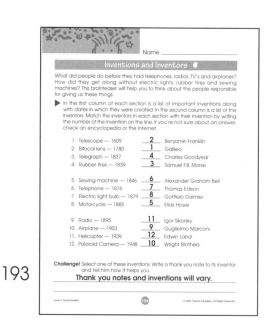

What did people do before they had telephones, radios, TV's and airplanes? How did they get along without electric lights, rubber tires and sewing machines? This brainteaser will help you to think about the people responsible for giving us these things.

▶ In the first column of each section is a list of important inventions along with dates in which they were created. In the second column is a list of the inventors. Match the inventors in each section with their invention by writing the number of the invention on the line. If you're not sure about an answer, check an encyclopedia or the Internet.

1. Telescope — 1609   **2** Benjamin Franklin
2. Bifocal lens — 1780   **1** Galileo
3. Telegraph — 1837   **4** Charles Goodyear
4. Rubber tires — 1839   **3** Samuel F.B. Morse

5. Sewing machine — 1846 **6** Alexander Graham Bell
6. Telephone — 1876   **7** Thomas Edison
7. Electric light bulb — 1879 **8** Gottlieb Daimler
8. Motorcycle — 1885   **5** Elias Howe

9. Radio — 1895   **11** Igor Sikorsky
10. Airplane — 1903   **9** Guglielmo Marconi
11. Helicopter — 1939   **12** Edwin Land
12. Polaroid Camera — 1948 **10** Wright Brothers

Challenge! Select one of these inventions. Write a thank-you note to its inventor and tell him how it helps you.

Thank you notes and inventions will vary.

194

Page 195 — Great Land Masses

Name _____

Great Land Masses

There are seven continents in the world: North America, South America, Europe, Asia, Africa, Australia and Antarctica. All but the last two of these continents are divided into countries.

▶ Use the outline map below to help you decide on which continent each of the countries listed below belongs. Then, check your answers on a globe or world map.

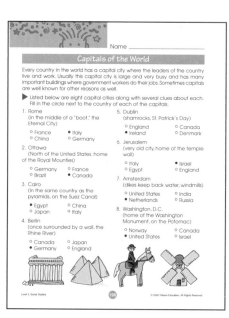

1. Argentina **South America**
2. Japan **Asia**
3. Italy **Europe**
4. United States **North America**
5. Egypt **Africa**
6. Russia **Asia**
7. Spain **Europe**
8. China **Asia**
9. England **Europe**
10. Brazil **South America**
11. Canada **North America**
12. Germany **Europe**
13. Mexico **North America**
14. Chile **South America**
15. Kenya **Africa**

195

Page 196 — Capitals of the World

Name _____

Capitals of the World

Every country in the world has a capital city where the leaders of the country live and work. Usually this capital city is large and very busy and has many important buildings where government workers do their jobs. Sometimes capitals are well known for other reasons as well.

▶ Listed below are eight capital cities along with several clues about each. Fill in the circle next to the country of each of the capitals.

1. Rome (in the middle of a "boot," the Eternal City)
   ○ France ● Italy
   ○ China ○ Germany

2. Ottawa (North of the United States, home of the Royal Mounties)
   ○ Germany ○ France
   ○ Brazil ● Canada

3. Cairo (in the same country as the pyramids, on the Suez Canal)
   ● Egypt ○ China
   ○ Japan ○ Italy

4. Berlin (once surrounded by a wall, the Rhine River)
   ○ Canada ○ Japan
   ● Germany ○ England

5. Dublin (shamrocks, St. Patrick's Day)
   ○ England ○ Canada
   ● Ireland ○ Denmark

6. Jerusalem (very old city, home of the temple wall)
   ○ Italy ● Israel
   ○ Egypt ○ England

7. Amsterdam (dikes keep back water, windmills)
   ○ United States ○ India
   ● Netherlands ○ Russia

8. Washington, D.C. (home of the Washington Monument, on the Potomac)
   ○ Norway ○ Canada
   ● United States ○ Israel

196

---

197 — A Taste of Italy

Name _____

A Taste of Italy

Italy is famous for its good food. Chances are that you have enjoyed Italian pizza at one time or another yourself.

▶ Unscramble the letters to spell three different toppings on each pizza.

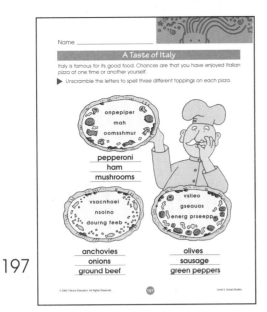

onpepiper
mah
oomsshmur

pepperoni
ham
mushrooms

vsacnhoei
nsoino
dourng feeb

vslieo
gseauas
energ prseepp

anchovies
onions
ground beef

olives
sausage
green peppers

197

198 — Parthenon Pillars

Name _____

Parthenon Pillars

Greece is one of the countries of southern Europe. It is a very mountainous country. Its most famous mountain is Mount Olympus, the highest in Greece. It stands 9,576 feet above the sea. Athens is the capital and best-known city in Greece. High above Athens are the ruins of the Parthenon, an ancient temple. People from all over the world climb to the heights over Athens to visit this wonderful building. It was built around 400 B.C. and dedicated to the goddess Athena. Beautiful statues and sculptures once filled this magnificent structure. The Parthenon measures 237 feet in length and 110 feet in width. It stands about 60 feet tall. Forty-six Doric columns surround the outer edge of the temple.

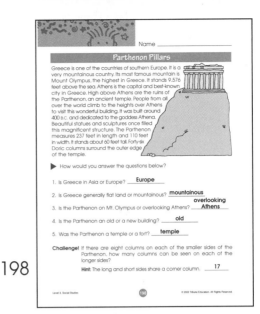

▶ How would you answer the questions below?

1. Is Greece in Asia or Europe? __**Europe**__

2. Is Greece generally flat land or mountainous? __**mountainous**__

3. Is the Parthenon on Mt. Olympus or overlooking Athens? __**overlooking Athens**__

4. Is the Parthenon an old or a new building? __**old**__

5. Was the Parthenon a temple or a fort? __**temple**__

Challenge! If there are eight columns on each of the smaller sides of the Parthenon, how many columns can be seen on each of the longer sides?

Hint: The long and short sides share a corner column. __**17**__

198

199 — Chinese Cyclists

Name _____

Chinese Cyclists

China is a large country in Asia. About one-fifth of the world's population lives in China. There is less than one automobile for every 500 people, so people generally use simple means of transportation, such as walking and riding bicycles.

▶ Think about these three problems and see if you can solve them.

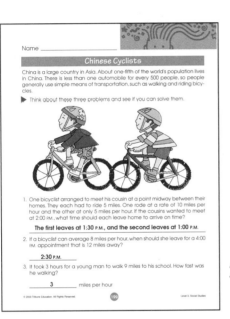

1. One bicyclist arranged to meet his cousin at a point midway between their homes. They each had to ride 5 miles. One rode at a rate of 10 miles per hour and the other at only 5 miles per hour. If the cousins wanted to meet at 2:00 P.M., what time should each leave home to arrive on time?

The first leaves at 1:30 P.M., and the second leaves at 1:00 P.M.

2. If a bicyclist can average 8 miles per hour, when should she leave for a 4:00 P.M. appointment that is 12 miles away?

2:30 P.M.

3. It took 3 hours for a young man to walk 9 miles to his school. How fast was he walking?

__**3**__ miles per hour

199

200 — The Lion Dance

Name _____

The Lion Dance

The Lion Dance, which started in China, became a Japanese folk dance. In this dance many people line up under a long piece of colorful cloth. The person in front wears a mask of a lion's head. As a group, the line of people dance in the streets around the town.

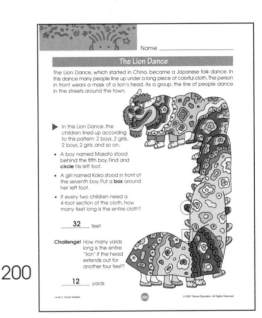

▶ In this Lion Dance, the children lined up according to this pattern: 2 boys, 2 girls, 2 boys, 2 girls, and so on.

• A boy named Masato stood behind the fifth boy. Find and **circle** his left foot.

• A girl named Koko stood in front of the seventh boy. Put a **box** around her left foot.

• If every two children need a 4-foot section of the cloth, how many feet long is the entire cloth?

__**32**__ feet

Challenge! How many yards long is the entire "lion" if the head extends out for another four feet?

__**12**__ yards

200

201 — Oriental Origami

Name _____

Oriental Origami

Japan is an island country in Asia. It is sometimes called "The Land of the Rising Sun." One of the things Japan is famous for is the art of origami. This is the art of folding paper to create beautiful shapes and figures.

Suppose Masato and five of his friends fold sheets of paper to create the figures below.

▶ Read the clues and decide who made each origami figure. Write the correct name on the line below each figure.

Clues: • Masato's figure and Yoshiko's figure are both in the middle.
• Both Kenichi's and Takashi's figures are on the ends.
• Yukiko's figure is directly to the right of Kenichi's.
• Masato's figure is separated from Kenichi's by two other figures.
• Manami's figure is separated from Yukiko's figure by two others.

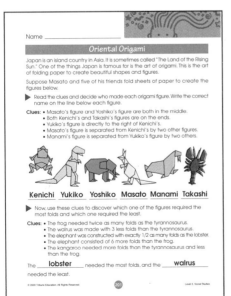

Kenichi **Yukiko** **Yoshiko** **Masato** **Manami** **Takashi**

▶ Now, use these clues to discover which one of the figures required the most folds and which one required the least.

Clues: • The frog needed twice as many folds as the tyrannosaurus.
• The walrus was made with 3 less folds than the tyrannosaurus.
• The elephant was constructed with exactly 1/2 as many folds as the lobster.
• The elephant consisted of 6 more folds than the frog.
• The kangaroo needed more folds than the tyrannosaurus and less than the frog.

The __**lobster**__ needed the most folds, and the __**walrus**__ needed the least.

201

202 — Kenya's Kingdom

Name _____

Kenya's Kingdom

Kenya is a beautiful country on the continent of Africa. Large areas of Kenya have been set aside as national parks and wildlife preserves. Tourists come from all over to see many unusual animals in their natural settings. In these parks and preserves, the animals are protected from those who might harm them.

▶ Try your hand at these tricky problems about the animals of Kenya.

1. An ostrich traveled forty miles at a rate of 20 miles per hour. What was its rate of speed?

20 miles per hour

2. A crocodile laid 34 eggs and buried them in the mud. Three large lizards found the eggs and carried them away. The first lizard carried 3 eggs every 10 minutes. The second carried 5 eggs every 15 minutes. The third carried 1 egg every 2 minutes. How long did it take the lizards to carry off all the eggs?

30 minutes

3. Three giraffes nibbled on the leaves of a tree that was 35 feet tall. The first giraffe was 1/5 the height of the third giraffe. The second giraffe was 5 times the height of the first giraffe. The third giraffe's head reached 3/7 of the height of the tree. What are the heights of the three giraffes?

First giraffe __**3 feet**__

Second giraffe __**15 feet**__

Third giraffe __**15 feet**__

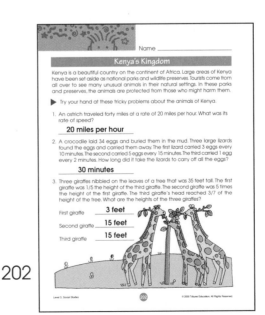

202

335

Page 203

Name _____

"True" Tales

Three men claimed to have taken a photograph of the mysterious Sasquatch, also known as Bigfoot. Information collected from previous reports states that Bigfoot is from 7 to 10 feet tall, weighs over 500 lbs., has thick fur and long arms, and walks upright on two feet, leaving footprints over 16 inches long.

Mr. T. Rapper's Story

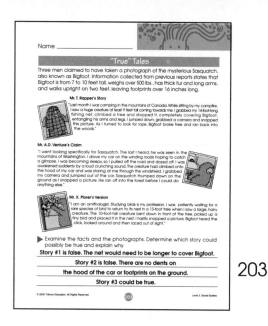

"Last month I was camping in the mountains of Canada. While sitting by my campfire, I saw a huge creature at least 9 feet tall coming towards me. I grabbed my 14-foot-long fishing net, climbed a tree and dropped it, completely covering Bigfoot, entangling his arms and legs. I jumped down, grabbed a camera and snapped this picture. As I turned to look for rope, Bigfoot broke free and ran back into the woods."

Mr. A.D. Venture's Claim

"I went looking specifically for Sasquatch. The last I heard, he was seen in the mountains of Washington. I drove my car on the winding roads hoping to catch a glimpse. I was becoming sleepy, so I pulled off the road and dozed off. I was awakened suddenly by a loud crunching sound. The creature had climbed onto the hood of my car and was staring at me through the windshield. I grabbed my camera and jumped out of the car. Sasquatch thumped down on the ground as I snapped a picture. He ran off into the forest before I could do anything else."

Mr. X. Plorer's Version

"I am an ornithologist. Studying birds is my profession. I was patiently waiting for a rare species of bird to return to its nest in a 13-foot tree when I saw a large, hairy creature. The 10-foot-tall creature bent down in front of the tree, picked up a tiny bird and placed it in the nest. I hastily snapped a picture. Bigfoot heard the click, looked around and then raced out of sight."

▶ Examine the facts and the photographs. Determine which story could possibly be true and explain why.

Story #1 is false. The net would need to be longer to cover Bigfoot.

Story #2 is false. There are no dents on

the hood of the car or footprints on the ground.

Story #3 could be true.

© 2000 Tribune Education. All Rights Reserved. Level 3, Social Studies

Page 204

Name _____

Beaches 'n' Bonnets

The Bahamas are a chain of about 3,000 coral islands and reefs in the West Indies. If you visit the Bahamas, you probably will spend some time on the beach. So put on your swimming suit, grab a beach towel and prepare to soak up some rays.

The temperatures might seem perfect to you. It will be 85°F by 10:00 A.M. in the morning. It will then rise 1 degree every hour until about 2:00 P.M., when it will begin to decrease 2 degrees every hour until about 7:00 P.M.

1. What will the thermometer read at 4:00 P.M.? __85°__

2. What will the temperature be at 7:00 P.M.? __79°__

You will probably want to get a sun hat for the rest of your stay. An open-air market sells a variety of straw hats. The prices vary depending on their structure and design.

▶ What is the actual price of each kind of hat? Add the additional cost to the basic hat price. Write the actual price on the line below each hat.

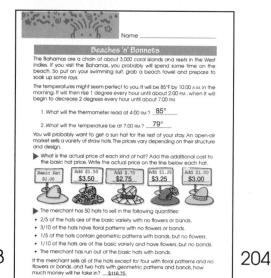

Basic Hat $2.00 | Add $1.50 **$3.50** | Add $.75 **$2.75** | Add $1.25 **$3.25** | Add $1.00 **$3.00**

The merchant has 50 hats to sell in the following quantities:

• 2/5 of the hats are of the basic variety with no flowers or bands.
• 3/10 of the hats have floral patterns with no flowers or bands.
• 1/5 of the hats contain geometric patterns with bands, but no flowers.
• 1/10 of the hats are of the basic variety and have flowers, but no bands.
• The merchant has run out of the basic hats with bands.

If the merchant sells all of the hats except for four with floral patterns and no flowers or bands, and two hats with geometric patterns and bands, how much money will he take in? __$116.75.__

Level 3, Social Studies

Page 206

Name _____

Birds of a Feather

Birds are the only animals that have feathers. All birds have wings, but not all can fly. They all hatch from eggs, have backbones and are warm-blooded.

▶ Fill in the puzzle with the names of the birds you see on the eggs. The last letter of one name becomes the first letter of the next name. Start at the outside edge and spiral in toward the center. The first three names are written for you.

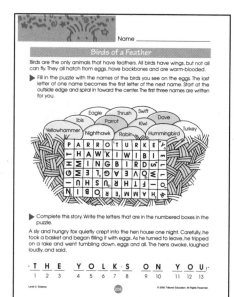

Eagle · Thrush · Swift · Ibis · Parrot · Dove · Yellowhammer · Nighthawk · Kiwi · Robin · Hummingbird · Turkey

▶ Complete this story. Write the letters that are in the numbered boxes in the puzzle.

A sly and hungry fox quietly crept into the hen house one night. Carefully, he took a basket and began filling it with eggs. As he turned to leave, he tripped on a rake and went tumbling down, eggs and all. The hens awoke, laughed loudly, and said.

__T H E   Y O L K S   O N   Y O U !__
  1 2 3   4 5 6 7   8 9   10 11 12 13

Level 3, Science © 2000 Tribune Education. All Rights Reserved.

Page 207

Name _____

No Speed Limits

All animals exhibit some movement during the course of their lives.
The chart below indicates the comparative speeds of various animals:

Animals in the Air

Housefly	5 mph	Dragonfly	50 mph
Robin	30 mph	Peregrine Falcon	180 mph

Animals on Land

Turtle	1/10 mph	Gazelle	50 mph
African Elephant	25 mph	Cheetah	70 mph

Animals in the Water

Goldfish	4 mph	Dolphin	25 mph
Sea Turtle	20 mph	Sailfish	30 mph

▶ Answer the following questions by stating possible explanations.

1. What is there about a peregrine falcon that helps it to fly faster than a common housefly? __Possible answers: body size;__ __muscle mass; light, hollow but strong bones; wing size__

2. If a tall person can frequently outrun a short person, why can't an elephant outrun a cheetah? __Possible answers: different amount of body fat__ __versus muscle mass, leg structure, weight distribution__

3. What factors allow a peregrine falcon to move faster than a cheetah? __Possible answers: can ride in air drafts; does much gliding,__ __thus conserving energy; less obstacles in the air; wing efficiency__

4. Although many land turtles are slow, lumbering creatures, the sea turtle can move rather swiftly. What might explain this? __Possible answers: has a flatter, more streamlined shell; long,__ __paddle-like flippers work efficiently in water currents__

© 2000 Tribune Education. All Rights Reserved. Level 3, Science

Page 208

Name _____

Animals on Guard

Wild animals in their natural habitats often face many different enemies and dangers. Each species has its own special way of defending itself.

▶ Use the words in the Word Bank to complete the analogies about animal defenses.

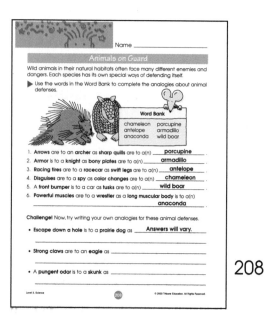

Word Bank
chameleon · porcupine
antelope · armadillo
anaconda · wild boar

1. Arrows are to an archer as sharp quills are to a(n) __porcupine__
2. Armor is to a knight as bony plates are to a(n) __armadillo__
3. Racing tires are to a racecar as swift legs are to a(n) __antelope__
4. Disguises are to a spy as color changes are to a(n) __chameleon__
5. A front bumper is to a car as tusks are to a(n) __wild boar__
6. Powerful muscles are to a wrestler as a long muscular body is to a(n) __anaconda__

Challenge! Now, try writing your own analogies for these animal defenses.

• Escape down a hole is to a prairie dog as __Answers will vary.__

• Strong claws are to an eagle as _____

• A pungent odor is to a skunk as _____

Level 3, Science © 2000 Tribune Education. All Rights Reserved.

Page 209

Name _____

Self-Preservation

Here are some more examples of how some plants and animals protect themselves.

Plants

The **teasel** is a plant that forms a moat between two leaves, collects rainwater at that point, and then drowns unsuspecting snails and insects.

The **screw pine**, a tropical plant, has tough, sword-shaped leaves with sharp barbs that can capture curious animals.

The **nettle** has leaves covered with hairs that act like needles that puncture and release irritating chemicals.

The **acacia tree** has hollow thorns that provide both a home and a sugary food for ants that, in turn, attack other animals endangering the tree.

The **sticky sundew** has leaves covered with sticky, glue-like hairs that trap insects.

The **octopus tree** has spines that extend beyond its leaves, providing it with protection from large animals.

Animals

The **armadillo** has a bumpy, worm-shaped tongue and gummy saliva with which to catch its prey.

The **markhor**, one of the largest species of goats, has great corkscrew horns to use as swords against enemies.

The **archer fish** shoots aim at insects in the air and shoots water from its mouth to drown them. It then eats the insects when they fall to the ground.

The **spined spider**, a tropical short-legged spider, has sharp, brightly colored spines sticking out from its body to discourage predators from attacking it.

The **clownfish** lives near sea anemones. The clownfish provides food for the anemones and the anemones remove parasites from the clownfish.

The **gaboon viper**, with the longest fangs of any snake, can inject a deadly poison into its victim.

▶ Use the information above and the clues below to pair one plant with one animal that show a similar means of self-preservation. Write their names under the correct clue.

We like to "fence" with our enemies.
screw pine
markhor

Always practice water safety near us.
teasel
archer fish

We've been in many a "sticky situation."
sticky sundew
armadillo

We follow a buddy system.
acacia tree
clownfish

Our message to intruders has a point!
octopus tree
spined spider

Be careful! That's poison.
nettle
gaboon viper

© 2000 Tribune Education. All Rights Reserved. Level 3, Science

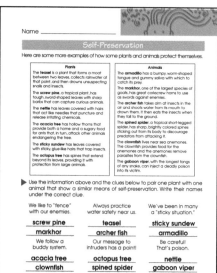

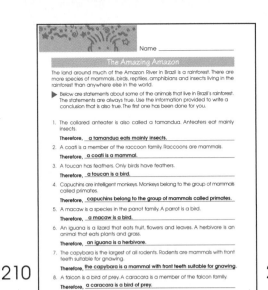

The Amazing Amazon

The land around much of the Amazon River in Brazil is a rainforest. There are more species of mammals, birds, reptiles, amphibians and insects living in the rainforest than anywhere else in the world.

▶ Below are statements about some of the animals that live in Brazil's rainforest. The statements are always true. Use the information provided to write a conclusion that is also true. The first one has been done for you.

1. The collared anteater is also called a tamandua. Anteaters eat mainly insects.
   Therefore, __a tamandua eats mainly insects.__

2. A coati is a member of the raccoon family. Raccoons are mammals.
   Therefore, __a coati is a mammal.__

3. A toucan has feathers. Only birds have feathers.
   Therefore, __a toucan is a bird.__

4. Capuchins are intelligent monkeys. Monkeys belong to the group of mammals called primates.
   Therefore, __capuchins belong to the group of mammals called primates.__

5. A macaw is a species in the parrot family. A parrot is a bird.
   Therefore, __a macaw is a bird.__

6. An iguana is a lizard that eats fruit, flowers and leaves. A herbivore is an animal that eats plants and grass.
   Therefore, __an iguana is a herbivore.__

7. The capybara is the largest of all rodents. Rodents are mammals with front teeth suitable for gnawing.
   Therefore, __the capybara is a mammal with front teeth suitable for gnawing.__

8. A falcon is a bird of prey. A caracara is a member of the falcon family.
   Therefore, __a caracara is a bird of prey.__

210

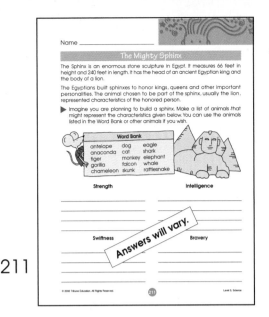

The Mighty Sphinx

The Sphinx is an enormous stone sculpture in Egypt. It measures 66 feet in height and 240 feet in length. It has the head of an ancient Egyptian king and the body of a lion.

The Egyptians built sphinxes to honor kings, queens and other important personalities. The animal chosen to be part of the sphinx, usually the lion, represented characteristics of the honored person.

▶ Imagine you are planning to build a sphinx. Make a list of animals that might represent the characteristics given below. You can use the animals listed in the Word Bank or other animals if you wish.

Word Bank
antelope   dog   eagle
anaconda   cat   shark
tiger   monkey   elephant
gorilla   falcon   whale
chameleon skunk   rattlesnake

Strength   Intelligence

Swiftness   *Answers will vary.*   Bravery

211

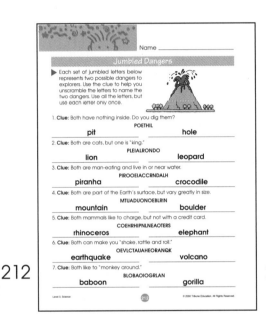

Jumbled Dangers

▶ Each set of jumbled letters below represents two possible dangers to explorers. Use the clue to help you unscramble the letters to name the two dangers. Use all the letters, but use each letter only once.

1. **Clue:** Both have nothing inside. Do you dig them?
   POETHIL
   pit   hole

2. **Clue:** Both are cats, but one is "king."
   PLEIALRONDO
   lion   leopard

3. **Clue:** Both are man-eating and live in or near water.
   PIROOEIACCRNDALH
   piranha   crocodile

4. **Clue:** Both are part of the Earth's surface, but vary greatly in size.
   MTUADUONOEBLRIN
   mountain   boulder

5. **Clue:** Both mammals like to charge, but not with a credit card.
   COEHRHIPNLNEAOTERS
   rhinoceros   elephant

6. **Clue:** Both can make you "shake, rattle and roll."
   OEVLCTAUAHEORANQK
   earthquake   volcano

7. **Clue:** Both like to "monkey around."
   BLOBAOIOGRLAN
   baboon   gorilla

212

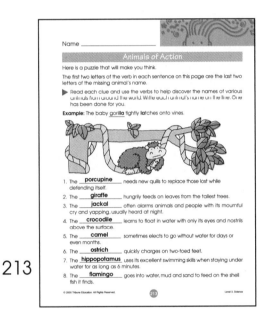

Animals of Action

Here is a puzzle that will make you think.

The first two letters of the verb in each sentence on this page are the last two letters of the missing animal's name.

▶ Read each clue and use the verbs to help discover the names of various animals from around the world. Write each animal's name on the line. One has been done for you.

Example: The baby **gorilla** tightly **la**tches onto vines.

1. The __porcupine__ needs new quills to replace those lost while defending itself.
2. The __giraffe__ hungrily feeds on leaves from the tallest trees.
3. The __jackal__ often alarms animals and people with its mournful cry and yapping, usually heard at night.
4. The __crocodile__ learns to float in water with only its eyes and nostrils above the surface.
5. The __camel__ sometimes elects to go without water for days or even months.
6. The __ostrich__ quickly charges on two-toed feet.
7. The __hippopotamus__ uses its excellent swimming skills when staying under water for as long as 6 minutes.
8. The __flamingo__ goes into water, mud and sand to feed on the shell fish it finds.

213

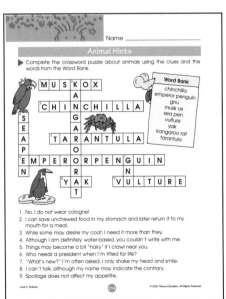

Animal Hints

▶ Complete the crossword puzzle about animals using the clues and the words from the Word Bank.

Word Bank
chinchilla
emperor penguin
gnu
musk ox
sea pen
vulture
yak
kangaroo rat
tarantula

Crossword answers: MUSKOX, CHINCHILLA, TARANTULA, EMPERORPENGUIN, YAK, VULTURE, SEAPEN, KANGAROORAT

1. No, I do not wear cologne!
2. I can save unchewed food in my stomach and later return it to my mouth for a meal.
3. While some may desire my coat, I need it more than they.
4. Although I am definitely water-based, you couldn't write with me.
5. Things may become a bit "hairy" if I crawl near you.
6. Who needs a president when I'm titled for life?
7. "What's new?" I'm often asked. I only shake my head and smile.
8. I can't talk, although my name may indicate the contrary.
9. Spoilage does not affect my appetite.

214

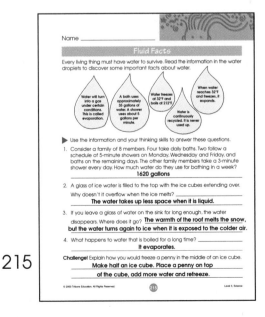

Fluid Facts

Every living thing must have water to survive. Read the information in the water droplets to discover some important facts about water.

- Water will turn into a gas under certain conditions. This is called evaporation.
- A bath uses approximately 36 gallons of water. A shower uses about 5 gallons per minute.
- Water freezes at 32°F and boils at 212°F.
- When water reaches 32°F and freezes, it expands.
- Water is continuously recycled. It is never used up.

▶ Use the information and your thinking skills to answer these questions.

1. Consider a family of 8 members. Four take daily baths. Two follow a schedule of 5-minute showers on Monday, Wednesday and Friday, and baths on the remaining days. The other family members take a 3-minute shower every day. How much water do they use for bathing in a week?
   __1620 gallons__

2. A glass of ice water is filled to the top with the ice cubes extending over. Why doesn't it overflow when the ice melts?
   __The water takes up less space when it is liquid.__

3. If you leave a glass of water on the sink for long enough, the water disappears. Where does it go? __The warmth of the roof melts the snow, but the water turns again to ice when it is exposed to the colder air.__

4. What happens to water that is boiled for a long time? __It evaporates.__

Challenge! Explain how you would freeze a penny in the middle of an ice cube.
__Make half an ice cube. Place a penny on top of the cube, add more water and refreeze.__

215

Page 216

Name _____

Record-Setting Weather

Even though the people who predict weather use all sorts of complicated instruments, their forecasts are never 100% accurate.

▶ Here are some record-setting weather conditions. Look them over carefully. Then, answer the questions below.

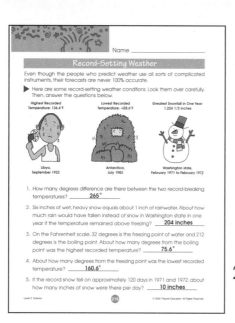

Highest Recorded Temperature: 136.4°F

Lowest Recorded Temperature: -128.6°F

Greatest Snowfall in One Year: 1,224 1/2 inches

Libya, September 1922

Antarctica, July 1983

Washington state, February 1971 to February 1972

1. How many degrees difference are there between the two record-breaking temperatures? **265°**

2. Six inches of wet, heavy snow equals about 1 inch of rainwater. About how much rain would have fallen instead of snow in Washington state in one year if the temperature remained above freezing? **204 inches**

3. On the Fahrenheit scale, 32 degrees is the freezing point of water and 212 degrees is the boiling point. About how many degrees from the boiling point was the highest recorded temperature? **75.6°**

4. About how many degrees from the freezing point was the lowest recorded temperature? **160.6°**

5. If the record snow fell on approximately 120 days in 1971 and 1972, about how many inches of snow were there per day? **10 inches**

Page 217

Name _____

"Association" Power

"Learning all these scientific terms is hard!" said Brad.

"I have an idea!" exclaimed Vonda brightly.

"Let's make up associations for the scientific terms that we want to learn. That will help us remember the terms for tomorrow's test."

▶ Use the Word Bank to help Vonda and Brad choose scientific terms that fit into the situations below.

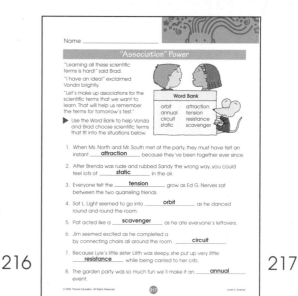

Word Bank

orbit
annual
circuit
static

attraction
tension
resistance
scavenger

1. When Ms. North and Mr. South met at the party, they must have felt an instant **attraction** because they've been together ever since.

2. After Brenda was rude and rubbed Sandy the wrong way, you could feel lots of **static** in the air.

3. Everyone felt the **tension** grow as Ed G. Nerves sat between the two quarreling friends.

4. Sat L. Light seemed to go into **orbit** as he danced round and round the room.

5. Pat acted like a **scavenger** as he ate everyone's leftovers.

6. Jim seemed excited as he completed a by connecting chairs all around the room. **circuit**

7. Because Lyle's little sister Lilith was sleepy, she put up very little **resistance** while being carried to her crib.

8. The garden party was so much fun we'll make it an **annual** event.

Page 218

Name _____

Space Lingo

▶ Carefully follow each direction on this and the next page to form words that are important for successful space travel.

1. Write a 3-letter word that means a rule we must obey. **L A W**
Add the name of the meal you eat at noon. **L U N C H**
Remove two letters to form a word that marks the beginning of a space trip. **L A U N C H**

2. Write a 4-letter word that refers to a bottle stopper. **C O R K**
Jumble those letters to form a word that means "a stone." **R O C K**
Add "et" for the power source for a spaceship. **R O C K E T**

3. Write a 2-letter word hidden in "that." **A T**
Add the abbreviation of Missouri. **M O**
Add a 6-letter word that means "a globe." **S P H E R E**
Combine the letters to form a word for the space around Earth.
A T M O S P H E R E

4. Write a 5-letter verb that shows how you might cook turkey or chicken. **R O A S T**
Add a fish often used in sandwiches. **T U N A**
Jumble the letters and you will have the name of a space crew member.
A S T R O N A U T

Page 219

Name _____

(continued) ### Space Lingo

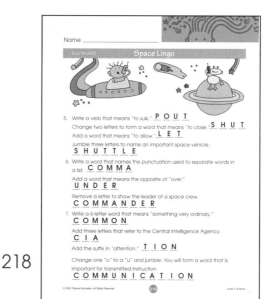

5. Write a verb that means "to sulk." **P O U T**
Change two letters to form a word that means "to close." **S H U T**
Add a word that means "to allow." **L E T**
Jumble three letters to name an important space vehicle.
S H U T T L E

6. Write a word that names the punctuation used to separate words in a list. **C O M M A**
Add a word that means the opposite of "over."
U N D E R
Remove a letter to show the leader of a space crew.
C O M M A N D E R

7. Write a 6-letter word that means "something very ordinary."
C O M M O N
Add three letters that refer to the Central Intelligence Agency.
C I A
Add the suffix in "attention." **T I O N**
Change one "o" to a "u" and jumble. You will form a word that is important for transmitted instruction.
C O M M U N I C A T I O N

Page 220

Name _____

Kaleidoscope of Letters

A **kaleidoscope** is a small tube that contains tiny pieces of glass. When the kaleidoscope is turned, different arrangements of the glass are made. The results are beautiful designs.

▶ Each of the pieces of glass in this kaleidoscope contain a letter. These letters can spell a number of valuable treasures.

How many treasures can you form using only letters that are attached to each other by the sides of their triangular shapes? List them on the lines below.

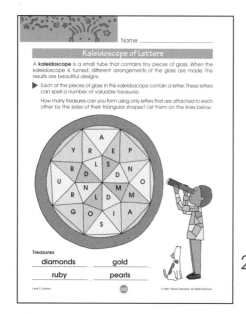

Treasures

diamonds   gold

ruby   pearls

Page 222

Name _____

You Oughta Be in Pictures!

Photographs are pictures that capture images at a precise moment. **Movies**, on the other hand, appear to show continuous action. Actually, movies give us the **illusion of movement**. A movie contains thousands of still pictures that move before our eyes so quickly that we cannot detect the individual pictures! The photographs are in sequence with only a tiny change from one to the next. When they are flashed very quickly before our eyes, we see what we think is movement.

▶ Examine the twelve pictures below. Only the first and last pictures are in the correct places in the sequence. Number the other pictures from 2 to 11 so that they are also in the correct order.

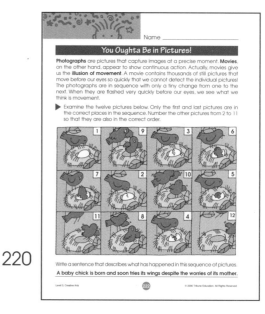

Write a sentence that describes what has happened in this sequence of pictures.
A baby chick is born and soon tries its wings despite the worries of its mother.

Body Language

Mimes are easily distinguished from other actors by their appearance. They wear white make-up on their entire face with dark lines drawn around their eyes and red paint on their lips. A mime's clothing is simple—often white or black pants with a T-shirt and sometimes a hat.

▶ Here is a list of short skit ideas for a single mime to perform. Study the suggestions carefully. Then, number them from 1 to 10 in their order of difficulty with 1 being the easiest to perform.

_____ An astronaut landing on Mars
_____ Walking your stubborn dog to the vet's office.
_____ Directing traffic at rush hour
_____ Running a relay on the moon
_____ Climbing the steps in the Empire State
_____ Feeding a playful baby
_____ Being a wind-up doll
_____ Making pizza at a restaurant
_____ Driving on a tall mountain
_____ Eating spaghetti that contains one long noodle _____

Answers will vary.

▶ Listed below are words that express feelings and emotions. Use these words or others of your choice to describe the feelings a mime might convey in each skit above. Write your choices on the lines above.

anger
astonishment
boredom
competitiveness
complacency
determination

diligence
discontentment
disgust
displeasure
exhaustion
giddiness

hesitancy
hostility
impatience
innocence
light-heartedness
obstinance

persistency
relentlessness
resignation
rigidity
surprise
uncertainty

223

Level 3, Creative Arts

With Expression

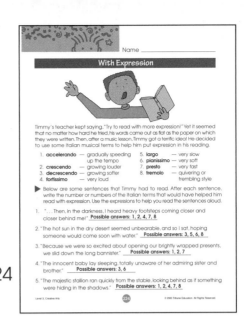

Timmy's teacher kept saying, "Try to read with more expression!" Yet it seemed that no matter how hard he tried, his words came out as flat as the paper on which they were written. Then, after a music lesson, Timmy got a terrific idea! He decided to use some Italian musical terms to help him put expression in his reading.

1. **accelerando** — gradually speeding up the tempo
2. **crescendo** — growing louder
3. **decrescendo** — growing softer
4. **fortissimo** — very loud
5. **largo** — very slow
6. **pianissimo** — very soft
7. **presto** — very fast
8. **tremolo** — quivering or trembling style

▶ Below are some sentences that Timmy had to read. After each sentence, write the number or numbers of the Italian terms that would have helped him read with expression. Use the expressions to help you read the sentences aloud.

1. "...Then, in the darkness, I heard heavy footsteps coming closer and closer behind me!" **Possible answers: 1, 2, 4, 7, 8**

2. "The hot sun in the dry desert seemed unbearable, and so I sat, hoping someone would come soon with water." **Possible answers: 3, 5, 6, 8**

3. "Because we were so excited about opening our brightly wrapped presents, we slid down the long bannister." **Possible answers: 1, 2, 7**

4. "The innocent baby lay sleeping, totally unaware of her admiring sister and brother." **Possible answers: 3, 6**

5. "The majestic stallion ran quickly from the stable, looking behind as if something were hiding in the shadows." **Possible answers: 1, 2, 4, 7, 8**

224

Level 3, Creative Arts

Fancy "Feets"

*The feeling spreads
As the music flows,
It makes you want
to tap your toes!*

If watching a professional tap dancer makes it look easy, try it yourself! It looks like fun, but you need a lot of muscle control and stamina to dance so quickly.

▶ Four dancers decided to have a contest to see who could tap-dance the fastest. Use the chart below to answer the questions.

> Tommy — 10 taps per second
> Rhonda — 150 taps every 15 seconds
> Sammy — 540 taps per minute
> Chris — 3,300 taps in 5 minutes

Which two people tapped at the same rate? **Tommy and Rhonda**
Which dancer could tap the fastest? **Chris**

▶ The answer to the riddle below is hidden in the letters. Each vowel equals 1/2 beat and each consonant equals 1 beat. Circle the letters (from left to right) that represent each 5th beat. Then, write them in order on the blanks to solve the riddle.

A G L I S C S E M P Q O X Z N B
R O U D S N E I G O C A S F H
U J K O P S X Y N T I M H J I Q
B A V W O H L B C N E S D O J S

What two vegetables did the tap dancer grow?

C O R N S and "B" **O N I O N S**

225

Level 3, Creative Arts

Shapes Within

Some artists paint very realistic pictures—apples that look real enough to eat, people who look as though they could walk off the canvas, and other objects so authentic-looking that a person touches them to see if they are real. Other artists' paintings are more abstract. They paint pictures that give the idea of an object, not a duplication of it. **Cubism** is one type of abstract art. Geometric shapes are a part of these pictures.

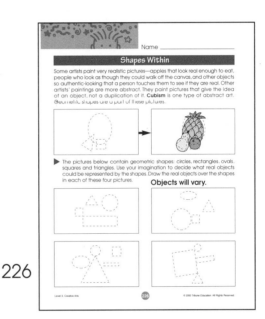

▶ The pictures below contain geometric shapes: circles, rectangles, ovals, squares and triangles. Use your imagination to decide what real objects could be represented by the shapes. Draw the real objects over the shapes in each of these four pictures. **Objects will vary.**

Level 3, Creative Arts **226**

Bits and Pieces

▶ Below are some collages. Each one represents a favorite children's story. This could be tricky! One item is added to each collage that doesn't belong in it. Cross out that thing. Then, write the name of the story on the line. Choose the names from the Word Bank.

Hansel and Gretel   **Peter Pan**   **Cinderella**

Three Little Pigs   **Jack and the Beanstalk**   **Wizard of Oz**

Aladdin   **Pinocchio**

Word Bank
Jack and the Beanstalk
Pinocchio
Hansel and Gretel
Wizard of Oz
Three Little Pigs
Peter Pan
Aladdin
Cinderella

227

Level 3, Creative Arts

An Array of Art

Mr. Art Curator was very excited. Today, the new shipment of artwork arrived. Every piece needed to be placed in the correct gallery. Read the title of each piece of art and decide in which gallery the artwork should be placed.

▶ Write the number of each art title in the correct room.

Gallery of Portraits	Gallery of Seascapes
8, 11, 17	3, 7, 10

Gallery of Still Life
2, 6, 16

Gallery of Primitive Arts
1, 12, 18

Gallery of Landscapes	Gallery of Textiles
5, 13, 15	4, 9, 14

Art Titles

1. African Drum
2. Fruit in a Bowl
3. A Breeze Along the Coast
4. Rug of Twisted Braids
5. Spring Meadow
6. The Golden Violin
7. Adventure on High Seas
8. Chief of Sioux Nation
9. Knotted Wool Weaving
10. The Danube on a Summer Day
11. John Glenn, Astronaut
12. Brazilian Ceremonial Cup
13. Conquering the Peak
14. French Lace
15. City Congestion
16. Purple Vase with Primrose
17. Young Child with Mother
18. Cameroon Mask

Level 3, Creative Arts **228**

Brainteaser Answer Keys

Page 229

Name _____

Mobility at Its Best

Each mobile below needs related items to hang from each string. Choose things from the Word Bank that fit together. Write their names at the end of each string in their mobile. After each mobile is complete, write a title that explains why all of the objects in that mobile are related.

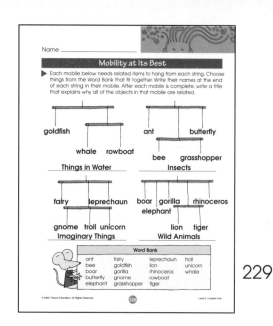

goldfish

whale   rowboat

Things in Water

ant   butterfly

bee   grasshopper

Insects

fairy   leprechaun

elephant

gnome   troll   unicorn

Imaginary Things

boar   gorilla   rhinoceros

lion   tiger

Wild Animals

Word Bank			
ant	fairy	leprechaun	troll
bee	goldfish	lion	unicorn
boar	gorilla	rhinoceros	whale
butterfly	gnome	rowboat	
elephant	grasshopper	tiger	

229

Page 230

The World Is Not Flat!

By adding a few lines to a square, an artist can make it look like a cube.

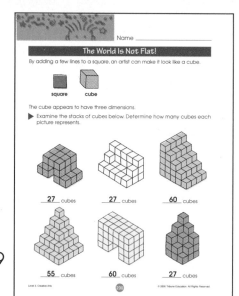

square   cube

The cube appears to have three dimensions.

Examine the stacks of cubes below. Determine how many cubes each picture represents.

__27__ cubes   __27__ cubes   __60__ cubes

__55__ cubes   __60__ cubes   __27__ cubes

230

Page 231

"Riddled" With Instruments

In these riddles about musical instruments, one important word is missing in each. Find the word in the Word Bank and write it on the line. Then, in each box, write the letter of the instrument that fits the description.

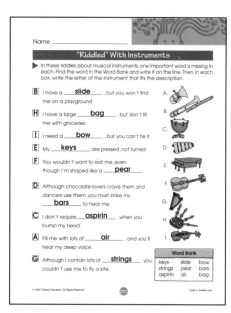

B I have a __slide__ , but you won't find me on a playground.

H I have a large __bag__ , but don't fill me with groceries.

I I need a __bow__ , but you can't tie it.

E My __keys__ are pressed, not turned.

F You wouldn't want to eat me, even though I'm shaped like a __pear__ .

D Although chocolate-lovers crave them and dancers use them, you must strike my __bars__ to hear me.

C I don't require __aspirin__ when you bump my head.

A Fill me with lots of __air__ , and you'll hear my deep voice.

G Although I contain lots of __strings__ , you couldn't use me to fly a kite.

Word Bank		
keys	slide	bow
strings	pear	bars
aspirin	air	bag

231

Page 232

Banding Together

Six friends decide to form a band to play for special occasions. Read the clues to decide which instrument each musician plays. Use the chart to help organize the clues. Each musician plays only one instrument.

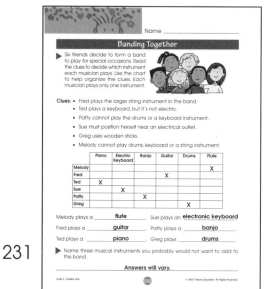

Clues:
- Fred plays the larger string instrument in the band.
- Ted plays a keyboard, but it's not electric.
- Patty cannot play the drums or a keyboard instrument.
- Sue must position herself near an electrical outlet.
- Greg uses wooden sticks.
- Melody cannot play drums, keyboard or a string instrument.

	Piano	Electric Keyboard	Banjo	Guitar	Drums	Flute
Melody						X
Fred				X		
Ted	X					
Sue		X				
Patty			X			
Greg					X	

Melody plays a __flute__ .   Sue plays an __electronic keyboard__

Fred plays a __guitar__ .   Patty plays a __banjo__ .

Ted plays a __piano__ .   Greg plays __drums__ .

Name three musical instruments you probably would not want to add to this band.

Answers will vary.

232

Page 233

The Prince and the Dragon

In what could be a typical folk tale, the prince came to save the princess who was trapped in a cave by a huge, ferocious, fire-breathing dragon. The prince brought only a rope, a rock and a bucket of sand, but he could also do excellent voice imitations.

Can you think of ways to save the princess from the dragon?

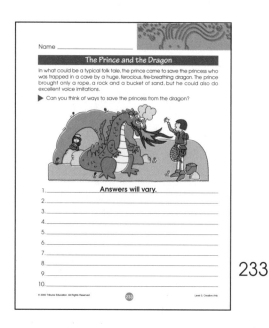

Answers will vary.

1. _____
2. _____
3. _____
4. _____
5. _____
6. _____
7. _____
8. _____
9. _____
10. _____

233

Page 234

Curtain's Going Up

Every play has three important elements: characters, setting and plot. The **characters** are the people who act out the play and recite the lines. The **setting** is the location and time in which the play takes place. The **plot** is what happens to the characters or what the characters do in the setting.

There are six plays listed below. Each one has a catchy title. Your job is to briefly list the main characters, the setting and a short description of the plot of each play. The first one has been done for you. Use your own creativity.

1. **Title:** *Blizzard Blindness*
   Main Character: Sam Bravehart and his dog Mack
   Setting: Winter in the Maine woods
   Plot: Sam and his dog are lost in a blizzard. They are rescued by an unexpected twist in the plot.

2. **Title:** *What's Cooking?*
   Main Character: _____
   Setting: _____
   Plot: _____

3. **Title:** *In Search of the Blue Diamond*
   Main Character: _____
   Setting: _____
   Plot: _____

4. **Title:** *Capturing the Great Shark*
   Main Character: _____
   Setting: _____
   Plot: _____

Answers will vary.

6. **Title:** *Mystery of the Sinking Potion*
   Main Character: _____
   Setting: _____
   Plot: _____

234

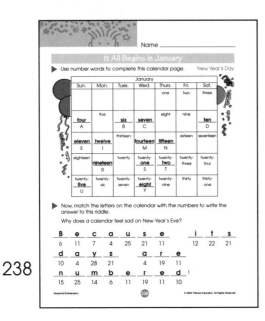

238

It All Begins in January — New Year's Day

Use number words to complete this calendar page.

January

Sun.	Mon.	Tues.	Wed.	Thurs.	Fri.	Sat.
				one	two	three
four A	five	six B	seven C	eight	nine	ten D
eleven E	twelve	thirteen	fourteen M	fifteen N	sixteen	seventeen
eighteen	nineteen R	twenty	twenty-one S	twenty-two T	twenty-three	twenty-four
twenty-five U	twenty-six	twenty-seven	twenty-eight V	twenty-nine	thirty	thirty-one

Now, match the letters on the calendar with the numbers to write the answer to this riddle.

Why does a calendar feel sad on New Year's Eve?

B e c a u s e   i t s
6 11 7 4 25 21 11   12 21 21

d a y s   a r e
10 4 28 21   4 19 11

n u m b e r e d !
15 25 14 6 11 19 11 10

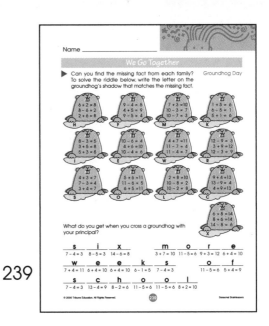

239

We Go Together — Groundhog Day

Can you find the missing fact from each family? To solve the riddle below, write the letter on the groundhog's shadow that matches the missing fact.

What do you get when you cross a groundhog with your principal?

s i x   m o r e
7 − 4 = 3   8 − 5 = 3   14 − 8 = 6   3 + 1 = 4   11 − 5 = 6   9 + 3 = 12   6 + 4 = 10

w e e k s   o f
7 + 4 = 11   5 + 10 = 6   4 + 6 = 10   6 + 4 = 10   3 + 4 = 7   11 − 5 = 6   5 + 4 = 9

s c h o o l
7 − 4 = 3   13 − 4 = 9   8 − 6 = 2   11 − 5 = 6   8 + 2 = 10

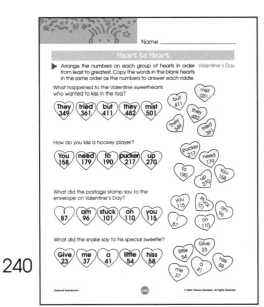

240

Heart to Heart — Valentine's Day

Arrange the numbers on each group of hearts in order from least to greatest. Copy the words in the blank hearts in the same order as the numbers to answer each riddle.

What happened to the Valentine sweethearts who wanted to kiss in the fog?

They 349   tried 361   but 411   they 482   mist 501

How do you kiss a hockey player?

You 158   need 179   to 190   pucker 217   up 270

What did the postage stamp say to the envelope on Valentine's Day?

I 87   am 96   stuck 101   on 110   you 115

What did the snake say to his special sweetie?

Give 23   me 37   a 41   little 54   hiss 58

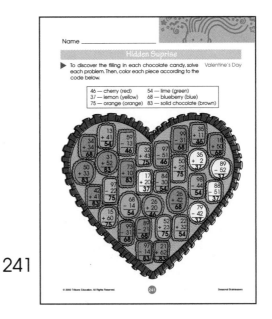

241

Hidden Surprise — Valentine's Day

To discover the filling in each chocolate candy, solve each problem. Then, color each piece according to the code below.

46 — cherry (red)	54 — lime (green)
37 — lemon (yellow)	68 — blueberry (blue)
75 — orange (orange)	83 — solid chocolate (brown)

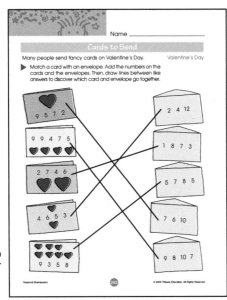

242

Cards to Send — Valentine's Day

Many people send fancy cards on Valentine's Day.

Match a card with an envelope. Add the numbers on the cards and the envelopes. Then, draw lines between like answers to discover which card and envelope go together.

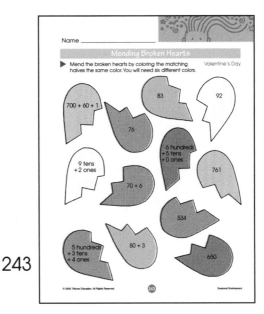

243

Mending Broken Hearts — Valentine's Day

Mend the broken hearts by coloring the matching halves the same color. You will need six different colors.

700 + 60 + 1   83   92
9 tens + 2 ones   76   6 hundreds + 5 tens + 0 ones
70 + 6   761
534
5 hundreds + 3 tens + 4 ones   80 + 3   650

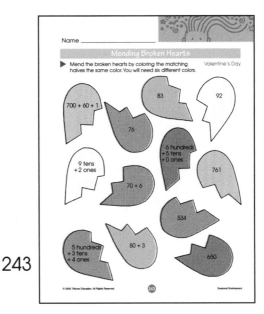

A Presidential Family — Presidents Day

Solve the subtraction problems. Then, match the letters with the answers beneath each line to find out which president had the most children.

A $\begin{array}{r}18\\-9\\\hline 9\end{array}$	B $\begin{array}{r}6\\-6\\\hline 0\end{array}$	C $\begin{array}{r}10\\-2\\\hline 8\end{array}$	E $\begin{array}{r}8\\-7\\\hline 1\end{array}$
F $\begin{array}{r}11\\-9\\\hline 2\end{array}$	G $\begin{array}{r}15\\-9\\\hline 6\end{array}$	H $\begin{array}{r}12\\-9\\\hline 3\end{array}$	I $\begin{array}{r}10\\-5\\\hline 5\end{array}$
N $\begin{array}{r}14\\-7\\\hline 7\end{array}$	O $\begin{array}{r}9\\-5\\\hline 4\end{array}$	R $\begin{array}{r}20\\-10\\\hline 10\end{array}$	S $\begin{array}{r}16\\-3\\\hline 13\end{array}$
T $\begin{array}{r}14\\-2\\\hline 12\end{array}$	U $\begin{array}{r}15\\-0\\\hline 15\end{array}$	W $\begin{array}{r}18\\-7\\\hline 11\end{array}$	Y $\begin{array}{r}16\\-2\\\hline 14\end{array}$

W a s h i n g t o n,
11 9 13 3 7 5 6 12 4 7

b e c a u s e   h e
0 8 9 15 13 1

w a s   t h e   f a t h e r
11 9 13   12 3 1   2 9 12 3 1 10

o f   o u r   c o u n t r y
4 2   4 15 10   8 4 15 7 12 10 14

244

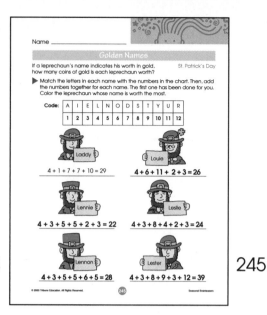

Golden Names — St. Patrick's Day

If a leprechaun's name indicates his worth in gold, how many coins of gold is each leprechaun worth?

Match the letters in each name with the numbers in the chart. Then, add the numbers together for each name. The first one has been done for you. Color the leprechaun whose name is worth the most.

Code:

A	I	E	L	N	O	D	S	T	Y	U	R
1	2	3	4	5	6	7	8	9	10	11	12

Laddy: $4 + 1 + 7 + 7 + 10 = 29$

Louie: $4 + 6 + 11 + 2 + 3 = 26$

Lennie: $4 + 3 + 5 + 5 + 2 + 3 = 22$

Leslie: $4 + 3 + 8 + 4 + 2 + 3 = 24$

Lennon: $4 + 3 + 5 + 5 + 6 + 5 = 28$

Lester: $4 + 3 + 8 + 9 + 3 + 12 = 39$

245

Pure Gold — St. Patrick's Day

Help the leprechaun sort his genuine gold coins from the fake ones. Color the coin **golden** (yellow) if the number on it is even. Color the coin **brown** if the number is odd.

246

Pots O'Gold — St. Patrick's Day

How many coins does each leprechaun have in his pot? Read the clues and write the numbers on the pots.

The number of my coins is an even number. It is greater than 50 and less than 62. The sum of its two digits is 13. — 58

My coins are a factor of 5. I have less than 60 coins. The sum of its two digits is 10. — 55

I'm glad I have 3 more coins than the second highest leprechaun. — 77

I have saved an odd number of coins. It is half of 100 plus 17. — 67

I've collected more than 65 coins but less than 75. The sum of its two digits is 11. The first digit is larger than the second. — 74

247

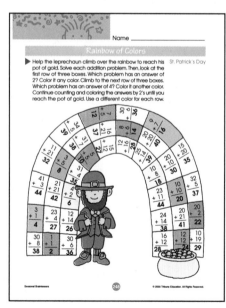

Rainbow of Colors — St. Patrick's Day

Help the leprechaun climb over the rainbow to reach his pot of gold. Solve each addition problem. Then, look at the first row of three boxes. Which problem has an answer of 2? Color it any color. Climb to the next row of three boxes. Which problem has an answer of 4? Color it another color. Continue counting and coloring the answers by 2's until you reach the pot of gold. Use a different color for each row.

248

Count the Coins — St. Patrick's Day

Each whole pot of gold contains $1.00. Count the money in each half on the pot. Then, write the amount on the pot, and draw a line to connect the two halves that equal $1.00.

76¢   33¢   67¢

30¢   24¢

80¢

70¢   58¢   20¢   42¢

249

Brainteaser Answer Keys

342

250

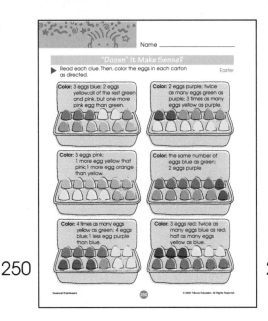

"Dozen" It Make Sense?

Read each clue. Then, color the eggs in each carton as directed.

Easter

Color: 3 eggs blue; 2 eggs yellow; all of the rest green and pink, but one more pink egg than green.

Color: 2 eggs purple; twice as many eggs green as purple; 3 times as many eggs yellow as purple.

Color: 3 eggs pink; 1 more egg yellow that pink; 1 more egg orange than yellow.

Color: the same number of eggs blue as green; 2 eggs purple.

Color: 4 times as many eggs yellow as green; 4 eggs blue; 1 less egg purple than blue.

Color: 3 eggs red; twice as many eggs blue as red; half as many eggs yellow as blue.

251

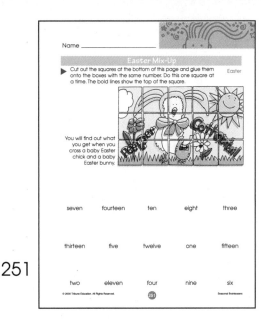

Easter Mix-Up

Cut out the squares at the bottom of this page and glue them onto the boxes with the same number. Do this one square at a time. The bold lines show the top of the square.

Easter

You will find out what you get when you cross a baby Easter chick and a baby Easter bunny.

seven	fourteen	ten	eight	three
thirteen	five	twelve	one	fifteen
two	eleven	four	nine	six

253

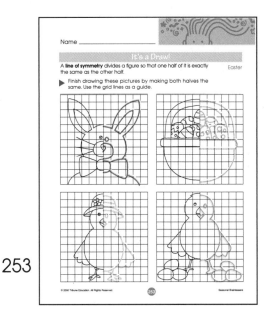

It's a Draw!

A **line of symmetry** divides a figure so that one half of it is exactly the same as the other half.

Easter

Finish drawing these pictures by making both halves the same. Use the grid lines as a guide.

254

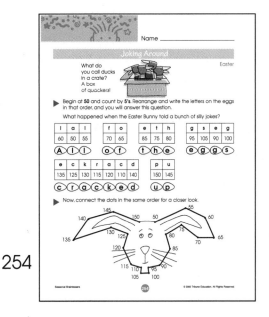

Joking Around

What do you call ducks in a crate? A box of quackers!

Easter

Begin at **50** and count by **5's.** Rearrange and write the letters on the eggs in that order, and you will answer this question.

What happened when the Easter Bunny told a bunch of silly jokes?

| l | a | l | | f | o | | e | t | h | | g | s | e | g |
| 60 | 50 | 55 | | 70 | 65 | | 85 | 75 | 80 | | 95 | 105 | 90 | 100 |

A l l   o f   t h e   e g g s

| e | c | k | r | a | c | d | | p | u |
| 135 | 125 | 130 | 115 | 110 | 140 | | 150 | 145 |

c r a c k e d   u p

Now, connect the dots in the same order for a closer look.

255

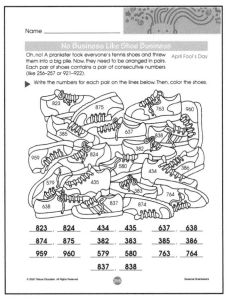

No Business Like Shoe Business

Oh, no! A prankster took everyone's tennis shoes and threw them into a big pile. Now, they need to be arranged in pairs. Each pair of shoes contains a pair of consecutive numbers (like 256–257 or 921–922).

April Fool's Day

Write the numbers for each pair on the lines below. Then, color the shoes.

823	824	434	435	637	638
874	875	382	383	385	386
959	960	579	580	763	764
		837	838		

256

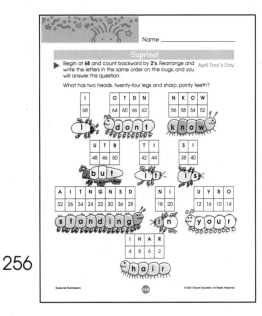

Suprise!

Begin at **68** and count backward by **2's.** Rearrange and write the letters in this same order on the bugs, and you will answer this question.

April Fool's Day

What has two heads, twenty-four legs and sharp, pointy teeth?

| I | | O | T | D | N | | N | K | O | W |
| 68 | | 64 | 60 | 66 | 62 | | 56 | 58 | 54 | 52 |

I   d o n t   k n o w

| U | T | B | | T | I | | S | I |
| 48 | 46 | 50 | | 42 | 44 | | 38 | 40 |

b u t   i t   i s

| A | I | T | N | G | N | S | D | | N | I | | U | Y | R | O |
| 32 | 26 | 34 | 24 | 22 | 30 | 36 | 28 | | 18 | 20 | | 12 | 16 | 10 | 14 |

s t a n d i n g   i n   y o u r

| I | H | A | R |
| 4 | 8 | 6 | 2 |

h a i r

Brainteaser Answer Keys

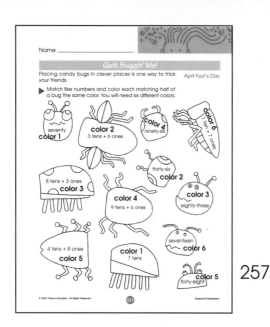

Quit Buggin' Me!

April Fool's Day

Placing candy bugs in clever places is one way to trick your friends.

▶ Match like numbers and color each matching half of a bug the same color. You will need six different colors.

- seventy — color 1
- color 2 — 3 tens + 6 ones
- color 4 — ninety-six
- color 6 — ten + 7 ones
- 8 tens + 3 ones — color 3
- thirty-six — color 2
- color 4 — 9 tens + 6 ones
- color 3 — eighty-three
- 4 tens + 8 ones — color 5
- color 1 — 7 tens
- seventeen — color 6
- color 5 — forty-eight

257

Love Our Planet

Earth Day

▶ Use a blue crayon to color all of the spaces with odd numbers. Then begin at the star. Write the letters that you did not color in the spaces below. Move clockwise around the circle.

S A V E   O U R   E A R T H.
G E T   R I D   O F
P O L L U T I O N.

258

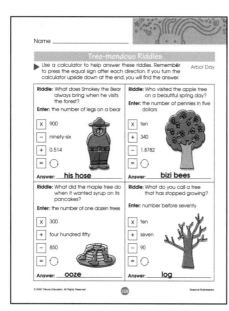

Tree-mendous Riddles

Arbor Day

▶ Use a calculator to help answer these riddles. Remember to press the equal sign after each direction. If you turn the calculator upside down at the end, you will find the answer.

Riddle: What does Smokey the Bear always bring when he visits the forest?
Enter: the number of legs on a bear
- × 900
- − ninety-six
- + 0.514
- = ○
Answer: his hose

Riddle: Who visited the apple tree on a beautiful spring day?
Enter: the number of pennies in five dollars
- × ten
- + 340
- − 1.8782
- = ○
Answer: bizi bees

Riddle: What did the maple tree do when it wanted syrup on its pancakes?
Enter: the number of one dozen trees
- × 300
- + four hundred fifty
- − 850
- = ○
Answer: ooze

Riddle: What do you call a tree that has stopped growing?
Enter: number before seventy
- × ten
- + seven
- − 90
- = ○
Answer: log

259

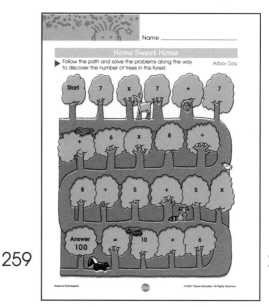

Home Sweet Home

Arbor Day

▶ Follow the path and solve the problems along the way to discover the number of trees in this forest.

Start 7 × 7 + 7
+ 6 × 8 +
8 + 5 ×
Answer 100 = 10 + 6

260

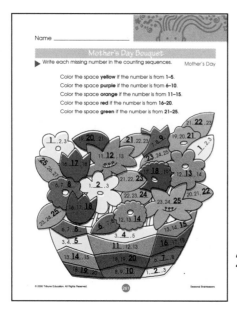

Mother's Day Bouquet

Mother's Day

▶ Write each missing number in the counting sequences.

Color the space **yellow** if the number is from 1–5.
Color the space **purple** if the number is from 6–10.
Color the space **orange** if the number is from 11–15.
Color the space **red** if the number is from 16–20.
Color the space **green** if the number is from 21–25.

261

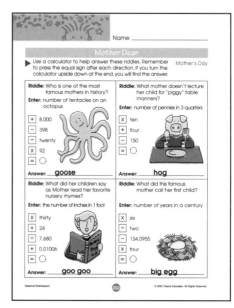

Mother Dear

Mother's Day

▶ Use a calculator to help answer these riddles. Remember to press the equal sign after each direction. If you turn the calculator upside down at the end, you will find the answer.

Riddle: Who is one of the most famous mothers in history?
Enter: number of tentacles on an octopus
- + 8,000
- − 398
- ÷ twenty
- × 92
- = ○
Answer: goose

Riddle: What mother doesn't lecture her child for "piggy" table manners?
Enter: number of pennies in 3 quarters
- × ten
- + four
- − 150
- = ○
Answer: hog

Riddle: What did her children say as Mother read her favorite nursery rhymes?
Enter: the number of inches in 1 foot
- × thirty
- + 24
- ÷ 7,680
- + 0.01006
- = ○
Answer: goo goo

Riddle: What did this famous mother call her first child?
Enter: number of years in a century
- × six
- ÷ two
- − 134.0955
- × four
- = ○
Answer: big egg

262

263

Name _____

Honor Our Veterans
Memorial Day

▶ Solve these addition problems. Next, write the letter on each star that matches the answer on the line below. Then, answer the question.

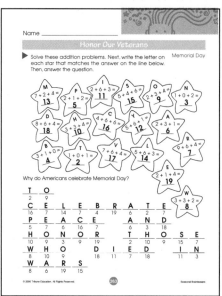

Stars:
- M 7 + 2 + 4 = **13**
- P 2 + 1 + 2 = **5**
- (blank) **11**
- S 5 + 4 + 2 = **15**
- O 2 + 3 + 4 = **9**
- N 1 + 0 + 2 = **3**
- D 8 + 6 + 4 = **18**
- H 4 + 3 + 3 = **10**
- E   = **16**
- V   = **12**
- Y 2 + 3 + 1 = **6**
- A 3 + 1 + 0 = **4**
- ? 1 + 0 + 1 = **2**
- T 7 + 6 + 4 = **17**
- L 5 + 6 + 3 = **14**
- R 9 + 4 + 4 = **7**
- E 2 + 1 + 4 = **19**
- W 3 + 3 + 2 = **8**

Why do Americans celebrate Memorial Day?

```
 T  O
 2  9
 C  E  L  E  B  R  A  T  E
16  7 14  7 19  4 19  2  7
 P  E  A  C  E        A  N  D
 5  7  6  3 18        3 18
 H  O  N  O  R        T  H  O  S  E
10  9  3  9 19        2 10  9 15  7
 W  H  O        D  I  E  D        I  N
 8 10  9       18 11  7 18       11  3
 W  A  R  S
 8  6 19 15
```

264

Name _____

Salute to Our Flag
Flag Day

▶ Think big! Find the answer to each problem. Then, check it with a calculator.

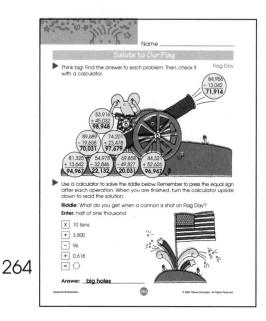

```
84,956
-13,042
71,914

53,916      89,689     74,201
+45,032    -19,658    +23,478
98,948     70,031     97,679

81,325     54,978     69,858     44,321
+13,642   -32,846   -49,827    +52,626
94,967     22,132     20,031     96,947
```

▶ Use a calculator to solve the riddle below. Remember to press the equal sign after each operation. When you are finished, turn the calculator upside down to read the solution.

Riddle: What do you get when a cannon is shot on Flag Day?

Enter: half of one thousand
- ✕ 10 tens
- + 3,800
- − 96
- + 0.618
- = ◯

Answer: ___big holes___

265

Name _____

An "Outta This World!" Tie
Father's Day

Dad thinks his tie is very special—because it's from you!
▶ Solve the problems and write the answers.

Color the space **purple** if the answer is **1–3**.
Color the space **green** if the answer is **4–6**.
Color the space **blue** if the answer is **7–9**.
Color the space **orange** if the answer is **10–12**.
Color the space **yellow** if the answer is **13–15**.

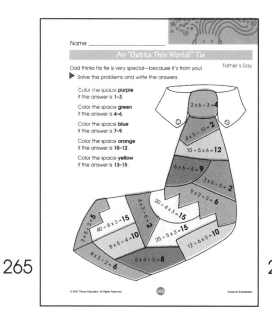

- 2 × 6 − 3 = **4**
- 4 × 5 − 10 = **2**
- 10 ÷ 5 × 6 = **12**
- 6 × 6 − 4 = **9**
- 3 × 6 − 9 = **2**
- 9 × 2 − 3 = **5**
- 20 ÷ 4 × 3 = **15**
- 4 × 3 ÷ 3 = **5**
- 3 × 5 ÷ 3 = **5**
- 40 ÷ 8 × 3 = **15**
- 8 × 5 ÷ 4 = **10**
- 25 ÷ 5 × 3 = **15**
- 12 ÷ 6 × 5 = **10**
- 4 × 3 ÷ 2 = **6**
- 6 × 4 ÷ 3 = **8**

266

Name _____

Fishing With Dad
Father's Day

▶ Use a calculator to help answer these riddles. Remember to press the equal sign after each direction. If you turn the calculator upside down at the end, you will find the answer.

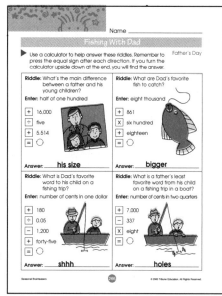

Riddle: What's the main difference between a father and his young children?
Enter: half of one hundred
- + 16,000
- ÷ five
- + 5.514
- = ◯

Answer: ___his size___

Riddle: What are Dad's favorite fish to catch?
Enter: eight thousand
- + 861
- ✕ six hundred
- + eighteen
- = ◯

Answer: ___bigger___

Riddle: What is Dad's favorite word to his child on a fishing trip?
Enter: number of cents in one dollar
- + 180
- ÷ 0.05
- − 1,200
- + forty-five
- = ◯

Answer: ___shhh___

Riddle: What is a father's least favorite word from his child on a fishing trip in a boat?
Enter: number of cents in two quarters
- + 7,000
- − 337
- ✕ eight
- = ◯

Answer: ___holes___

267

Name _____

Superstar
4th of July

▶ Connect the dots starting at **100** and counting by **10's**.

(dot-to-dot: 100, 110, 120, 130, 140, 150, 160, 170, 180, 190, 200, 210, 220, 230, 240, 250, 260, 270, 280, 290, 300)

▶ Arrange the numbers in order for each word below. Write the letters that go with the numbers in the empty boxes. You should get the solution to this riddle.

What should you do if the Statue of Liberty sneezes?

```
G  S  N  I         O  D  G          L  B  S  E  S
350 320 340 330    370 390 380     400 390 430 410 420
 S  I  N  G          G  O  D          B  L  E  S  S
```

```
R  A  C  E  I  A  M
470 440 490 460 480 500 450
 A  M  E  R  I  C  A
```

268

Name _____

Rocket's Red Glare
4th of July

▶ Write the answers for these multiplication facts. Match the letters to the answers on the lines below. You will discover the answer to this question.

What did one firecracker say to the other firecracker?

- A 7 × 7 = **49**
- B 3 × 2 = **6**
- E 6 × 4 = **24**
- G 9 × 8 = **72**
- H 5 × 8 = **40**
- I 3 × 7 = **21**
- M 5 × 3 = **15**
- N 4 × 4 = **16**
- O 8 × 7 = **56**
- P 3 × 4 = **12**
- R 10 × 5 = **50**
- S 7 × 6 = **42**
- T 9 × 9 = **81**
- U 4 × 7 = **28**
- Y 5 × 6 = **30**

```
 M  Y        P  O  P        I  S
15 30       12 56 12       21 42
 B  I  G  G  E  R        T  H  A  N
 6 21 72 72 24 50       81 40 49 16
 Y  O  U  R  S
30 56 28 50 42
```

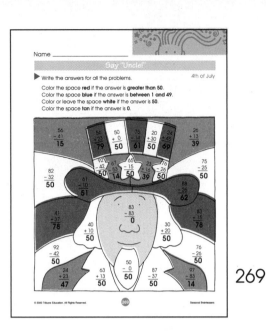

269

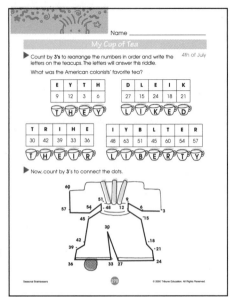

270

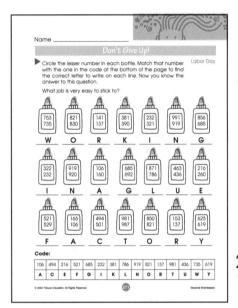

271

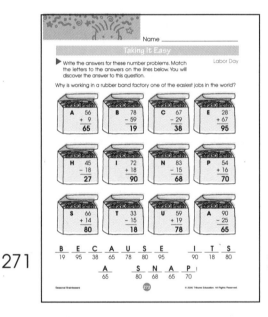

272

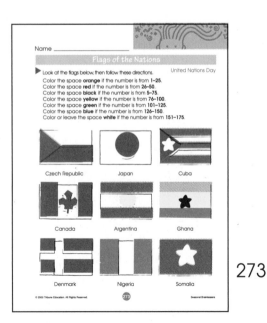

273

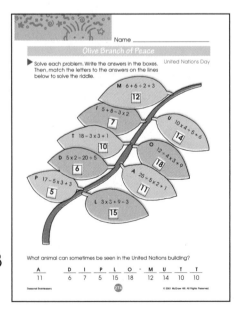

274

275

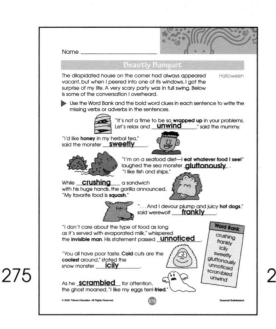

Name _____

Beastly Banquet

Halloween

The dilapidated house on the corner had always appeared vacant, but when I peered into one of its windows, I got the surprise of my life. A very scary party was in full swing. Below is some of the conversation I overheard.

▶ Use the Word Bank and the bold word clues in each sentence to write the missing verbs or adverbs in the sentences.

"It's not a time to be so **wrapped up** in your problems. Let's relax and **unwind**," said the mummy.

"I'd like **honey** in my herbal tea," said the monster **sweetly**.

"I'm on a seafood diet—I **eat whatever food I see!**" laughed the sea monster **gluttonously**. "I like fish and ships."

While **crushing** a sandwich with his huge hands, the gorilla announced, "My favorite food is **squash**."

"...And I devour plump and juicy **hot dogs**," said werewolf **frankly**.

"I don't care about the type of food as long as it's served with evaporated milk," whispered the **invisible man**. His statement passed **unnoticed**.

"You all have poor taste. **Cold** cuts are the **coolest** around," stated the snow monster **icily**.

As he **scrambled** for attention, the ghost moaned, "I like my eggs terri-**fried**."

Word Bank
crushing
frankly
icily
sweetly
gluttonously
unnoticed
scrambled
unwind

276

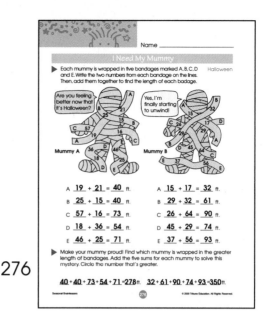

Name _____

I Need My Mummy

Halloween

▶ Each mummy is wrapped in five bandages marked A, B, C, D and E. Write the two numbers from each bandage on the lines. Then, add them together to find the length of each bandage.

Mummy A   Mummy B

A __19__ + __21__ = __40__ ft.   A __15__ + __17__ = __32__ ft.
B __25__ + __15__ = __40__ ft.   B __29__ + __32__ = __61__ ft.
C __57__ + __16__ = __73__ ft.   C __26__ + __64__ = __90__ ft.
D __18__ + __36__ = __54__ ft.   D __45__ + __29__ = __74__ ft.
E __46__ + __25__ = __71__ ft.   E __37__ + __56__ = __93__ ft.

▶ Make your mummy proud! Find which mummy is wrapped in the greater length of bandages. Add the five sums for each mummy to solve this mystery. Circle the number that's greater.

__40__ + __40__ + __73__ + __54__ + __71__ = __278__ ft.   __32__ + __61__ + __90__ + __74__ + __93__ = __350__ ft.

277

Name _____

A Boo-tiful Parade

Halloween

▶ Follow the directions. Begin with the leader ghost on the left.

1. Color a **red number 1** on the **first** ghost.
2. Draw **silly orange hats** on the **fifth** and **seventh** ghosts.
3. Color **purple polka-dots** on the **ninth** ghost.
4. Color **green stripes** on the **third** ghost.
5. Write "**Boo!**" on the **tenth** ghost.
6. Draw a **big tooth** in the **second** ghost's mouth.
7. Draw **funny yellow hair** on the **fourth** ghost's head.
8. Draw **black beards** on the **sixth** and **eighth** ghosts.

278

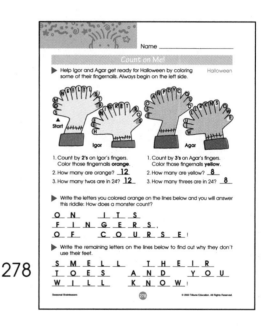

Name _____

Count on Me!

Halloween

▶ Help Igor and Agar get ready for Halloween by coloring some of their fingernails. Always begin on the left side.

Start

Igor   Agar

1. Count by **2's** on Igor's fingers. Color those fingernails **orange**.
2. How many are orange? __12__
3. How many twos are in 24? __12__

1. Count by **3's** on Agar's fingers. Color those fingernails **yellow**.
2. How many are yellow? __8__
3. How many threes are in 24? __8__

▶ Write the letters you colored orange on the lines below and you will answer this riddle: How does a monster count?

O N   I T S
F I N G E R S,
O F   C O U R S E !

▶ Write the remaining letters on the lines below to find out why they don't use their feet.

S M E L L   T H E I R
T O E S   A N D   Y O U
W I L L   K N O W !

279

Name _____

Monster Treats

Halloween

Frank and Stein have sorted their Halloween treats into groups. If the treats are shared equally, how many pieces of each kind will each monster get?

▶ Circle every two treats. Write the division problem that represents this and solve it. The first one has been done for you.

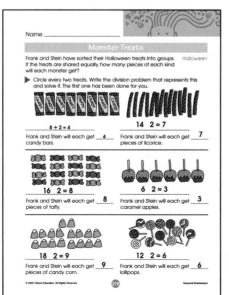

8 ÷ 2 = 4   14   2 = 7

Frank and Stein will each get __4__ candy bars.   Frank and Stein will each get __7__ pieces of licorice.

16   2 = 8   6   2 = 3

Frank and Stein will each get __8__ pieces of taffy.   Frank and Stein will each get __3__ caramel apples.

18   2 = 9   12   2 = 6

Frank and Stein will each get __9__ pieces of candy corn.   Frank and Stein will each get __6__ lollipops.

280

Name _____

Down to the Bones

Halloween

▶ Solve the addition problems. Then, color each bone as directed.

34 – orange   97 – red   56 – green
75 – black   48 – yellow   83 – purple

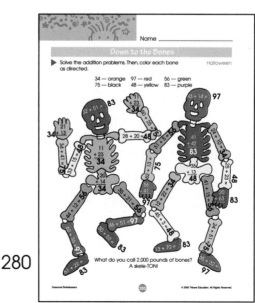

What do you call 2,000 pounds of bones? A skele-TON!

Brainteaser Answer Keys

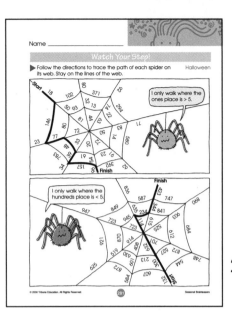

281

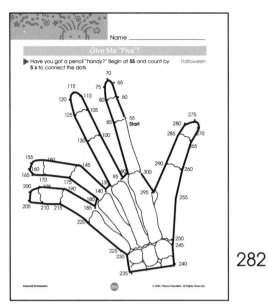

282

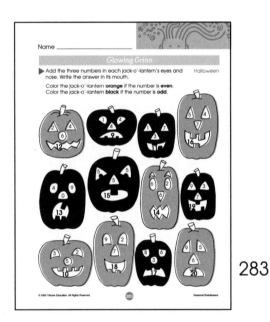

283

284

285

Ticklish Situation

How many feathers does each turkey have?
Read the clues. Write the numbers on the lines.

This even number is between 380 and 390. If you add the 3 digits, the answer is 15.
I have **384** feathers.

This number is between 500 and 550. It has a 5 in the ones place. The sum of the digits is 13.
I have **535** feathers.

This odd number is less than 790 and more than 770. The sum of the digits is 22.
I have **787** feathers.

Just between us turkeys . . .

Question: What has feathers on its body, feathers under its head and feathers floating on top of it?

Answer: A turkey sleeping on a feather pillow, snuggling under a feather comforter.

286

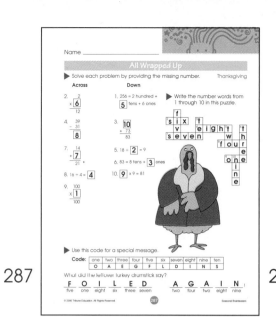

Page 287

Name

All Wrapped Up   Thanksgiving

Solve each problem by providing the missing number.

Across   **Down**

2. 2   1. 256 = 2 hundred +
    x 6   [5] tens + 6 ones
    ---
    12   ► Write the number words from
                                  1 through 10 in this puzzle.
4. 39
    - 31   3. 10
    ----   + 73
    8   ----
                                   83

7. 14   5. 18 – [2] = 9
    + 7
    ----   6. 83 = 8 tens + [3] ones
    21

8. 16 ÷ 4 = [4]   10. [9] x 9 = 81

9. 100
    x 1

    100

Number word puzzle grid:
f
s i x t
v   eight t
seven   w h
     f o u r e
        o n e
          n i n e

► Use this code for a special message.

Code:

one	two	three	four	five	six	seven	eight	nine	ten
O	A	E	G	F	L	D	I	N	S

What did the leftover turkey drumstick say?

F O I L E D   A G A I N !
five one eight six three seven two four two eight nine

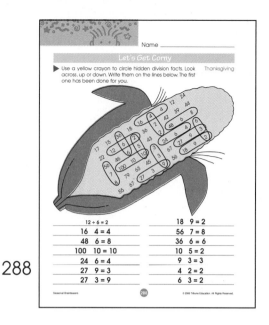

Page 288

Name

Let's Get Corny   Thanksgiving

Use a yellow crayon to circle hidden division facts. Look across, up or down. Write them on the lines below. The first one has been done for you.

12 ÷ 6 = 2		18 9 = 2
16 4 = 4		56 7 = 8
48 6 = 8		36 6 = 6
100 10 = 10		10 5 = 2
24 6 = 4		9 3 = 3
27 9 = 3		4 2 = 2
27 3 = 9		6 3 = 2

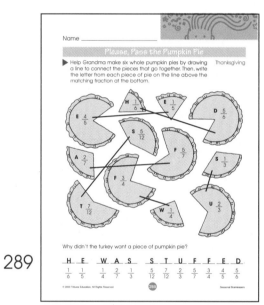

Page 289

Name

Please, Pass the Pumpkin Pie   Thanksgiving

Help Grandma make six whole pumpkin pies by drawing a line to connect the pieces that go together. Then, write the letter from each piece of pie on the line above the matching fraction at the bottom.

Pie pieces: H 1/6, E 1/5, D 5/6, E 4/5, S 5/12, F 5/7, A 2/7, F 3/4, S 1/3, T 7/12, W 1/4, U 2/3

Why didn't the turkey want a piece of pumpkin pie?

H E   W A S   S T U F F E D
1/6 1/5 1/4 2/7 5/12 7/12 2/3 5/7 3/4 4/5 5/6

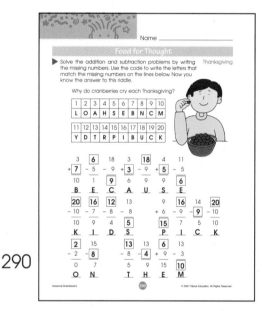

Page 290

Name

Food for Thought   Thanksgiving

Solve the addition and subtraction problems by writing the missing numbers. Use the code to write the letters that match the missing numbers on the lines below. Now you know the answer to this riddle.

Why do cranberries cry each Thanksgiving?

1	2	3	4	5	6	7	8	9	10
L	O	A	H	S	E	B	N	C	M

11	12	13	14	15	16	17	18	19	20
Y	D	T	R	P	I	B	U	C	K

B E C A U S E
K I D S   P I C K
O N   T H E M

Page 291

Name

M-m-m-mmm Good!   Thanksgiving

Help the Native Americans and Pilgrims calculate how much food they need to prepare for their feast. Write each answer on the line below the problem.

78 + 20 ÷ 10 + 15
95 turkeys

5 x 9 + 27 – 12
60 ears of corn-on-the-cob

75 + 55 x 2 – 100
85 carrots

15 ÷ 10 ÷ 5
17 deer

99 – 52 ÷ 2
73 loaves of bread

25 x 4 + 100 ÷ 2
150 potatoes

100 x 10 ÷ 2 – 150
350 beans

20 x 5 ÷ 2 + 6
56 apples

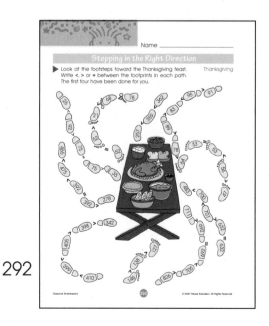

Page 292

Name

Stepping in the Right Direction   Thanksgiving

Look at the footsteps toward the Thanksgiving feast. Write <, > or = between the footprints in each path. The first four have been done for you.

Brainteaser Answer Keys

293

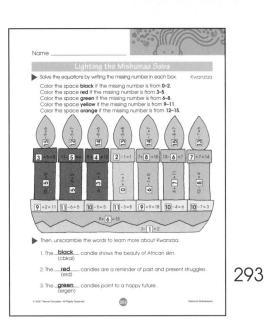

Name _____

Lighting the Mishumaa Saba
Kwanzaa

Solve the equations by writing the missing number in each box.

Color the space **black** if the missing number is from **0–2**.
Color the space **red** if the missing number is from **3–5**.
Color the space **green** if the missing number is from **6–8**.
Color the space **yellow** if the missing number is from **9–11**.
Color the space **orange** if the missing number is from **12–15**.

Then, unscramble the words to learn more about Kwanzaa.

1. The **black** candle shows the beauty of African skin.
   (cbkal)

2. The **red** candles are a reminder of past and present struggles.
   (erd)

3. The **green** candles point to a happy future.
   (ergen)

294

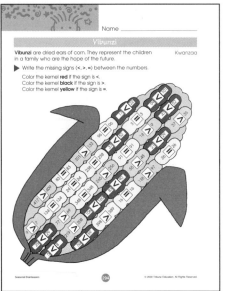

Name _____

Vibunzi
Kwanzaa

Vibunzi are dried ears of corn. They represent the children in a family who are the hope of the future.

Write the missing signs (<, >, =) between the numbers.

Color the kernel **red** if the sign is <.
Color the kernel **black** if the sign is >.
Color the kernel **yellow** if the sign is =.

295

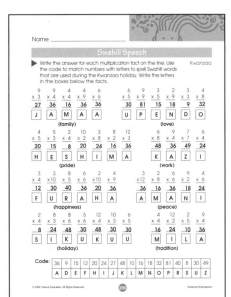

Name _____

Swahili Speech
Kwanzaa

Write the answer for each multiplication fact on the line. Use the code to match numbers with letters to spell Swahili words that are used during the Kwanzaa holiday. Write the letters in the boxes below the facts.

JAMAA (family) UPENDO (love)
HESHIMA (pride) KAZI (work)
FURAHA (happiness) AMANI (peace)
SIKUKUU (holiday) MILA (tradition)

Code:
36	9	15	12	20	24	27	48	10	16	18	32	81	40	8	30	49
A	D	E	F	H	I	J	K	L	M	N	O	P	R	S	U	Z

296

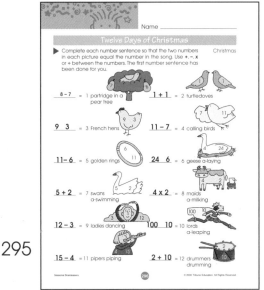

Name _____

Twelve Days of Christmas
Christmas

Complete each number sentence so that the two numbers in each picture equal the number in the song. Use +, –, x or ÷ between the numbers. The first number sentence has been done for you.

8 – 7 = 1 partridge in a pear tree
9 – 3 = 3 French hens
11 – 6 = 5 golden rings
5 + 2 = 7 swans a-swimming
12 – 3 = 9 ladies dancing
15 – 4 = 11 pipers piping
1 + 1 = 2 turtledoves
11 – 7 = 4 calling birds
24 ÷ 6 = 6 geese a-laying
4 x 2 = 8 maids a-milking
100 ÷ 10 = 10 lords a-leaping
2 + 10 = 12 drummers drumming

297

Name _____

Frosty the Snowman
Christmas

Frosty the Snowman and his friends need a few items. Start at the top left and follow the directions carefully, but don't take too long or the page may melt!

1. Draw three coal buttons on the 1st, 3rd, 4th and 7th snowmen.
2. Put a baseball cap on the 2nd, 5th and 8th snowmen.
3. Wrap a big scarf around the necks of the 4th, 6th and 10th snowmen.
4. Color orange carrot noses on the snowmen that follow the 3rd, 7th and 9th snowmen.
5. Draw a coal nose on the rest of the snowmen.
6. Place a black top hat on Frosty's head. (**Hint:** He already has a scarf, three buttons and a carrot nose.)

298

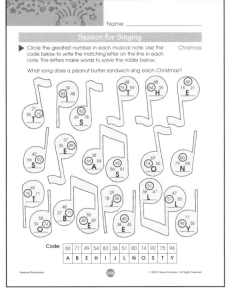

Name _____

Season for Singing
Christmas

Circle the greatest number in each musical note. Use the code below to write the matching letter on the line in each note. The letters make words to solve the riddle below.

What song does a peanut butter sandwich sing each Christmas?

Code:
66	71	49	54	83	36	51	80	74	92	75	96
A	B	E	H	I	J	L	N	O	S	T	Y

299

Name _____

Calculating Santa

▶ Use a calculator to solve these riddles. Remember to press the equal key after each operation. Then, turn the calculator upside down at the end to read the answer.

Christmas

Riddle: What does Santa say as he plants snow peas in his garden?

Enter: the number of pounds in 3 short tons (1 short ton = 2,000 pounds)

- [x] five hundred
- [+] 40,000
- [+] four hundred
- [+] 4
- [=] ◯

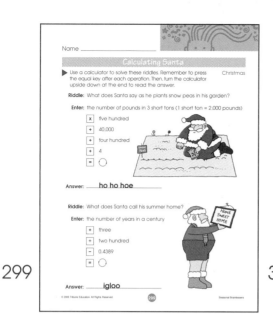

Answer: ho ho hoe

Riddle: What does Santa call his summer home?

Enter: the number of years in a century

- [+] three
- [+] two hundred
- [−] 0.4389
- [=] ◯

Answer: igloo

300

Name _____

Calculating Santa (continued)

▶ Use a calculator to answer the questions. Remember to press the equal key after each operation. Then, turn the calculator upside down at the end to read the answer.

Christmas

Riddle: How does Santa's voice change when he's getting a sore throat?

Enter: one thousand

- [+] 656
- [+] 0.1656
- [+] four thousand
- [=] ◯

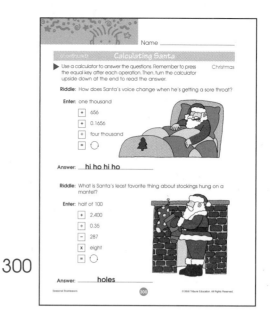

Answer: hi ho hi ho

Riddle: What is Santa's least favorite thing about stockings hung on a mantel?

Enter: half of 100

- [+] 2,400
- [+] 0.35
- [−] 287
- [x] eight
- [=] ◯

Answer: holes

301

Name _____

Trip Up North

▶ Trace the safest way to the North Pole. Finish the clues and connect the dots in the order of the missing numbers. Be careful! Not all the numbers will be used.

Christmas

Clues: 1. 6 tens = **6U**
2. The number in the hundreds place in 849 **8**
3. 900 + 50 + 6 = 9**5**6
4. 7 hundreds = **700**
5. The number in the tens place in 934 **3**
6. 400 + 60 + 1 = 46**1**
7. 2 ones = **2**
8. 2 hundreds + 9 tens + 5 ones = 200 + **90** + 5

302

Name _____

Smart Tree

▶ Solve the subtraction problems. Then, match the letters to the answers to solve the riddle.

Christmas

What is the name of the world's smartest Christmas tree?

A L B E R T
31 424 115 202 11 321

P I N E S T E I N
527 67 112 202 199 321 202 67 112

A	B	E	I
156 − 125 **31**	262 − 147 **115**	325 − 123 **202**	565 − 498 **67**

L	N	P	R
878 − 454 **424**	732 − 620 **112**	655 − 128 **527**	904 − 893 **11**

S	T	E	N
395 − 196 **199**	826 − 505 **321**	468 − 266 **202**	590 − 478 **112**

303

Name _____

While Visions of ...

▶ Solve the addition problems. Then, match the letters to the answers to solve the riddle.

Christmas

How do the children all nestled in bed sleep on Christmas Eve?

T H E Y   H A V E
912 839 639 990   839 379 469 639

P R E S E N T
809 699 639 836 639 889 912

D R E A M S !
983 699 639 379 904 836

A	D	E	H
256 + 123 **379**	856 + 127 **983**	364 + 275 **639**	516 + 323 **839**

M	N	P	R
726 + 178 **904**	267 + 622 **889**	482 + 327 **809**	376 + 323 **699**

S	T	V	Y
706 + 130 **836**	427 + 485 **912**	275 + 194 **469**	875 + 115 **990**

304

Name _____

A Special Glow

▶ Find the missing part of each candle below to make it a whole candle. Color it the same color as the part shown in the candle holder.

Hanukkah

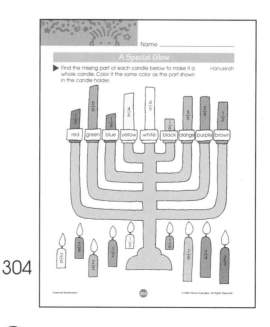

Brainteaser Answer Keys